5-24-73

Studies in Comparative Politics

THE NEW POLITICS OF EUROPEAN INTEGRATION

THE NEW POLITICS
OF EUROPEAN
INTEGRATION

edited by

GHIŢA IONESCU
Professor of Government at the
University of Manchester

MACMILLAN
ST. MARTIN'S PRESS

First published 1972 by
THE MACMILLAN PRESS LTD
London and Basingstoke
Associated companies in New York Toronto
Dublin Melbourne Johannesburg and Madras

Library of Congress catalog card no. 72–80483

SBN 333 13322 6

Printed in Great Britain by
BIDDLES LTD · MARTYR ROAD · GUILDFORD

Contents   1757303

Ghiţa Ionescu   *Foreword*   vii

Altiero Spinelli   *European Union and the Resistance*   1

Denis de Rougemont   *The Campaign of the European Congresses*   10

Richard Mayne   *The Role of Jean Monnet*   32

Étienne Hirsch   *Relations between the Officials of the European Communities and the Governments of the Member-States*   56

Stephen Holt   *British Attitudes to the Political Aspects of Membership of the European Communities*   64

Michael A. Wheaton   *The Labour Party and Europe 1950–71*   80

Émile Noel and Henri Étienne   *The Permanent Representatives Committee and the 'Deepening' of the Communities*   98

H. Vredeling   *The Common Market of Political Parties*   124

Michael Steed   *The European Parliament: the Significance of Direct Election*   138

J.-R. Rabier   *Europeans and the Unification of Europe*   153

Stanley Henig   *The Mediterranean Policy of the European Community*   178

Helen S. Wallace   *The Impact of the European Communities on National Policy-Making*   196

Terkel T. Nielsen   *European Groups and the Decision-Making Processes: The Common Agricultural Policy*   215

Michael A. Wheaton   *Literature on the Political Problems of European Integration*   235

Appendix   249

Contributors   270

Index   271

Ghiţa Ionescu

Foreword

THIS BOOK CONTAINS MATERIAL FROM THE COLLECTION OF STUDIES published in two separate issues, at five years' interval, of the journal of comparative politics *Government and Opposition*. The first issue was published in July 1967 under the title 'The Politics of European Integration', and the second in October 1971 under the title of 'The New Politics of European Integration'.

Three of the four articles which we reproduce from the 1967 issue are historical. The history of European integration, that is of the actual events which led to the establishment, consolidation and expansion of this unique organization, is not sufficiently known. Moreover, the general impression of the man in the street is that the organization was the by-product of international government schemes, produced by chancelleries and technocrats, and super-imposed upon the national institutions amidst the ignorance or indifference or even objections of the peoples.

Three of the historical studies reprinted here retrace the initial phases of the movement towards integration, and by doing so show that, contrary to the widespread belief that it was the re-sult of official initiative and inspiration, it was the consequence of grass roots initiatives which, after a time, won so much popu-lar support that governments and bureaucracies had to sit up and take notice. It is noteworthy that each of the chroniclers of the three phases were also direct witnesses of the events which they describe.

Thus, to begin with the very beginning, few people remember now that the idea of European Union originated in the crucible of war, among the particularly exposed men of the Resistance and of the concentration camps. Altiero Spinelli, who was one of them, and is now one of the high officials of the Communities, describes how this occurred, recalling also the part played in this luminous prologue by Albert Camus, the great French writer and philosopher.

Denis de Rougemont, who joined this early group immediately after the war and who is now rightly considered as the Sage of

European Federalism, takes up the story where Spinelli leaves off. He describes how during what he calls 'the campaign of the congresses' a handful of non-political initiators – Henri Brugmans, Spinelli, Salvador de Madariaga, Retinger, Jean Monnet, Stephen Spender and himself – carried on the work of mobilizing public opinion, governments and politicians out of their inertia.

One of these initiators, Jean Monnet, went further by actually organizing a European pressure-group, formed by politicians of all parties, industrialists, writers, scientists and all men of good will, in order to channel the popular impulse into political action. Richard Mayne, who was one of Jean Monnet's closest collaborators and who has published a particularly illuminating history of the European Revival, shows how Jean Monnet succeeded in winning over European political circles and bringing about the first of the three communities: the European Coal and Steel Community, which was then to expand into the present institutional complex established by the Treaty of Rome in 1957.

A fourth historical article by Stephen Holt retraces the parallel history of the British impulses and hesitations, advances and withdrawals, offers and refusals – until, finally, on 28 October 1971 the House of Commons in an historical vote declared the willingness of Britain to join Europe. Michael Wheaton, in a fifth historical study, concentrates on the ever fluctuating attitudes of the Labour Party towards Britain's entry, until, on the day itself, the party split into two opposed groups – Europeans and anti-Europeans.

M. Étienne Hirsch, who was President of Euratom, and who, though himself a Frenchman, had the specific honour of being dismissed from his position as a high European official at the request of General de Gaulle's government, discusses the relations between the officials of the European Communities and the governments of the member-states during that initial period.

The remaining articles are concerned with the political process of European integration, or more precisely with the new politics of European integration. The basic political process of the Communities, as set up by the Treaty of Rome, can be best illustrated by the diagram on page ix; they consist, in theory, of the dialogue between the Commission (the *supra*-national organism) and the Council of Ministers (the *inter*-national organism). So far the theory: in practice in the *new* politics of European integration there has been a change from within. It is this that the political studies, which form the bulk of this book, try to discuss. But here a word should be said about the approach of these studies. We place our interests between those of the students of all aspects of European integration so well represented in this country by the *Journal of Common Market Studies* and the publications of PEP and RIIA, and those of the political scientists, who especially in the USA, have studied the problems of integration according to different systems, and with different purposes (from K. Deutsch and D. Easton to Haas, Lindberg and Puchala).

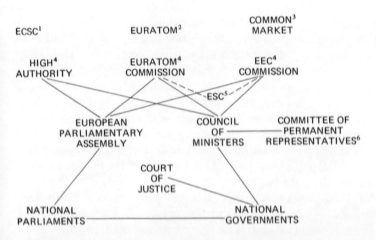

Political Process in the European Communities

1 European Coal and Steel Community 2 European Atomic Energy Community 3 European Economic Community 4 Executives 5 Economic and Social Committee 6 Committee of Permanent Representatives

Our approach could perhaps be best defined by paraphrasing the title of the important study by L. N. Lindberg and S. A. Scheingold, *Europe's Would-be Polity*,[1] into the 'actual European polity'. Actual, because in the first place we acknowledge the great changes which have taken place in the politics of European integration since 1966; and secondly, because we are more interested in what is actually happening than in what could happen if. . . . To give an example, Mr Lindberg's conception of the European polity, incomplete and wanting as it might be found to be under analysis, is more *actual*

---

[1] Subtitled *Patterns of Change in the European Community* (Prentice-Hall, New Jersey, 1970). See also J. A. Caporaso and A. L. Pelowski, 'Economic and Political Integration in Europe: A Quasi-Experimental Analysis', in *American Political Science Review*, Vol. LVX (June 1971) p. 418.

than Sir Derek Walker-Smith's conception of the sovereign European state.

This also explains why we invited experts from within and without the Communities, namely officials and parliamentarians of the European institutions, and scholars from British and other universities to express their views on various aspects of the present politics of European integration, and on the changes which have taken place since 1966.

Their individual contributions warrant some general observations. It is commonly agreed that the two major changes to reckon with are the twist given to the working of the institutions of the Communities and to their decision-making processes by the French Fifth Republic; and the geopolitical, not to speak of economic, expansion which will result from the coming increase in membership from six to ten European countries, including Great Britain. It is also commonly agreed that the second development is a consequence of the first. The British governments which applied for membership found the post-Gaullist style consonant with their own conceptions of sovereignty, and their entry will further consolidate it.

It can be assumed on the other hand that European opinion expects the entry of Britain into the EEC to have more far-reaching consequences on the political plane than even in the fields of technology, industry, commerce and finance. Her new partners hope and believe that the stability of the British parliament and of British parliamentary life will permeate their own representative institutions, many of which have had a more chequered history. It is also expected that British participation in the further shaping of the institutions of the Communities will result in a speeding up of the emergence of the European Parliament. Some British marketeers have already proposed that London should be the seat of this future institution.

The authors who examine in this volume the relations between the national and the supranational factors in the European political process tend to concentrate either on the direct or on the mediated aspects of these relations. In other words they dwell either on relations between any government of any member nation-state and the Communities as a whole, or on the relations between the Commission and the Council within the Communities.

After analysing the ways in which European decision-making affects that of the member-states, Helen Wallace concludes in her article that the present trend towards consultation through given national channels by 'diplomatic' means has come to stay, unless and until the present structures are given an opposite 'integrationist' twist. Stanley Henig's case-study on the emergence of a Mediterranean policy in the Communities indirectly confirms the supposition that the institutional contact established between the foreign ministries of the Six would facilitate collaboration in diplomatic matters.

From the second standpoint, that of the mediated relations between the supranational Commission and the international Council of Ministers a pessimistic or a relatively more optimistic attitude can be adopted. The pessimists, mostly federalists and early officials of the Communities, are inclined to think that since integration was not achieved on proper institutional foundations, all other functional forms of cooperation or coordination are only palliatives. The present arrangements are too frail and could not survive in really adverse conditions or when put to really severe tests. They see the recent evolution as a continuing deterioration and the progressive subordination of the Commission to the Council (i.e. of Europe to the nation-states) as a betrayal of the purpose of the Communities. The more optimistic attitude derives its wisdom from a basic scepticism. It takes the view that as long as the European Parliament does not exist, in reality, as the European Legislative Power, relations between the two executives: the supranational executive, the Commission, and the international executive, the Council of Ministers, are bound to be fraught with difficulties. It is in the nature of things that each of these executives, with different origins and motivations, should pull the processes of decision-making in opposite directions. The Commission, at its most enthusiastic, that is in the heyday of the Hallstein period, might well have frightened governments, members and non-members alike, by its Eurocratic single-mindedness. The spectre of the omnipotent Brussels bureaucracy was frequently conjured up by British anti-marketeers as late as 1971-2. In any case, it could not be expected that the nation-states should voluntarily relinquish their own, precarious enough powers of decision-making; rather would they rally with a vengeance around de Gaulle's nationalistic positions.

The post-Hallstein general staff of the Commission, oscillating between these two views have endeavoured, to keep the Communities working and, when and if possible to improve their functioning. A quite new dimension would be added, however, to the political institutions of the Community, should the plans for a political secretariat over the appointment of national ministers for EEC affairs be put into effect. One could conclude that by now it is easier to go ahead than to reverse, and that the organization itself has produced its own, albeit haphazard, functional solutions and transitional organs.

Of one of these committees, the Medium-Term Economic Policy Committee, more should have been said from a political point of view in this book,[2] and more will probably soon be heard. (The Medium-Term Economic Policy Committee has suffered not only from the dislike of the Council of Ministers for 'integrative' institutions – it has also suffered from internal rivalries and dissensions within the Commission itself, which have hampered its progress. Like all major bureaucracies, that of the Communities is not immune from such ills.) For it is the model for the kind of concertations which it is Utopian to believe that the groups, institutions and governments of the European nation-states can produce on their own. It is realistic on the contrary to see that such concertations make sense and are possible only when they are extended over an interdependent unit. The multinational corporations, and their future counterparts, the multinational professional organizations, are not fully accountable to the nation-state. From another angle, the interaction between the initial French idea of planning and the initial German idea of liberalism has been influenced by thinking in European terms. The concertation required between groups, corporations, sectional interests, professional representations and the organs of national representation in the individual European nation-states, is in any case conditioned by its European validity and applicability. As the problems of monetary and other financial and economic unions become more pressing, the Medium-Term Economic Policy Committee, if it were to be given new powers and guidance, might turn out to be one of the most effective instruments for the government of industrial Europe.

MM. Noel and Étienne go straight for the institution of the Committee of Permanent Representatives, which has grown considerably in importance since 1966. For the committed federalist, this committee is the very embodiment of the opposed concept of *l'Europe des nations*. From inside, MM. Noel and Étienne take a more *nuancé* view. They see the CPR as a bureaucratic outgrowth of the Council (and therefore likely to be considered as a rival to the Commission itself, which David Coombes, among others, described

---

[2] The committee is alluded to in several articles, notably in Helen Wallace, p. 231 and Noel–Étienne, p. 101. See also G. Denton, *Planning in the EEC. The Medium-Term Economic Policy Programme of the EEC* (PEP, RIIA, 1967).

as the European bureaucracy). But they see it also as a new and useful organ of mediation, or to use the Brussels expression, of 'concertation' within the institutions of the EEC. For those who, like this writer, are prepared to accept that one *raison d'être* of the EEC in the future technological society of Europe is to organize, foster, and implement concertation it is not criticism of the EEC that it should aim at, or obtain, less power of decision than the national governments had in their heyday. It is, on the contrary, a recognition that probably more than the national governments, the embryo-government of Europe sees its role from the beginning as one of concertation. Thus, these institutionalized mediators between the governments and the Communities, and between the Council and the Commission, foster the concertation needed for the elaboration of European decisions and policies, by seeing both the national and the European view-points. The committees which have been set up, with the Commission represented as the seventh (eventually eleventh) member, are specific European institutional improvisations.

Hence there is so much variety in the nature of the committees, according to their origins, their objects, and to whom they report. Most of the Committees have been set up by and are responsible to either the Council or the Commission and not to the Parliament. But while for instance the Davignon Committee was formed by the foreign offices of the member states, and directly linked with the European Parliament (to which it reports) the Comités de Concertation which group, for purposes of long term policy high, officials of the various branches of the civil services of the six states, are set up by and responsible to the CPR, i.e. to the Council. It may well be that the experimental activity of the committees will provide the transition to the future institutions and procedures of the Communities, or what Dahrendorf has called the second generation of European institutions.

MM. Noel and Étienne do not conceal their anxiety lest these organs of indirect European decision-making by concertation might delay the appearance of the institution of direct European deliberation – the European Parliament. H. Vredeling, in his understandably impatient article, pins his hopes on the political parties as the vehicles for the political unification of the continent. These informal, non-constitutional, and yet all-powerful organs of political representation of the European nation-states might cut across obstacles more easily than the massive constitutional institutions, surrounded by superstitious formalities. Michael Steed speculates on the

possibilities of European elections. But, as he points out, it is only
with great caution that one can assess how far functions familiar
at the national level can be reproduced on the European level.

Parliaments have aged in the European nation-states; some of
their functions have been successfully duplicated by informal organizations, groups, media; their relations with the executives are
now submerged in complex consultations with political groups, but
also with sectional interests and multinational organizations – both
beyond the criteria of accountability familiar to the institutions of
national representation. The modern institutions of European representation should be seen in this projection. The same applies to
the political parties which, in industrial-technological societies, may
well be threatened by the emancipation from their political tutel-
age of the institutions of functional representation (thus especially
the socialist parties and the trades unions). Should the organs of
decision-making in the Communities be discouraged from including
national, inter-, multi- and supra-national groups in their concertations for the sake of the political parties, jealous of their roles as
spokesmen? Or should the European Parliament be envisaged as a
multi-cameral assembly, with different kinds of representation?

From this point of view the work done by the Vedel Commission
on 'the enlargement of the powers of the European Parliament'
(see Appendix, pp. 249 ff. below) represents an important step towards the immediate displacement of some of the decision-making
processes from the European Executive to the European Legislative, or Legislative-to-be.

Yet, when one comes to the study by T. Nielsen of the best-
organized European group, COPA, and of its endeavour to influence
the decision-making processes of the EEC in the one integrated
sector, agriculture, the picture changes again, particularly in relation
to 1966,[3] when the collaboration between the EEC and the groups
seemed to open up new political avenues. Mr Nielsen's conclusion,
that COPA has been more successful in influencing the way in which
the agricultural policy has been implemented, than in defining the
strategic policy options, seems to prove, as in a parable, the need
for the groups to be politically buttressed.

The importance of groups and of public opinion in industrial-
technological polities is analyzed by M. Rabier, with the help of a
collection of first hand data. The ingenious trans-European ques-

---

[3] See especially D. Sidjanski, 'Pressure Groups and the European Economic
Community' in *Government and Opposition*, Vol. 2, No. 3, p. 397.

tionnaire pinpoints the conflict between imagination and parochialism. When European communications are properly organized, politicians and administrators will profit considerably from such revealing inquiries into public attitudes as those organized by M. Rabier.

Altiero Spinelli

European Union and the Resistance*

EVEN BEFORE THE END OF THE FIRST WORLD WAR, DURING THE inter-war years and right up to the outbreak of the second world war, a vein of political thought ran through Europe which condemned national sovereignties and set up against them the idea of a European federation.

In reality, the federalist trend of thought in the inter-war years remained marginal to the main political currents, and partook more of the nature of prophecy than of politics. In the 1920s and 1930s politics in Europe were both tense and varied, culminating in the emergence of many political-ideological tyrannies. But in spite of the violent divergencies over political problems in those years, politics itself, of the right and of the left, of moderates and radicals, of conservatives and revolutionaries, were based on the profound experience which the peoples had lived through during the first world war, namely of the solidity of the nation state. This experience led to the conviction that only on this rock could anything be built.

One exception to this spreading idolatry of the state could perhaps at first be found in the Russian revolution and in Lenin's powerful condemnation of imperialist wars. But for the communists, it was not the states as such, but the capitalists who ruled the states, who were responsible for wars. If the capitalists were to be expelled, the nation states themselves were to be respected and adopted as powerful instruments in the hands of revolutionary parties. Russia emerged from the collapse of tsarism and the ensuing civil war as a new and still more compact state, even more determined to assert its unity and independence.

To the west of Russia, the new ideology, advancing from year to year and from country to country was fascism, or nazism. Its purpose was to bring about again the total war-time mobilization of the

* Vol. 2, No. 3, April–July 1967.

nation, in the belief that only such a politico-military totalitarian structure would enable the states to gird themselves for the eternal struggle for primacy among themselves. In these two decades more or less totalitarian regimes spread over Europe, harshly nationalistic, burdened with all kinds of claims, determined to resort to war again at the first favourable occasion.

The surviving democracies were not suffering from numbers of unsatisfied claims; they did not succumb to the temptation of limiting the freedom of their citizens in order to re-create the powerful unity of a state prepared for total war. But their international policy was also based on national selfishness, and did not differ in substance from that of the totalitarian states. Of the 26 states in Europe in 1938, seventeen had become authoritarian, and almost half of these fascist. Democracy survived in only nine.

THE SECOND WORLD WAR

The European states embarked on the second world war having to outward appearances concentrated to the maximum all power in their hands, secured the complete obedience of all citizens, and transformed their peoples into immense armed forces. And yet the very violence of the ideological contrasts between democracy, fascism and communism had served to undermine the sense of national solidarity at least in the more politically mature strata of the populations. For a long time, communists everywhere in Europe had focused their loyalty on their party, and through the party on the Soviet Union, at the expense of loyalty to their own nation state.

In the totalitarian countries on the other hand, the democratic enemies of the regime plotted continuously against it; some conducted clandestine propaganda inside their countries against tyranny and in favour of a democratic regime, newer and better than that which fascism had destroyed. Others had been forced into exile, and led from abroad the agitation against the regime in power in their own country. Still others were in prison, banished to penal islands, held in concentration camps. The desperate struggle, in which all the resources of the state were used against the conspirators, had reduced the national loyalty of the anti-fascists to vanishing point. Since fascism and nazism had identified themselves so completely with the state, to oppose these tyrannies meant necessarily to oppose the state itself. The necessity was ever more clearly conceived, not merely of removing the state from the control of its fascist rulers, but of destroying it and replacing it with another better one. When the fascist powers launched the war, these anti-fascist plotters sided with those who were fighting against fascism, and hoped for the defeat of their own countries, seeing in defeat the means for the overthrow of tyranny.

This rejection of the principle 'my country right or wrong', the decision to support what was 'right' even against one's country, amounted to defeatism when confined to words, but became high treason if translated into deeds. Some of the enemies of tyranny, more deeply imbued with national traditions, suffered soul-searching agonies before taking this stand. Others, of a more radical temperament, broke through the taboo of national loyalty to their own state without difficulty and without remorse.

Thus this time the war turned out quite differently. The model of the state which successfully organizes the nation and yet maintains its independence was valid only for Britain, and with far greater sacrifices, for the Soviet Union. All the other states proved incapable of guaranteeing the independence and the security, and even more the eventual conquests, of their peoples. In order to fulfil their tasks, the European states had demanded and obtained from their citizens total obedience, the complete sacrifice of their liberty, their property, their lives. And now they all collapsed, ignominiously enough, under the blows of Hitler. And the German state, which had first brought down its enemies, then crushed its own allies, was burdened with so many and such crimes that when in turn it was invaded by Americans, Russians and British, it ceased to exist as a sovereign state, and Germany became simply occupied territory, administered by the victors.

THE PART PLAYED BY THE PEOPLES

In this catastrophic eclipse of the civil order created by the nation states, people were now reduced to thinking of themselves first, and deciding for themselves to which laws, noble or base, they should grant or withhold their allegiance. The nation state had become, for those who sought guidance, a compass which had ceased to give any bearings. In these circumstances, those who had been regarded as insignificant political deviationists became, for good or ill, the only true guides of their peoples. At first, while Hitler had been building his ephemeral racist empire, the fifth columns of his supporters furnished the central nucleus in the occupied states for the political

organization of these countries in the orbit of the 'New Order'. But
the ferocity of the new order aroused more and more opposition, and
the growing power of the Anglo-Russian-American allies began to
give grounds for hope that nazism and fascism could be overthrown.
Then, those who had previously been regarded as the 'scum of the
earth', the pre-war Italian and German anti-fascists, and the members
of the Resistance in all countries, those who had placed other political
and moral values above those of the nation state, came into their own.
They became the natural nucleus around which gathered those who
did not want to wait passively for liberation from outside, but who
wished to participate actively with the allies in the restoration of
liberty in their countries and in the whole of Europe.

Not all that happened after the destruction of Hitler's empire
conformed to the dream of the Resistance – indeed the Resistance
itself was split by the contradictions between the three great ten-
dencies, communists, moderates and radicals, into which it had been
articulated. The fundamental choice between evolution towards
communism or towards democracy did not depend on the strength
of one or the other trend, but on whether the country concerned was
in the American or the Russian zone of influence.

In Western Europe, the restoration of democracy was carried out
with extreme caution to the disappointment of the radical wing.
But if power fell to the moderates, the 'great design' of the reborn
democracies was nevertheless the one which had been formulated
by the radical wing in the Resistance: a democratic state which would
establish regional autonomy in modern terms; an economic system,
based on the free market, contained within a planning system capable
of ensuring continuous economic development and at the same time
taking increasing account of the requirements of social justice; a
federal power to which the conduct of foreign policy, defence and
the economic system should be transferred – the conduct in fact
of those three fields of government activity in which the national
states had most signally failed.

FEDERALISM AND ANTI-FASCISM

These three aims of the radical 'great design' of the Resistance have
by no means been achieved. But there can be no doubt that they
are fundamental to the democratic experience in Western Europe –
indeed that the level of their realization is a measure of the success
or failure of this experience.

Of the three, the federal aim was the most novel, the furthest removed from European political traditions. It was the most difficult to achieve because it implied common supranational action, to which neither the peoples nor the political forces had as yet adjusted themselves. What is more, before action could take place, the supranational ideal had to be developed in peoples' minds, an evolution which seemed almost impossible during the war.

As soon as it was formulated, the democratic anti-fascists easily acceded to the idea that after the fall of Hitler it would be wiser not to restore the previous national sovereignties. They accepted that it would be preferable to give a federal structure to Europe, since this would also solve the problem of co-existence in peace and freedom with Germany. The difficulty, however, of organizing effective co-ordinated action in Europe suddenly appeared so great that nearly all ceased to plan far ahead, and came to agree that the question could only really arise after the democratic reconstruction of Europe had been completed in all the relevant countries.

FEDERALISM IN THE RESISTANCE

When we recall today the emergence of this federal idea during the war, not as a distant ideal, but as the cornerstone of the new democratic post-war world, we may fail to do justice to the originality and vigour of this vision, if we do not also remember that those who dreamed of it were exiles on penal islands, or in concentration camps, or members of the Resistance in a number of countries. What they wrote on the subject circulated illegally among small local circles of conspirators, and with difficulty crossed any frontier. Groups in each country were ignorant of the existence of similar groups elsewhere. And yet as was later to be known, here and there members of the French, German, Italian, Dutch, Czech, Yugoslav or Polish Resistance movements had developed the same conception, expressing in almost identical words the same feelings and ideas, and were already promoting a first, still illegal, movement or committee for European federation.[1]

The first practical moves from local to European activity were

[1] Federalist documents of the European resistance were published for the first time in *Europe de demain*, ed. La Baconnière, Neuchâtel, 1944, edited by Ernesto Rossi, an Italian federalist who was then in Switzerland. Dr W. Lipgens, of the University of Heidelberg, is about to publish a study which will contain a good deal of source material on European federalism during the war.

taken by the Italian federalists. The initial nucleus, composed of some
four or five people, had been formed in the summer of 1941, on the
island of Ventotene, on which we were detained along with hundreds of other political prisoners. The outcome of frequent and
lengthy discussions in the group was that we undertook to prepare a
trial manifesto. The 'Ventotene Manifesto' as it is known today,[2]
written between 1940 and 1941 by this group, headed by Ernesto
Rossi and myself, stated among other things:

> The problem which must be solved in the first place, and with-
> out whose solution there will be no real progress, is the definitive
> abolition of the division of Europe into national sovereign states.
> . . . The minds of people are already much better disposed than
> in the past towards federal reorganization of Europe. All reason-
> able men recognize now that it is impossible to maintain a balance
> between independent European states. . . . The dividing line
> between progressive and reactionary parties no longer falls be-
> tween more or less democracy, a more or less socialist approach,
> but along a new line which separates those who conceive the
> conquest of national political power to be the essential aim of the
> struggle . . . and those who see as their main aim the creation of
> a solid international state . . . This is a time for a new task and
> it is also the time for the new men of the MOVEMENT FOR A
> FREE AND UNITED EUROPE.

We managed to circulate these pages clandestinely among anti-
fascist groups in Italy.

When Mussolini fell and the group was liberated, we founded
the European Federalist Movement illegally on 27 August 1943 in
Milan, and two of us were deputed to go to Switzerland and get in
touch with federalists from other countries. We did not know them;
we did not even know if they existed. But our faith in the correct-
ness of our analysis, the optimism of conspirators who do not
discern clearly the magnitude of the obstacles in their path, and the
habit of illegality, all contributed to convince us that other federalists
existed and that we would find them in Switzerland where all the
illegal organizations had some kind of clandestine representation.

Slowly, and in spite of great difficulties caused by the fact that the
Swiss authorities, out of respect for Swiss neutrality, did not allow
foreigners to organize public political manifestations, we arranged

[2] See complete text of the *Manifesto* in *Piccola antologia federalista*, Giovani
Europa editrice, Rome, 1956, pp. 9–15.

a first meeting. A federalist resolution was approved, which began as follows: 'Several militants of the Resistance movements of Denmark, France, Italy, Norway, the Netherlands, Poland, Czechoslovakia and Yugoslavia, and the representatives of a group of militant anti-nazis in Germany have met together in a city in Europe on 31 March, 29 April and 7 July 1944.' The unnamed city was Geneva, the meeting place was the house of Dr Visser 't Hooft, the future secretary general of the Ecumenical Council of Churches.

In July 1944 a 'Draft Declaration of the European Resistances' was issued which stated that:

> The resistance to the nazi oppression which unites the peoples of Europe in the same struggle has brought about a solidarity and a community of aims and interests which acquire their full significance with the fact that the delegates of the movements of European Resistance have met to draft the following declaration. . . .
>
> The peace of Europe is the cornerstone of the peace of the world. Within the span of a single generation Europe has been the epicentre of two world wars which have originated above all in the existence on this continent of thirty sovereign states. This anarchy can be solved only by the creation of a Federal Union among the European peoples. . . .
>
> This Federal Union should be endowed with:
>
> (1) A government which would be responsible not to the governments of the various member-states, but to their peoples, through which it would be able to exercise a direct authority within the limits of its attributions;
>
> (2) An army placed under the orders of this government and excluding all national armies;
>
> (3) A Supreme Court which will judge all questions arising from the interpretation of the Federal Constitution and any disputes between the member states or between those states and the Federation.[3]

AFTER THE LIBERATION

After the liberation of France the French Committee for European Federation, which had been set up some time before in the

---

[3] See complete text of the Declaration in *L'Europe de demain*, *loc. cit*, pp. 71–3.

Resistance, and of which Albert Camus[4] was a member, took the initiative of calling the first European Federalist Conference in Paris.
The organization of this conference was entrusted to those same
Italian federalists who had prepared the meetings in Geneva, and
who once again clandestinely crossed the Alps and arrived in Paris.
The conference took place in March 1954, and those who attended
included Albert Camus, André Philip, Emanuel Mounier, Altiero
Spinelli and François Bondy among others. Noteworthy also was
the presence of George Orwell and the Labour MP John Hynd.

These two conferences, held before the end of the war, provided
the first occasion when members of the Resistance in different countries were able to compare the conclusions they had separately come
to, and to discover their similarity. Thus they launched a European-
wide movement supported by those who, in the concluding words
of the Geneva declaration, 'were resolved to consider their respective
national problems as partial aspects of the general European problem'
and 'to promote the federal organization of the European peoples'.[5]

Two years were to pass before, as a consequence of these early
appeals, the Union Européenne des Fédéralistes was born on 27
August 1947 in Montreux. Other currents of ideas, which had not
originated in the Resistance, now flowed into this new organization.
Parallel to the federalist current, there had emerged during the war a
functionalist current, incarnated above all in Jean Monnet. This
trend believed that European unity could be achieved, not by
means of a direct attack on national sovereignties, as the federalists
believed, but by means of the creation of specialized European
administrative bodies around which concrete interests would gather.
A third current of ideas came to join the federalists and the
functionalists, namely the 'unionist' current promoted by Winston
Churchill. Many statesmen adhered to this last trend, attracted by

---

[4] Indeed ever since December 1943, *Combat*, the clandestine paper edited by
Camus in the Resistance, contained (e.g. no. 53, 1943) such passages: 'France's
place is in the Europe of the Resistance. There is her mission. . . . Not in the
theoretical Europe carved upon green tables by the diplomats of the "Great
Powers", but in this Europe of sorrows, waking at dawn in anguish, in this
underground Europe of the maquis and false papers, in this Europe of blood,
which has been wounded and gives back blow for blow . . . The European
resistance will remake Europe. A free Europe composed of free citizens, because we have all known slavery. A Europe politically and economically united
because we have paid the full price of division. A Europe armed, because we
have paid the ransom of weakness.' See text in *L'Europe de demain, loc. cit.*,
pp. 94–5.

[5] *Ibid.*, p. 75.

Churchill's prestige, and it received great publicity as a result of The Hague Congress of 1948 and the creation of the European Movement. Prominent statesmen and politicians in many countries became leaders of this movement; they felt the urgency of taking some step in the direction of European unity, but were not committed to any previously established programme.

The first concrete results in the European field emerged in the 1950s as a result of the alternation of strenuous debate between these three trends, and of the collaboration of the basically Europeanist statesmen (Schuman, Adenauer, de Gasperi, Spaak, Beyen, Bech); of Jean Monnet and his functionalist followers; and of the federalists of the Union Européenne des Fédéralistes. The statesmen brought their decision-making power; the functionalists their administrative experience, the federalists their vision of the ultimate goal. The federalists had deceived themselves with regard to the speed with which the resistance of national traditions could be overcome. But without their fundamental criticism of the nation-state, without their faith in European federal democracy, the slow, difficult and tortuous process of unification would probably soon have petered out. And federalism had had its roots in that crucible of passions and dreams which was the Resistance. It was not by accident that the men who led the Union Européenne des Fédéralistes in the 1950s, during the creative period of Europeanism, were all veterans of the various resistance movements: Henri Frenay, Eugen Kogón, Hendrik Brugmans, Alfred Mozer and the author of these lines.

(Translated from the Italian)

Denis de Rougemont

The Campaign of the European Congresses*

JUST AS THE REVOLUTION OF 1848 WAS PRECEDED BY A CAMPAIGN of banquets, so, a hundred years later, the European revolution was announced by a 'campaign of congresses' spread over the years 1947–9. These congresses expressed the state of mind and stimulated the major trends of a heterogenous and many-sided movement – a movement curiously inefficient in its tactics, and direct in its strategy, but to which the Council of Europe owes its existence and because of which the Community of the Six has been able to take shape and to win the acceptance of public opinion, and hence of the parliaments and governments responsible to public opinion.

Historians may argue that the congresses achieved nothing – and indeed we do not normally expect congresses to achieve much. Members of the same profession meet together to sit through tedious sessions and enjoy themselves all the better afterwards. But in those days a strange driving passion unknown to this generation, inspired the militants of Europeanism and induced them to prefer the nightly labours of commissions to receptions and operas. It is the sense of this driving passion which must be communicated, if we are to convey the psychological and historical reality of the campaign of congresses, and to pay due tribute to the influence it exerted. Their action should not be considered as that of a general seizing a military position, a law-giver imposing a legal structure, or even a medicine effecting a cure. Rather should it be regarded as a concerted concentration of psychic and psychological factors which prepare the ground and enable the organism to resorb certain poisons, overcome certain inhibitions and liberate new energies. It is such profound metamorphoses which really deserve the name of revolution.

The era of the congresses opened in August 1947 in Montreux and ended in Lausanne in December 1949. Its history has not yet

* Vol. 2, No. 3, April–July 1967.

been written and, unless a start is soon made, it may never be fully and accurately written. The rare printed documents[1] do not reveal the true nature of events which took place in minds and hearts; manuscripts, or duplicated texts, closer to the truth, have not been systematically collected, and they will not last for long on the poor quality post-war paper. And lastly, the actors of the period are leaving the stage. There is a photograph, taken at The Hague, of Churchill, resuming his seat after his inaugural speech, wiping away a tear with a forefinger, surrounded by the ex-ministers Raoul Dautry and Paul Ramadier, J. Retinger, the *éminence grise* of the Congress, the Dutch senator Kerstens, who took the chair on that occasion, and one of the three rapporteurs of the Congress. Of them all, the only survivor is the rapporteur, the author of these lines.

This is no attempt at a history, but an effort to bring to life the atmosphere of the time, the hopes, failures and problems of those who were responsible for some of the congresses. The historical evocation will thus necessarily be incomplete and the approach deliberately subjective, though I shall check my recollections against a personal journal kept at the time (unfortunately only too scanty as always in periods of activity) and with letters, drafts, minutes of committees, collected at the Centre européen de la culture in Geneva. What I hope to bring out here is precisely what the objective study of reports and resolutions will never reveal to authors of doctoral theses: a certain creative freshness, inspiring the whole undertaking, and which might have enabled it to succeed by surprise attack had not the calculations of prudent realism bored into it as the worm in the bud. For it was the very *naïveté* of some few federalists which almost 'made Europe' in 1948; but the skill of politicians, embracing our cause the better to suffocate it, dragged it down to the level of the 'possible' where they were sure that no miracles could occur.

THE CONGRESS OF MONTREUX

I had just returned to Europe after six years in the USA, and had settled at Ferney-Voltaire, in France, but near Geneva, when

---

[1] Reports and collected Resolutions of Montreux, The Hague, Westminster, Lausanne; and two small books: *Europe Unites* (*The Hague Congress and After*), and *European Movement and the Council of Europe*, edited by the secretariat of the European Movement, London, 1949. On The Hague, see also *Le Problème de L'Union Européenne* by O. Philip, 1950, and my *Europe en jeu*, 1940.

Alexandre Marc called to tell me of the existence of a European Union of Federalists, with headquarters in Geneva, which was about to hold a congress in Montreux. Recalling that we had been active colleagues in the 'personalist movement' centred around *Esprit* and *l'Ordre Nouveau* in 1932–9, he asked me to address the congress. And indeed, while in America, I had not ceased to think of the union of Europe, should I ever be able to return there. But I was taken aback. I had not yet even unpacked, and before speaking in public, I needed time to take my bearings. Two days later Raymond Silva, the French journalist and secretary general of the European Union of Federalists turned up in the evening, and took up the same theme. When I objected, he replied; 'All I ask is that you should read out to the congress what you wrote in 1940 on the "Way of Federalism".[2] Those pages contain the doctrine our militants need. We shall be about thirty, around a table, we shall talk, and you will have the opportunity to make contact with a group of friends and disciples.'

I jotted that same evening in my journal, 6 August 1947: 'How to refuse this time? I was thinking of just such a movement when I decided to return to Europe. An end? A new beginning? The fact that A.M. and R.S. were my first visitors gives meaning perhaps to my settling here.'

On 26 August in the evening, in the Pavillion des Sports, facing the Montreux Palace, there were the thirty people foretold by Silva, sitting around a table indeed, but on a stage facing an overflowing hall! Panic rose in me. I had prepared a short and precise text for a round-table discussion. Henri Brugmans, the chairman, introduced me as one of the authors whose works were read in the detention camp in which he had been confined in Holland. If the young people in our countries, he said, had been unable to translate into action the ideas which I had put forward, it was because they could not as yet find the outlet for their efforts in the only suitable framework, a federalist, federated Europe . . . I had to speak.

Notes from my journal: 'spoke – very quickly, thinking that I was going to bore them a great deal Surprised by applause for I don't know what, after some ten minutes, then more, and more again, particularly when I made a point by point contrast between totalitarianism and federalism; at the end, an "ovation" (I think it

[2] Published in London by Federal Union, British Branch of the World Movement for Federal Government.

is called) it seemed to last quite a long time. "You have made the congress," said Silva, as we left, "we shall only need to quote you." An odd character, leaning on a stick, drags me away from the seekers after interviews, sits me down before a *fine a l'eau* in the Montreux Palace, and says: "That's all very fine, but now we must work." He is a Pole, some sixty years old, Dr Retinger, with a lot of ideas about bringing together the numerous groups which have emerged from the Resistance, or from the governments in exile in London; they all want a united Europe, he told me, you have given them the doctrine, to-night, now we come to the main business, practical work. . . .'

The next day I left Montreux to meet some friends arriving in Sion from Paris. I was not yet committed. Having made the key-note speech, I seemed to feel that I had done enough. Notes from my journal: 28 August, evening. 'Yesterday evening, in Sion, my eye was attracted by a poster of the *Gazette de Lausanne*: "Montreux: Important statements on Europe". I thought to myself that I had been wrong to leave the congress, I must have missed the main part. I decide to return at once. Read the *Gazette* in the train. The "important statements" . . . were mine . . . Went this morning to the Economic Commission, out of curiosity. The chairman, Hopkinson (parliamentary secretary of the conservative group) invites me to sit on the platform. Five minutes later I am summoned to join in a discussion before the microphone of the Swiss radio with Brugmans, Robert Aron, Silva and Duncan Sandys, representing the movement inaugurated by Churchill. Sandys declares that the movement for European unity must be based on the Marshall Plan, and that economic integration must necessarily lead to military integration. According to him, we should confine ourselves to modest measures of cooperation arising out of consultations between governments. I speak immediately after Sandys, and urge that European action should arise from the militant movements, should hustle the cautious governments and should demand no less than a political federation, without which there could be no concerted economy or defence. Our disagreement is so blatant that the producer interrupts the recording to enable us to bring some harmony into our statements. (Which we manage to achieve, more or less, before resuming the debate in front of the microphone in the afternoon.)'

Twenty years later, I can see clearly that the difficulties and frustrations from which our movement was to suffer in the next

three years were all implicit already in this first confrontation between the revolutionary drive of the federalists and the realistic
tactics of the unionists. 'Nothing can be done without the governments' they say, and the others reply, 'But the governments do not
want to do anything. It is up to us to point out the goal, and afterwards we shall seek the roads which will lead us there.' I believe
that it is because I was thrown, publicly and without notice, into
this debate that I felt committed from that moment to the service
of European federalism.

It would however be untrue to say that I was deeply impressed
by the content of the discussions or the texts of the resolutions at
that time. I have just re-read the principal speeches and conclusions
of the congress.[3] Yet the reports of Henri Brugmans on the politics
of Europe, of Maurice Allais on economic organization, and of
Theo Chopard on trade unionism, contained fruitful and more
precise proposals than did the final resolutions. The will to unite
all European peoples, including those of Eastern Europe, was re-
affirmed as the only means of fending off the danger of colonization
by a Party or a Currency; the myth of the ineluctable choice between
two great powers, the myth of absolute national sovereignty, both
were denounced and emptied of their terrifying content; and so
were also false contrasts, as between liberty and planning, patriotism
and universalism, federal authority and local autonomy. Finally a
remarkable report by Daniel Serruys proposed the following stages
in the economic organization of the continent: a customs union as
the final expression of an economic union, in other words a common
production plan; complete free trade to be achieved by the progressive reduction of tariffs, spaced out over 10 to 15 years; a 'plan
Monnet'[4] for Europe, necessary not only in order to achieve a
balance between German and French production (in coal and metal-
lurgy), but for the sake of production in the union as a whole; the
pooling of resources of atomic and tidal energy; the regulation of
the agricultural problem of Europe, to be studied in terms of a
regional union, and 'constantly revised in terms of the world
economic situation'. One must admit that not much has since then
been added to this programme – indeed some vital elements, such
as economic union, have been dropped.

[3] *Rapport du premier congrès annuel del' UEF*, 27–31 August 1947, Montreux, published by UEF, Geneva, n.d. (1948) 142 pp.

[4] 'Plan Monnet' was then the name attached to the measures designed to restore
the *French* economy.

In the historical perspective which begins to emerge after twenty years, the Montreux congress now seems to me to hold a central and decisive place; it was here that most of the currents of European thinking, previously unknown to each other, flowed together; and here was born the idea of joining forces in a spectacular demonstration, which was to take place a few months later at The Hague.

A MEMORABLE CONVERGENCE

To tell the truth, though I left Montreux riding high on the tide of recovered comradeship and on the eve of a great adventure, I was far from an objective assessment of the importance of what had taken place in the huge, shabby Palace. For the sake of future historians, I will briefly outline the three main components of this episode. By a curious coincidence they all three emerged together in time and space, a year before, at the end of the summer, and in Switzerland.

First of all there took place a meeting in Hertenstein, near Lucerne, at the end of August, under the auspices of Europa Union (founded in 1925); representatives came from federalist groups in France, Italy, Belgium, Holland, Denmark and Great Britain and also from Germany, Austria and several Eastern European countries. This meeting was to give birth to the European Union of Federalists, which called the Montreux congress, following on two meetings at which the Union was set up, at Luxemburg (October 1946) and Amsterdam (April 1947). Behind the meeting at Hertenstein were the Resistance movements of all these countries which were now continuing their struggle by promoting European unity[5] and many of their leaders were present at Montreux. The ideas of most of the members of the Resistance had a common source, the 'personalist movement', formed at first in Paris in 1932 (around *Esprit* and *l'Ordre Nouveau*) and which had spread over the rest of Europe, including Germany (Harro Schulze-Boysen and the *Gegner* group) but not Italy, where federalism appeared independently in the detention camps on the Lipari islands. (Manifesto of Ventotene in 1942, and the journal *L'Unità europea*.) The personalist-resistance element was represented at Montreux by Robert Aron, Alexandre

[5] Delegates from the Resistance had already met secretly in Geneva in spring 1944, to draw up a European federalist manifesto; cf. *L'Europe de demain* ed. La Baconnière, Neuchâtel, 1946. The main ideas expressed in Montreux and the Hague, will already be found there.

Marc and others (who had, like myself belonged to the circles of
l'Ordre Nouveau and *Esprit*) and by Brugmans, who had expressed
his indebtedness to these groups elsewhere.

There had been the *Rencontres Internationales*, held from 1 to 12
September in Geneva in 1946. Leaving aside strictly political considerations, the *Rencontres* had stated in memorable fashion the
problem of the 'European spirit' in the turmoil of the post-war
world. A number of writers, Julien Benda, Georges Bernanos, Jean
Guéhenno, Karl Jaspers, Georgy Lukacz, Stephen Spender, F.
Flora, Jean de Salis, and myself attempted in the course of lectures
followed by public debates, to define Europe's sense of her own
destiny, confronted by the seemingly contradictory ambitions of
the Big Two. Supported particularly by Jaspers, I had urged the
political union of Europe according to the federalist formula. Some
of us, including a somewhat sceptical Jean Guéhenno, an enthusiastic Maurice Druon, Stephen Spender and myself, had even
attempted to draw up a federal charter – I have lost the drafts. The
Rencontres however did attract the attention of an elite to the European problem, and helped to create a favourable climate of opinion,
almost an intellectual fad.

Finally, a few days later, on 16 September, Winston Churchill in
his speech in Zurich boldly, yet cautiously launched his idea for 'a
kind of United States of Europe', at the same time quietly withdrawing both Great Britain and the Soviet Union into the wings,
as benevolent witnesses to a marriage of convenience between
France and Germany. He then proceeded to found the United
Europe Movement, represented in Montreux by his son-in-law,
Duncan Sandys.

There was yet a fourth component however; during the war,
the heads of the governments in exile, the Belgian, the Dutch, the
Polish governments, the governments of the Baltic states, of the
successor states of the Dual Monarchy, and of the Balkan states had
held talks, had prepared studies and common plans, had even signed
a number of pacts aiming at a future union of Europe. The main-
spring of this activity had been Dr Retinger, General Sikorski's
right-hand man. He had been parachuted into occupied Poland
at the age of 56, and had acquired a game leg as a result. Immediately after the war, with Paul van Zeeland, he founded the
European League of Economic Cooperation, and he represented it
in Montreux.

All this I discovered, little by little, during the congress and in the ensuing months; only now am I able to see it as a somewhat coherent picture. I had plunged into a new environment, and was testing its strangeness, consistency, unexpected currents and refreshing dynamism. In that autumn twenty years ago, I was not concerned to discover the complex origins of an organization of which I was not yet a member, and of a movement within which I could sense possibilities of action to be urgently developed.

FROM MONTREUX TO THE HAGUE: A DRAMATIC CHOICE

It was in fact during the intervals between meetings in the Montreux Palace that the idea of summoning the Estates-General of Europe the very next spring was launched. It was at once vehemently debated. We thought of quickly drafting those whom (taking the expression from *l'Ordre Nouveau* of 1933) we called the 'live-forces' of our countries: industrial, agricultural and employers' unions; co-operatives; magistrates and parliaments; youth movements, churches. Then of having them draw up their 'cahiers de revendications' and appoint their delegates, who would come together in vast deliberative assemblies which would gradually turn into constituent assemblies, as agreement emerged on the new forms of a federal Europe. Permanent committees would study problems – juridical, social, economic, colonial, etc. Their leaders would form the nucleus of a future European government.[6] We thought of Versailles as the seat of the assembly: this symbol of absolutism and later of the settlement of nationalist accounts in 1919 would in some way be redeemed by the coming of a federal Europe.

But while UEF dreamt of this, the observers from the non-federalist European movements who were present at Montreux were thinking on their side of calling a great conference of leading personalities under the awe-inspiring aegis of Churchill. A meeting was arranged to seek an agreement.

On 11 November 1947, in Paris, the delegates of Churchill's United Europe Movement, of the French Council for United Europe (president Raoul Dautry, vice-presidents P. Reynaud, P. Ramadier, A. Siegfried), and of the Economic League for European Cooperation (P. van Zeeland, D. Serruys) met those of the UEF (Brugmans, Silva, A. Voisin) and formed an International

---

[6] Unpublished document from the archives of the European Union of Federalists, 24 September 1947.

Joint Committee for the movements of European Unity, of which
J. Retinger was the secretary and prime mover.

On 15 November H. Brugmans reported on this meeting to the
central committee of UEF. The minutes which I have before me
make it possible to reconstruct exactly the dramatic *situation* in
which UEF had to play its part, or rather to shape it, taking great
risks whatever it did.

Brugmans recalls first the idea which had germinated in Montreux of 'summoning Europe' in a vast popular campaign, in order
to create the nucleus of a future government. The other organizations had decided for their part to call together at The Hague the
outstanding European personalities and were inviting us to join in.
'We have at once sensed the dangers for us in this spectacular
gathering; it could crush us or, at the very least, create confusion in
the public at large.' The leaders of the Socialist Movement for the
United States of Europe have refused to be associated with UEF
in the preparations for The Hague, because of Churchill's presence.
Sandys having successfully secured that his English committee and
the French committee should each have a vote, as well as the Economic League and the UEF, the latter finds itself alone against
three. 'However if we refuse, what will happen? It seems to me
difficult to call the Estates General against the congress of The
Hague. The others will have ample cover on the left (and others of
the same opinion will no doubt follow) and we shall soon have to
face serious financial difficulties. Very probably this would soon
paralyse our action in the immediate future, and it is the immediate
future which counts. . . . Our own movements will disintegrate if
we do not give them a clear goal. We would run the risk of becoming a sect. And in the meantime the others would act. The right is
enjoying an unexpected revival, the communists have deliberately
isolated themselves and the "third force" will either withdraw to
its tent or join the "great names" of "united Europe" and the
League. We could, doubtless, to a certain extent prevent the others
from winning a complete victory at The Hague but we could not
succeed either, and we should have paralysed each other mutually.'

Brugmans therefore proposed that the agreement prepared on 11
November should be ratified, provided however that the countries
of Eastern Europe were invited; that permanent organs should be
established at The Hague; and that the delegates should be chosen
by national committees without the Joint Committee having the
right of veto.

In the discussion which followed, one could feel that each of the 18 members of the central committee who spoke (out of the 20 present) had the same fears and contradictory desires, however unequally divided: breaking with the party of leading personalities, which held the purse strings and the press, meant, on one hand, to run the risk of courting rapid destruction or of becoming a sect, as Brugmans had said (but was it not by running just such a risk that Lenin finally won?) and on the other to condemn The Hague to be simply a *trompe l'oeil* congress, without any European future.

But to go to The Hague under the auspices of a union vaguely outlined by Churchill instead of calling the Estates-General – did this not involve running the risk of losing not only the benefit of numbers (UEF already grouped together 28 movements, comprising 100,000 subscribing members) but also the creative and revolutionary dynamism which the federalist doctrine brought with it?

Should we survive and risk losing the very reason for our existence (and not only the support of the socialists)? Or should we run the risk of isolation and dislocation and thus jeopardize the only chance perhaps for our federalist revolution to succeed? (The left, youth and the others would follow.)

UEF chose that day to take the risk of collaborating. It did so seemingly without enthusiasm, even with a certain pessimism among many as if the decision already implied more than a concession: a kind of admission of the relative weakness of 100,000 sincere militants faced with a few former British and French ministers, not all of them so certain of their right to speak in the name of the future.

FROM MONTREUX TO THE HAGUE II: WHO DEFINES THE PURPOSE?

The UEF expected that the Estates-General would give birth to a federal political life and form a nucleus of European government. But the Joint International Committee of 14 December in Paris laid down the following objectives for The Hague congress:

(1) to demonstrate in striking fashion the powerful and widespread support which already existed for the European idea;
(2) to produce material for discussion, propaganda and technical studies; and
(3) to provide a strong new impetus to the campaign in all countries.

One can see here the difference in level between the federalist ambitions and the unionist objectives. Can one say that the Joint Committee was nearer to the 'possible', to what political parties and their leaders would allow? This would amount to the admission that the federalists had at the same time given up trying to *create* the possible, which is the essential act of every revolution, political or spiritual. I think rather that UEF still hoped to make of The Hague congress something more than a congress. . . .

The Joint Committee had also decided to offer the chairmanship to Churchill; to accept the decision taken by the ELEC to present an economic report to the congress; to ask the British and French committees 'in collaboration with Dr Brugmans . . . to undertake responsibility for the preparation of a draft political report, for consideration by the Committee' (note the difference in procedure and the absence of any mention of UEF) and lastly Dr Retinger was asked to take steps 'to form a suitable group to prepare the necessary reports on the moral and cultural aspects of the European problem and, in this connection, Dr Retinger was asked to consult me'.

When Duncan Sandys, in January, and then Joseph Retinger, on 25 February, came to see me in Geneva and in Ferney to propose that I should form and lead the Cultural Commission of The Hague congress, I knew nothing of what had passed since Montreux in the inner circle of the committees. (I only had access much later to the minutes from which I have quoted.)

At Montreux, I had formulated the most radical federalist theses, but it was not my friends from the UEF who came to seek me out in my Voltairean retreat – it was precisely the men from London whom the federalists (rightly or wrongly) mistrusted the most: my innocence spared me the crises of conscience which they had just gone through. As soon as Retinger had asked me throw myself into the movement (I promised him to devote two years of my life and here I am still, after twenty years) I put very clearly the following conditions before I agreed to take charge of the cultural aspect of the proposed congress:

(1) The Cultural Commission, far from being a simple ornamental adjunct to the serious commissions (political and economic) must assume the decisive role in defining the purpose of the whole undertaking and its hoped for consequences.

(2) In order to prove that it shared this view, the Joint Committee should entrust to the Cultural Commission the draw-

ing up of the Preamble defining the long-term and short-term aims of the congress and of the movement.

(3) Since this Preamble should contribute also to the codification of the terminology of the resolutions, its contents, drawn up by the cultural section, should be debated before the Congress by the leaders of the political and economic sections.

Retinger gave me his word and promised to obtain the agreement of the Joint Committee and of the movements.

By the end of February I had already received promises of collaboration from fifty or so philosophers, scholars, writers and teachers, to whom I had submitted a first draft of the report which was to be the subject of the debates of the cultural section at The Hague, such as Nicolas Berdiaeff, Etienne Gilson, Jules Romains, Ignazio Silone, bishops, academicians, leading trade unionists, ministers of education (former and future). T. S. Eliot had written to me: 'I feel that at the present time one ought to do what one can to support a movement of this kind, however desperate the attempt.' And Salvador de Madariaga: 'I shall willingly devote (to the Commission) time which, to tell the truth, I do not have.'

The months of March and April were filled with some ten meetings of working committees in Paris, in l'Abbaye de Royaumont, and in the House of Commons. I kept in touch with the politicians and the economists; I had rows with the Joint Committee. I stirred up criticism and either took notice of it or threatened an open breach. I travelled widely, writing incessantly at all times of day and night, with the result that at the end of April, although I had neither secretariat nor any sort of budget for postage and travel, I had finished the Cultural Report, a draft of Resolutions and the text of the Preamble for the congress. And it had been agreed, with some difficulties, that I should read it immediately after Churchill's inaugural speech.

Retinger had supported me very skilfully. He wrote to me on 29 March ('copy to some of our colleagues') a letter which gave the document its full weight.

I consider that this declaration ought to form the starting point of our joint work and after the Congress it must become a manifesto of the whole international European movement. Just like the peace pledge in England a few years before the war was covered with some 13 million signatures – in the same way we

must endeavour to have this manifesto supported by millions of
signatures of Europeans, thus creating a very strong popular
movement as each signatory would not fail to remember his
signature and his pledge. It cannot fail also to produce an additional pressure on timid and recalcitrant governments.

The launching of such a manifesto ought to constitute one of
the principal and immediate objects of the Congress and of our
movement. It ought, by the work of collecting signatures, keep
our ideas constantly alive among the masses. Every meeting
organized by our affiliated bodies must end in collecting those
signatures (and eventually a few pence from each signatory to
keep the work going).

At the Joint Committee meeting of 8 April, in Paris, it was suddenly decided that 'the text until now entitled Preamble' would constitute a 'Message to the Europeans' to be approved by acclamation,
and would therefore be read at the closing session. Representatives
of three sections would examine it before the congress 'to ensure
the necessary homogeneity of the reports of the three commissions'.

This point noted and it was to be important, it remained to obtain
the *imprimatur* of the Joint Committee for the cultural report, the
political and economic reports being already at the printers. The
congress was ten days off.

In London, on 26 April, in a little room in the House of Commons, I found myself in the presence of an almost entirely British
group which displayed the greatest embarrassment: how to print
my report, because there were two others, by English authors,
which were also very deserving . . . I recalled that the Cultural
Commission had worked for two months on my text, and that I
had never heard of the two others. The reply was that my project
was 'too long', and that it spoke of federalism! 'It was felt that one
could not follow me as far as that. . . .' Consequently, and for lack
of time to shorten my text, incorporate the substance of the two
other reports, and send it to the printers (deadline: the next day
and I was leaving the same evening), they would propose the three
duplicated documents to the congress, *without* prior endorsement
by the Joint Committee . . . I felt that over the head of my report,
they were aiming at the 'Message' they were trying to break the
federalist point of the congress . . . I left the meeting in mid-afternoon
and went to Westminster Abbey to collect myself. Then on foot to
M. Retinger's house: I found him playing patience. He took me to

dine in a little restaurant opposite Victoria Station, where he used to meet Joseph Conrad. We agreed that I should not leave London until the next morning and that a secretary, advised by Retinger, should come at dawn to take my text to the printers. At the hotel a sullen waiter brought me kippers, beer and a table. At 6 in the morning I had finished, at 8 my plane took off, at midday I was asleep in Ferney. My cultural report, with the ink still wet, was distributed to the delegates on the second day of the congress. I was told that one of the authors who had been put up against me, on hearing at a dinner party in London that my text was being printed and not his, burst into tears. We were all nervous on the eve of battle.

THE HAGUE CONGRESS

Presidents and rapporteurs, we had crossed the hall in procession, Churchill and his wife leading the way up to the tribunal where Juliana and Prince Bernhard were already seated. There were flowers everywhere and fanfares in the courtyard of the palace. 'It might be a wedding' whispered Lord Layton who with me brought up the rear of the procession.

In the five days before this solemn session, the members of the Joint Committee, chairman and rapporteurs, had already gathered in The Hague, had met every day and every night, drawing up the procedure for the debates and above all, revising for the last time the proposed resolutions and the 'Message to the Europeans' of which I read in the minutes of 5 to 6 May (the meeting having lasted until 4 in the morning) that 'subject to certain passages which M. de Rougemont undertook to re-draft, *the text was approved*'. (We shall see presently why I single out this detail.)

From 8 May the members of the congress were divided into three sections. I could only take part in one, that of which I was in charge.

The debates on my report (creation of the European Centre of Culture, Charter of the Rights of Man) unfolded in the usual confusion, well illustrated by the following declarations: the novelist, Charles Morgan, wished matters of culture to be referred back to the governments, members of the Brussels Pact; the former minister Kenneth Lindsay thought on the contrary that 'our duty . . . is to set up a body competent to continue the work of the Congress'. Group Captain Cheshire, from Moral Rearmament, demanded first

a return to God and went on to denounce my report as
'anti-Christian'. Finally, Lord Russell, while stressing that 'there is no
reason to claim the superiority of Europe's heritage' said that 'a
Centre would assist men of different countries to maintain close
contact and learn to know each other's point of view' . . . In the
end, the whole positive content of the Report was passed in the
Resolution, voted unanimously. Centre, Charter of Rights and
Supreme Court, 'a Court above the States, to which individuals
and collective entities could appeal'. All this saw the light of day
from 1950 onwards with the application of the Resolutions of The
Hague.[7]

If one compares the introductory resolutions of the three sections, one is struck by the similarity of their way of stating the
European problem, of basing the efforts towards economic and
political union on the already existing cultural unity and on the
rights of the individual, anterior and superior to those of the state;
of asserting a form of federalist union appropriate to the safeguarding of the distinctive character of our peoples and of considering that this union would be the first step towards a world wide
federation.

The influence of federalist ideas is equally perceptible in key expressions such as 'to transfer certain sovereign rights of the nations
in order to exercise them in common' or 'the grant of a Common
Citizenship without loss of original nationality'.[8] The controversy
between federalists and unionists left a perceptible mark on the
political Resolution: the use, five times over, of the words 'the
union or the Federation' to designate the future Europe. However,
the rare detailed explanations given to the idea of union all indicated
a form of federal union, I mean: non-unitary with 'limited functions,
and real powers'.

But federalism triumphed only in the documents. Unionism, the
doctrine (or negation of doctrine) of those who hoped to make
Europe, without breaking eggs, remained the master of the field,
alone in a position to exploit the results of the dazzling demonstration at The Hague. On the one hand, those who called it were able
to prevent the congress from extending itself into a vast popular
movement; on the other hand the federalists did not know how to

---

[7] The political Resolution (paras 9–13) deals in very similar terms with the
same points, Charter and Supreme Court, as the cultural Resolution (paras. 4
and 5).

[8] Cf. Political Resolution, al. 3. and Political Report, III, 26, a.

impose their tactics: they allowed themselves to be fobbed off by promises of 'modest but concrete results'.

The federalists, as I have shown, hoped that the Estates-General would give birth – but how? – to a nucleus of European government whose powers were not outlined. Churchill had spoken of a 'Council of Europe' and no one knew whether it was to be something more or better than an alliance of absolute national sovereign powers. The political report (inspired by the unionists) proposed an extra-ordinary council, furnished with a permanent secretariat and a deliberative assembly, appointed by the national parliaments. The *political resolution* (voted also by the federalists) spoke only of an 'Assembly elected from within themselves – or outside' by the parliaments. Lastly, the final Message called for 'an Assembly . . . in which will be represented the living forces of all our nations' . . . the thesis of the integral federalists.

In fact, the European Movement, made up of the six organizations assembled in The Hague reached very rapidly a 'modest but concrete result': the creation in nine months of a Council of Europe, deprived of all powers and endowed with a purely consultative Assembly, formed of deputies appointed by their national parliaments. This was the triumph of the unionists, alone effective, but the federalists took part in all the delegations which obtained the agreements of the principal governments which were signatories of the Brussels Pact, Britain and France.

All this is common knowledge, but what is overlooked in general is the tiny and decisive incident which was to clip the wings of any hope of 'revolutionary action' by the movement.

The Message to the Europeans, having been debated for two months and passed by the Joint Committee on the eve itself of the congress, was printed on the upper part of a long roll of parchment. It was to be heard only at the end of the final session when I was to read it; all the members of the congress, led by Churchill, were to sign the document which was then to be circulated throughout Europe, to amass millions of signatures and to become the instrument of a powerful campaign agitating for Europe. But while I was giving a radio interview in the corridors, ten minutes before the time set for the session, someone came to find me: Sandys wanted to see me urgently in the Ridderzaal, where the plenary session of the economic committee was about to finish. I saw Churchill standing in front of the microphone, his hands on the lapels of his morning coat. At that moment a sudden freak storm caused all the lights to dim and to go out for a second. At the back of the hall, near the main entrance, I found Duncan Sandys and Randolph Churchill, who said to me: 'You want, I think, the congress to pass unanimously the text of commitment which ends your Message. Now I know at least thirty delegates who will oppose it because of the phrase "We want a common defence".' Sandys added: 'This phrase has not been debated by the Congress. I'm sorry, but we must forget about the Message.' My interviewer had followed me, his microphone in his hand, trailing the wire behind him. I signed to him and speaking into the microphone I repeated what had just been said to me and ended: 'OK! During the next European congress, Stalin who is stronger than you are, will send fifty delegates. *Et l'Europe ne se fera pas.*'

I think that I raised my voice a little. The ushers asked us to leave. I sent for Retinger and Paul van Zeeland, who were on the platform. In a little room near the entrance, we sat down six or seven of us, and after ten minutes of heated discussion, Paul van Zeeland who was to preside over the last meeting, proposed a compromise: I was to read the Message, leaving out the small incriminating phrase. This seemed sensible and harmless. In reality, it meant that the Message could no longer be signed, as that small phrase was part of it.[10]

I was still very pale, it seems, when van Zeeland asked me to read my text. When I began the final commitment, Sandys made an imperious sign with his hand that no one should rise in the hall. I had a small revenge (but only of self-respect) while Senator Kerstens was reading my message in English. I had returned to my seat on the platform, just behind Churchill who was tilting his chair backwards and forwards and I heard him say aloud: 'But why! We should stand up at that! We should all stand up!' No one moved, however, and the congress ended in a blaze of enthusiasm, but it had just killed the germs of any hope of a popular campaign, which would have reverberated throughout the whole of Europe.

And after. . . .

The European Movement, created in the months which followed and dominated by the unionists called firstly a political congress in

[10] Theoretically, Duncan Sandys was right: the Reports asked for a common defence, but the Resolutions no longer spoke of this. I notice that the theme of security therefore played no part at the Hague. And I add that two years later at the Strasbourg Assembly, Sandys made the first speech asking for a European army!

Brussels in February 1949, which saw no advance on that of The Hague, but which brought afterwards the full adherence and a powerful advocate, P. H. Spaak, during a mass meeting in the Place de la Bourse; then an economic congress in Westminster, in April 1949, which added nothing essential to the previous resolutions but stated that 'some permanent European Authority should be created to which governments would agree to entrust specific powers in certain defined spheres of economic activity.'[11] For the basic industries, such as coal, iron and steel, a European authority should be created with the view to suppressing customs duties, to defining the policy on investments, on production, on prices and on social rights. The influence of the socialists, and above all of André Philip came to be added to that of the liberals, who were the main authors of the analyses and projects drawn up by the first congresses. A year later, thanks to the creative genius of Jean Monnet and to the agreement between the christian democratic ministers of France, Germany and Italy, the creation of a High Authority for Coal and Steel was the start of a new strategy, which consisted of organizing at first the economy, with the idea that the political union should follow by virtue of the supranational machinery set up in certain key areas.

Lastly, the cultural conference of Lausanne (8–12 December 1949) arranged by our Bureau d'Etudes in Geneva and presided over by Salvador de Madariaga took up and developed all the suggestions, even those which had only been implicit in the texts of The Hague. It voted 21 Resolutions, of which 19 have been put into effect up to now, among them the European Centre of Culture, the College of Europe and the European Laboratory of Nuclear Research.

Thus, when the campaign of the congresses came to an end the unionists (the continental right and labour) had the Council of Europe; the economists (liberals and socialists) were to have the High Authority in Luxemburg, while awaiting the Common Market; those with cultural interests had the Centre in Geneva and a number of professional institutes and institutes of teaching and research. But the federalists, the initiators of the campaign, whose

[11] Summary of Recommendations, in *European Movement*, chapter on Westminster conference, p. 97. In the leaflets containing the texts of the congress, published in 1949, I read: 'It is urged that European organizations should be formed to which governments will agree to hand over some part of their sovereign powers in certain defined spheres of economic activities.'

great object was the political union of Europe as the safeguard of its diversities, what concrete results had they obtained?

VERY OPEN CONCLUSIONS

On 6 September 1949, the Consultative Assembly of the Council of Europe, born from the labours of the Congress of The Hague, proclaimed: 'The aim and the objective of the Council of Europe are the establishment of a European authority, endowed with limited functions but with real powers.'

This concept of limited, but real powers attributed to a state or to specialized authorities, had been the specific feature of any federalist regime in the eyes of the group around *l'Ordre Nouveau* since 1932. No one since then seems to me to have put forward any proposal going further than this modest but precise aim. It has only been very partially realized, in less than half of the western part of the continent, and only with reference to specific products such as coal and steel, vegetables and poultry. These are all very important in themselves. But Europe is composed of men and ideas too, let us say of spiritual, social and political forces, which are still awaiting the formulation, for each one of them, of the authority 'with limited but real powers' which would ensure their free exercise.

All the tactical and strategic means proposed or experimented with since 1946 have tended towards the same goal, by indirect ways and means. But in spite of partial achievements they have all failed to attain that goal.

The partial failure of the strategy of the European movement: the success of The Hague wore itself out in the creation of the Council of Europe, which soon lost sight of the aim which had been put before it at the start. OEEC and the Brussels Communities were dealing with economic matters; the Council was to deal with politics and culture. But when has it ever had real political aims? When one disposes of a Council of Ministers of seventeen countries, of an Assembly, and above all of a permanent secretariat, it should be possible to do more, if one really wanted to, than arrange cultural agreements and draw up a Charter of the Rights of Man.

The partial failure of the economic strategy: the success of the Common Market, remarkable as it is in its own field, has not been enough to set in motion the process of political union. There is no necessary link between an agreement on the price of wheat and a common policy with regard to the USA, the war in Vietnam, disarmament, or even a particular form of European government.

The failure of the 'Europe of the states': the Plan Fouchet with its pretence of 'starting from what is already there', that is to say from the nations, in fact never got started at all. This Europe was concerned above all to safeguard those famous 'national sovereignties' which, in the absence of any federal power able to give them a partial guarantee (as in the case of Switzerland and her cantons) are mere pretexts for rejecting that same federal power.

Finally *the failure of the strategy of direct agitation* in Europe and among the peoples of Europe, who have been unable to find the means for their end, a European Constituent Assembly.

'Is the European idea dying?' Last autumn, a leader writer on the *Figaro* replied to this question, the title of a series of three articles, first with percentages of production, which provide no evidence for or against an idea; and secondly by pointing to the undeniable political failure of the European plan.

And yet, in spite of all, *Europe advances*. From crises to fresh start it has been advancing relentlessly for twenty years. Strasbourg and Geneva, Luxemburg and Brussels, their treaties, statutes and councils, tens of teaching and research institutes, of professional associations, of 'twinned' cities, of industrial understandings, the hundred-fold increase in popular tourism – all this together is founding, structuring, building, weaving and nourishing a living substantive reality.

Europe advances, yes, but whither? Towards a 'closer union'? Or more 'integration'. These are vague words. Those who wish to lead minds, move the masses, and change the course of destiny, must be able to conjure up a clear, great and enthralling vision. They must be able to point to the goal. Above all, they must conceive and carry the living goal within themselves. Europe will be made wholly and quickly, when in all its countries, responsible people will have visualized it as it could be: a great federation of 25 nations and 500 million inhabitants. It should be able to ensure the autonomy of the nations and regions which compose it; and at the same time be able to exercise in the world that balancing power vested in such an immense conglomerate of values, traditions and inventiveness.

Without this vision, the union of Europe will always appear to be 'premature', and people will continue to repeat that since politics is the art of the possible, only the nations can be considered as the true objects of political will. What is really true, however, is that politics is the art of creating the possible, and all creation consists in anticipating, in the mind's eye, the act, the work of art, the monument which we are calling to life.

European federalists must therefore take up the task again where they let it drop, away from the hands of those who were only technicians. They must prepare (at last!) a plan, a model, of a *sui generis* union, starting from that vision of a total Europe which we must recover, and taking into account particular necessities which must be complied with. (In such an undertaking, one must deliberately neglect the famous 'existing possibilities', the only concern of politicians whose 'realism' amounts to neglecting both the final goal and the real needs.)

Such a model of a union will not necessarily take the form of a constitution. The deeply differing realities which make up Europe cannot all be handled in the same way. A multiplicity of Authorities will be needed to do justice to their specific purposes. To establish this model or plan of a federation seems to me to be the primary, long overdue, and decisive task, the real leap, the revolutionary and creative action without which we shall not leave the present plane of impossibilities. Those who will join in the work must be inspired by two guiding principles:

(1) Whereas the sovereign nation, in her grandeur, demands to be served by all her citizens until death, the Federation should be established to serve its members. Thus it should only be entrusted with those functions which by their *dimensions* go beyond the possibilities of the individual member. Such a principle of organization would render possible the definition, in each sector, not only of the *limits*, but also of the *reality* of the federal authority.

(2) From the start Europe must be conceived as a federation open to all the peoples of the continent who would fully accept its basic principles, and wish to associate themselves with all or *part* of its common enterprises. This means that the countries of Eastern Europe from Poland to Rumania must eventually be able to join, regardless of the political label on their regimes.

Sociologists and theologians, economists and philosophers, political scientists, town-planners and psychologists, the orthodox and the non-conformists of all schools should unite their efforts and draw up the model of a federated Europe. Then the politicians, the press and the pressure groups should undertake to have it adopted. Thus after twenty years of efforts, of researches, of partial successes and political failure, the task which the federalists wished to entrust to the Estates-General of Europe can be taken up again.

Indeed, the Common Market is now bringing its plan for a customs union to a successful conclusion. But then, how can further progress be made on the level of an economic union, which presupposes a political union? I think we are reaching the point where the demand for a federal union, embracing the whole reality of the whole of Europe while safeguarding its diversity, is the only realistic postulate. What is more, only such a federal union will be able to perpetuate the partial achievements, so hardly won, as for instance those of the Economic Communities.

(Translated from the French)

Richard Mayne

The Role of Jean Monnet[*]

THE FUTURE HISTORIAN OF EUROPEAN INTEGRATION IS LIKELY TO suffer from a surplus of documentation and a shortage of facts. If a certain kind of ignorance, as Lytton Strachey once remarked, is essential to the writing of intelligible history, it has little hope of survival amid the vast accumulation of newspaper cuttings, official statistics, policy speeches, annual reports and statesmen's memoirs with which the present-day scholar must contend. One expert has calculated that 'the volume of official documents produced by the United Kingdom Government and its agencies during the six war years 1939–45 equalled, in cubic content, the volume of all previous archives of the United Kingdom and of its constituent kingdoms England and Scotland that had survived down to the date of the outbreak of war.'[1] In another field, it has been said that if the American *Journal of the Fundamental Physical Sciences* continued to grow at the same rate as it has since 1945, by the year 2000 it would be heavier than the planet on which we live.[2] Documents on European unity are slightly less voluminous, but they already occupy imposing shelf-space in many languages. And yet, overwhelmed as he is by inert data and statistics, the historian still remains baffled. Reports and official documents reduce desperate efforts to bland, impersonal achievements and supposedly inevitable trends; memoirs are tainted by hindsight; newspapers summarize; speeches plead. Worst of all, the telephone leaves no record – unless in the sealed files of the security services or the imperfect notes that may be taken at either end. At once glutted and starved, the historian can only sketchily reconstruct what actually happened; and his account will often seem far too remote, well-ordered and reflectively analytical to those who took part in the muddle and drama of events.

These preliminary provisos, necessary to any treatment of the

[1] Arnold Toynbee, *A Study of History*, London, 1961, Vol. XII, p. 114, quoting W. K. Hancock; cf. M. R. D. Foot, *SOE in France*, London, 1966, p. 449.
[2] Léo Moulin, *La Société de demain dans l'Europe d'aujourd'hui*, Milan, 1966, p. 29.

* Vol. 2, No. 3, April–July, 1967.

effort to unite Europe, are more than ever essential in considering the role of Jean Monnet. It may well be that without Monnet something like the present European institutions would somehow have been established at some time since the second world war. But there can be no certainty either way. And those involved, however obscurely or modestly, in what seems to them a revolution in international affairs can hardly be blamed for their conviction that Monnet's role was vital, and still is. Would another man, in his place, have had his vision? Would another man, above all, have been able to secure the support for his ideas that Monnet managed to canvass? To the objective but distant historian, the answer to both questions may seem to be 'yes'. To those with even the slightest experience of working with Monnet, the issue is much more in doubt. They, with the advantage and disadvantage of personal involvement, have seen how often a given result has been achieved by chance combined with alertness, persistence, hard work and charm; they may be even unduly aware that, in Oliver Wendell Holmes's words, 'the mode whereby the inevitable comes to pass is effort'. If they go on record, as some of them have and others undoubtedly will, to stress the crucial role they ascribe to Jean Monnet, this is not a mere reflex of loyalty, but rather a sober recognition that this was how it happened, and that without Monnet's mercurial personality they doubt whether it would have happened at all.

In all this, naturally enough, there lurks a curious paradox. Monnet's own work has always been directed towards collective action. Accounts of it – and they are many – therefore attribute a large part to those whom he persuades to act collectively. This falls in line with Monnet's own express wishes: as one of his long-time collaborators put it to an American writer, 'an iron rule of those who work for him is, "Never take another fellow's place". People listen to Monnet – and there isn't a statesman in the free world who doesn't listen to him – because he isn't in competition with them: he doesn't want anything for himself.' The journalist in question pointed out the paradox: 'the evident flaw in this line of reasoning is that for almost anyone but Monnet the exact reverse would be more likely to be true'.[3] Thus it is that many writers on Jean Monnet have dealt brilliantly with every aspect of his work except the central enigma of Monnet himself. Who is he? What is his secret? Where lies the basis of his influence? Such questions are lost in thin air between facts and documents; and only a symposium

[3] John Brooks, *The European Common Market*, Buffalo, NY, 1963, p. 67.

of psychological novelists could possibly begin to answer them. It may be significant, indeed, that the three most revealing portraits of Monnet are from the pens or tongues of three imaginative writers – François Fontaine, François Duchêne, and the American already quoted, John Brooks.[4]

Monnet's own written words, oddly enough, are relatively unrevealing: they have the strength but also the limpidity of pure spirit. Fined and pared away until they achieve a stark simplicity, Monnet's speeches and articles give no sense of the endless struggle that lies behind them – the innumerable drafts, the interminable discussions, the solitary reflection, the last-minute changes, the exhausted secretaries, the annotations, the sheer donkeywork of research. To those who have traversed this anguished process, every word and comma in the ultimate smooth text has weight and meaning: to those who come to it without such background, its very clarity may make it seem banal. Only afterwards, when the text is subjected to exegesis by Monnet himself or his assistants, does the casual reader realize that the simplicity is Biblical and the naturalness the product of tortured art. Word for word, Monnet has probably produced as many epigrams as any living statesman: some of them have entered into the normal currency of 'European' discourse: many of them – like *'Nous ne coalisons pas les états, nous unissons des hommes'* – enshrine a revolutionary idea. But none by itself explains the hold that Monnet has so long exerted over men whose ostensible power is so much greater than his own.[5]

Who's Who, again, is just as unrevealing. It tells us that he was born in Cognac on 8 November 1888; that during the first world war he acted as French representative on the Inter-Allied Maritime Commission; that from 1919 to 1923 he was deputy secretary-general of the League of Nations; that he took part in the Austrian, Polish and Rumanian financial and economic stabilization; that he was sent to China by the League as advisor to the government on

[4] François Fontaine, 'L'Homme qui change le monde sous nos yeux', *Réalités* No. 203, December 1962, Paris, 1962, pp. 96–101; François Duchêne, quoted by Brooks, *op. cit.*, pp. 63–71. A study of Monnet's political ideas is included in Bino Olivi, *L'Europa Difficile*, Milan, 1964, pp. 69–101.
[5] Jean Monnet, *Les États-Unis d'Europe ont commencé*, Paris, 1955 is a symposium compiled from early 'European' speeches. Monnet's other speeches and articles exist in duplicated form in his secretariat; the statements of the Action Committee to date have been collected as Comité d'Action pour les États-Unis d'Europe 1955–65, *Recueil des Déclarations et Communiqués*, Lausanne, 1965. On methods, personal knowledge.

economic development; that he was chairman of the Franco-British Committee for Economic Co-ordination at the beginning of the second world war, then served on the British Supply Council in Washington; that he was commissioner for supplies, armament and reconstruction on the French National Liberation Committee in Algiers; that he was first commissioner of the French Plan after the war; that he led the French delegation to the Schuman Plan negotiations; that he was first president of the European Coal and Steel Community's High Authority; that he subsequently became president of the Action Committee for the United States of Europe. But these are the bare bones of an astonishing career.

What scarcely emerges from the public record, in fact, is that Jean Monnet is far from being the 'technocrat' or 'economic expert' that many writers have called him. He was educated in Cognac, and never attended a university – although he now has many honorary degrees. At eighteen, he was sent to Canada to sell brandy for the family firm; and he retains both a salesman's persuasiveness and a fondness for transatlantic freedom of manners – as well as a ready command of English. His year in China, likewise, seems to have left its mark. In appearance, Monnet is a stocky peasant: when he takes his regular morning walk near his small property outside Paris, he wears sturdy shoes, a dun-coloured windjacket and a wide-brimmed old-fashioned hat. He carries a stick, and frequently halts as he stumps along, turning to his companion, on the rare occasions when he is not alone, to make some abrupt remark, fruit of his continuing silent reflections. His face is ruddy, like a weather-beaten autumn apple: his eyes twinkle readily; his voice is dry and quick, breaking sometimes into a sharp staccato chuckle – '*C'est cocasse!*' he will exclaim. Photographs of him as a young man show him with a larger, dark moustache, somewhat saturnine: now, the moustache is clipped and grey, and the tiny lines on his face, with its watchful, hooded eyes and impassively raised eyebrows, sometimes give him a faintly Chinese air. From his days in China he recalls the advice of a friend who had lived there many years: 'Stop trying to understand these people – you never will. Just stick to what you want, and make your actions conform with your words.' It is a lesson Monnet often quotes to those who embark on undue exegesis of, say, Gaullist foreign policy: yet at times he is very adroit at fathoming other people's minds. A local peasant owned a field adjoining his property, which Monnet was anxious to buy. His predecessor as owner had been refused, and so was Monnet – until he bought a larger and better-hearted field elsewhere in the village, and offered it in exchange. His offer was instantly accepted: like had dealt with like.

A third influence on Monnet was his career in international banking. For a time, he was concerned in a Wall Street brokerage house, and made a fortune, which he lost in the 1929 crash. He was called in by the Polish government to plan a currency reform which it never carried out; he was also appointed one of the liquidators of the Kreuger match empire. From these experiences he derived a number of banker friendships; but he also acquired – if he did not possess already – something of the banker's judgement, feel and flair. Part of his skill lies in his ability to inspire confidence – and to gauge where and in whom he can place it. Many people, some very illustrious, confide in Monnet as they might confide in their bankers or in a solicitor who was a family friend. They know that their secrets are safe with him, and they know that his advice will be worth considering if he feels capable of giving it at all. His judgement is not always borne out by events, and he has failed in several of his ventures: but his instinct is always to try, since unless you try (he will repeat) you never know if you might not succeed.

The number of ventures that Monnet has inspired, indeed, is something that no official *curriculum vitae* has yet adequately described. An American scholar, John M. Haight, is in the process of re-counting Monnet's role in the purchase of American aircraft during the second world war;[6] but it is still not widely realized how crucial was Monnet's contribution to the allied war effort, or to many features of the postwar scene. It was he who helped persuade France and Britain to coordinate their strategic and other supplies within a few months of the outbreak of war, instead of waiting nearly three years, as in the first world war. It was he who instigated the drawing-up of a balance-sheet showing the respective strength and

[6] John M. Haight, 'France, the United States, and the Munich Crisis', *Journal of Modern History*, Vol. XXXII, No. 1, December 1960, pp. 340–58; 'Roosevelt and the Aftermath of the Quarantine Speech', *Review of Politics*. Vol, XXIV, No. 2, April 1962, pp. 233–59; 'Les Négociations françaises pour la fourniture d'avions américains (I)', *Forces Aériennes Françaises*, No. 198, December 1963, pp. 807–39; 'France's First War Mission to the United States', *The Air–power Historians*, Vol. XI, No. 1 (January 1964), pp. 11–15; 'Les négociations relatives aux achats d'av-ions américains par la France pendant la période qui précéda immédiatement la guerre', *La Revue de l'Histoire de la 2e. Guerre Mondiale*, No. 58, April 1965, pp. 1–34; 'Jean Monnet and the Opening of the American Arsenal', paper read to the Franco-American historical colloquium, September 1964.

prospects of the German and Allied air forces, thereby stimulating the American aircraft orders that so much helped Britain to withstand the blitz. It was Monnet, again, who played a leading part in Winston Churchill's 1940 proposal for Franco-British unity; he even flew to the seat of the French government in Bordeaux on the eve of the French armistice in a last effort to prevent collapse.[7] As a member of the British Supply Council in Washington, he is said to have conceived the idea of Lend-Lease and to have coined Roosevelt's slogan 'the arsenal of democracy'; and he certainly helped foster the 'Victory Program' which contributed so greatly to the winning of the war. In Algiers, he was largely responsible for the bringing together of General Giraud and General de Gaulle, preventing the serious rift in French unity that their rivalry threatened to create.[8] After the war, he proposed to de Gaulle the formation of the French Plan, which he inaugurated, and attempted to secure joint planning by Britain and France.[9]

But the achievement most firmly associated with Jean Monnet's name, and most manifestly due to his efforts, is the establishment of the three European Communities; and it is here that the qualities he had already proved brought their most spectacular results. Until his private papers enter the public domain, some details must be omitted from the story: but so much has already been printed from various sources that it may be legitimate to attempt a synthesis, discreet though it must be.

Throughout Monnet's career, one theme constantly recurs. This is the need for collective action to solve problems that no nation can deal with alone. It underlays his first public activity, on the Inter-Allied Maritime Commission in 1916: it became explicit in his work at the League of Nations. It recurred once more in the second

[7] Max Beloff, 'The Anglo-French Union Project of June 1940', *Mélanges Pierre Renouvin, Études d'Histoire des Relations Internationales (Publications de la Faculté des Lettres et Sciences Humaines de Paris, Série 'Études et Methodes' tome 13)*, Paris, 1966, pp. 199–219; Winston Churchill, *The Second World War*, Cassell paperback edition, London, 1964, Vol. III, pp. 183–7; Charles de Gaulle, *Mémoires de Guerre*, Livres de Poche edition, Paris, 1959, Vol. I, pp. 80 ff; J.-R. Tournoux, *Secrets d'État. Vol. II: Pétain et de Gaulle*, Paris, 1964, pp. 426–41, prints a contemporary account by René Pleven, who took part in the project.

[8] Cf. Robert Murphy, *Diplomat Among Warriors*, London, 1964, pp. 223 ff., for a somewhat partial account of this episode; on Monnet's career in general, cf. also 'Then Will It Live . . . ', *Time*, Vol. LXXVIII, No. 14, 6 October 1961, pp. 20–7.

[9] Étienne Hirsch, 'L'Angleterre fera-t-elle antichambre?', *Les Cahiers de la République*, No. 51, Paris, January 1963, pp. 9–16.

world war, in the Franco-British Committee for Economic Co-ordination, and it inspired the proposal for Anglo-French union. Monnet's experience of the League, in particular, had taught him a fundamental lesson. He was already convinced by 1944, that the League's successor, the United Nations, would 'be only a "switch-board" through which nations can communicate with each other. It will involve no real giving up of sovereignty. "This is not going to happen on a world scale . . . and let us not blind ourselves this time by the picture of impressive machinery to the really tough things that need to be done if we are to have peace."'

The journalist who reported these reflections of Monnet's went on: 'What are those tough things? For Monnet, as for most Euro-peans, the toughest questions of all are Germany and European unity. Monnet would like to see . . . the great Rhine coal and iron fields run by a European authority for the benefit of all participating nations. . . . But this in turn implies a Europe far more unified than before the war. Here he would like to see not merely a "switch-board" association, but a true yielding of sovereignty by European nations to some kind of central union – a union that could cut down tariffs, create a great internal European market and prevent that race of nationalism "which is the curse of the modern world". But where to begin? And how far to go? And could England be brought in?'[10]

The last two questions remain unanswered to this day: but the first found its answer six years after it was put. By the spring of 1950, in fact, the time was growing ripe for what was to be the European Coal and Steel Community. The International Ruhr Authority, set up two years earlier, was becoming less and less compatible with Germany's emergent status as a European nation in its own right, and the country was beginning to chafe at external control. What was more, the allies themselves profoundly disagreed about how the Authority should work: the Americans found it too stringent, the French too lax; while the British position lay some-where between these extremes. Germany, meanwhile, was becoming understandably restive. In Monnet's view, the continuance of such external control over her, treating her as an object of policy rather than an active participant in the rebuilding of Europe, was both unjust and unwise. Meanwhile, the broader context of events was beginning to emphasize the need for action. Shortly after the

[10] John Davenport, 'M. Jean Monnet of Cognac', *Fortune*, Vol. XXX, No. 2, August 1944, pp. 121–216.

CDE–CSU victory in the August 1949, elections – the first to be held freely in Germany for sixteen years – Konrad Adenauer announced to a press conference in Bonn that the new German Federal Republic would seek to join both NATO and the Council of Europe.[11] In October, the Foreign Ministers of France, Britain, the USA and the USSR once more failed to agree on a German peace treaty; and Franco-German relations remained uneasy not only because of the Ruhr, but also on account of the Saar – a problem whose solution was made little easier by the signature of the Franco-Saar Conventions of 3 March 1950.[12] As spring approached, the 'cold war' was likewise hardening; and the United States continued to press for a greater German contribution not only to Europe's economy, but also to her defence.[13] In mid-April, the United States Secretary of State, Dean Acheson, proposed to Britain and France a conference of experts in London to prepare a meeting of ministers to be held there on 12 and 13 May. No one knew what its outcome might be.

In this uneasy, uncertain, and shifting situation Monnet saw both danger and an opportunity. The danger was a danger to peace, through the growth of a 'cold war' mentality; the opportunity might be to sublimate the German question, as it were, in the beginnings of unity in Europe. A small step in this direction might lead to others, and at length transform the whole context of relations between East and West. As usual, Monnet committed his thoughts to paper. He first communicated them, in the form of memoranda, to Georges Bidault, French Prime Minister, at the end of April and the beginning of May: but Bidault failed to react.[14] Shortly afterwards, Monnet saw Bernard Clappier, *directeur de cabinet* to Robert Schuman, the Foreign Minister. It was through Clappier that Monnet's proposal reached Schuman and formed the basis of the 'Schuman Plan' rather than of a 'Bidault Plan', as it might otherwise have done.[15] Schuman studied it over the weekend at his small country house at Scy-Chazelles, near Metz. On the following Monday morning, back in Paris, he telephoned Monnet: 'I accept,' he said; 'For me, it's decided.' He wrote a short introduction, and

[11] Cf. Don Cook, *Floodtide in Europe*, New York, 1965, pp. 110–12, for a vivid description.

[12] Text in *L'Année Politique 1950*, Paris, 1951, pp. 355–59.

[13] On 7 May 1950, in New York, General Clay, former American Commander-in-Chief in Germany, proposed re-arming the Federal Republic.

[14] Pierre Gerbet, 'La Genèse du Plan Schuman', *Revue Française de Science Politique*, Paris, 1956, Vol. VI, No. 3, pp. 525–53 (p. 544).

[15] *Ibid.*, pp. 543 ff.

revised parts of the text with the aid of Monnet and his staff, which included in particular Pierre Uri and Étienne Hirsch. On the morning of Tuesday, 9 May, 1950, he presented the paper to the cabinet: with its approval, he went ahead. That same afternoon, with Monnet beside him, he held the press conference in the Salon de l'Horloge of the Quai d'Orsay at which the Schuman Plan was made known to the world.[16]

EUROPE AND BRITAIN

Schuman himself confirmed very emphatically Monnet's role in this 'conspiracy of surprise'. He also pointed out the difficulty that he and Monnet now had in explaining the Plan to the British.[17] This, in fact, was Monnet's next major task. First on a trip to London with Schuman, then later in an exchange of notes, arguments were deployed at length to try to persuade the British to join. Schuman's own account of British scepticism suggests that he himself quite quickly abandoned hope of Britain's full membership; indeed, he told the Anglo-French press in London on 15 May 1950, that France would go ahead with only one other country if necessary, and that others might be associated rather than full participants.[18] But the Franco-British exchange of notes, in the French side of which it may not be fanciful to detect Monnet's hand, suggests a far more determined effort to secure British adherence.[19] First, on 9 May 1950 itself, the French Ambassador in London, René Massigli, called on Ernest Bevin, British Foreign Secretary, with news of the Plan; later in the day, it was transmitted in full to the Foreign Office. During his subsequent visit to London with Schuman, Monnet made it clear that 'the French Government felt it desirable that the acceptance by other Governments of the principles set out in the French communiqué of 9th May should precede any working out of the practical application of their proposals'.[20] Thereafter, little happened for several days. Then, on 25 May the French govern-

---

[16] *Allocution de M. Jean Monnet à Scy-Chazelles le 3 octobre 1965;* for date of French cabinet decision, cf. HMSO, *Anglo-French Discussions regarding French proposals for the Western European Coal, Iron and Steel Industries, May–June, 1950* (Cmd. 7970), p. 3.

[17] Robert Schuman, *Pour l'Europe*, Paris, 1963, pp. 164–8.

[18] Raymond Racine, *Vers une Europe nouvelle par le Plan Schuman*, Neuchâtel, 1954, pp. 62 ff.

[19] Cmd. 7970 (cf. Note 16, above).

[20] *Ibid.*, p. 6.

ment was able to announce to the British that Germany had accepted – partly as a result of a visit which Monnet had paid to Adenauer two days earlier. The French government pointed out, echoing Monnet and Schuman, that 'if it were desired to reach concrete results it was necessary that the Governments should be in agreement from the beginning on the principles and the essential undertakings defined in the French Government's document, but that the numerous problems which would arise from putting the project into effect would require discussions and studies which would have to be pursued in common. . . .'[21]

By an unlucky coincidence, however, this message crossed with one from London sent on the same day. In this, Bevin rejected the whole idea of an international conference based on a prior commitment of principle: he proposed instead 'direct conversations between France and Germany' in which Britain would like 'to participate from the outset, with the hope that, by obtaining a clearer picture of how the proposals would operate in detail, they would be able to join the scheme'. The same point was made even more clearly two days later, when Britain replied to the French Note which its own had crossed. 'If the French Government', it said, 'intend to insist on a commitment to pool resources and set up an authority with certain sovereign powers as a prior condition to joining in the talks, His Majesty's Government would reluctantly be unable to accept such a condition.'[22]

Behind this refusal was a misunderstanding which may or may not have been partly deliberate.[23] From Monnet's point of view, coal and steel were means to an end: what was vital about the whole proposed enterprise was its fundamental principle. Unless the countries that engaged in the negotiation were prepared to accept this principle as the basis of discussion, there was little point in

[21] *Ibid.*, p. 7. On Monnet's visit to Adenauer, cf. Konrad Adenauer, *Erinnerungen 1945–1953*, Stuttgart, 1965, pp. 336–7.

[22] *Ibid.*, pp. 7, 8.

[23] In *The Road to Brighton Pier*, London 1959, pp. 12–13, Leslie Hunter reports a story told him by Ernest Bevin, according to which, when the Schuman Plan was announced, Kenneth Younger went with Herbert Morrison, then acting Prime Minister, to Bevin's sickbed to discuss it. 'Bevin, always keen to bring on junior ministers, turned to Younger and asked, "Well young, man, what do you think of it all?" Younger was all for Britain joining in. Bevin listened attentively and then heaved a sigh. "Splash about, young man, you'll learn to swim in time," he commented and then turning to Morrison began "Now, 'Erbert . . . " and got down to the details of how to keep out of this embarrassing offer.'

talking: on any other basis, indeed, negotiation would probably be counter-productive. This did not mean, however, that every country which joined in the talks would thereby be actually committing itself to pooling its coal and steel production under the proposed High Authority: only the signature of the eventual treaty could commit it to that – and even then the treaty would have to be ratified by Parliament. The commitment requested was a commitment of principle: it was not the signature of a blank cheque.

Seeking clarification of this issue, the French Ambassador in London called next day on Kenneth Younger, Minister of State at the Foreign Office; and as a result of their meeting, the French government on the following Monday, 30 May 1950, made one last effort to explain the point: 'there will be no commitment,' it repeated, 'except by the signature of a treaty between the states concerned and its parliamentary ratification'.[24]

While a reply to this communication was awaited in Paris, the Dutch government sent a *note verbale* which itself cast further light on the point in dispute. It stated that while accepting the principle of the Schuman Plan as a basis for negotiation, it reserved the right, during the course of negotiation, to retract this acceptance if the principle proved inapplicable in practice. Superficially, this appeared to confirm and justify the British reservation. In fact, it did the reverse. On the one hand, it made clear that the Netherlands initially accepted the Schuman Plan's basic principle of pooling sovereignty – at which Britain still demurred; on the other, it merely spelled out more explicitly the normal right of withdrawal which, as the French Note made plain, was available to any party in the talks.

On the evening of 31 May, however, the British die was cast: a further memorandum came from London, and the answer was still no. From then on, in the exchange of notes and communiqués that followed, each side seemed more concerned with cosmetics than with convincing the other; and Britain's European fate was sealed for many years.[25]

Monnet's next role in the story was as president of the French delegation at the Schuman Plan negotiations; and here again he proved himself exceptionally persuasive. His fundamental achievement, perhaps, was as much the manner of the negotiation as its ultimate success: as Robert Schuman later put it, 'the six delegations were in some sense allies, pooling their knowledge and their good-

[24] Cmd. 7970 (cf. Note 16, above), p. 10.
[25] *Ibid.*, pp. 11 ff.

will'.[26] 'During the nine months that it took to turn the Schuman declaration into a treaty of one hundred articles and a number of annexes,' said one of the participants, '(Monnet) saw to it that neither the central objective, a European community, nor the proposed method, delegation of powers to common institutions, got lost in the mass of details about coal, steel, scrap, transport, wages, cartels, distortions and discriminations. More than that, he never allowed the negotiations to become negotiations in the traditional sense. Apart from the basic objective and the method laid down in the Schuman declaration and accepted by each of the Six before negotiations began he showed great flexibility. The delegations were not confronted with French positions, as would have been normal and indeed as they expected, but were invited to discuss, to contribute, to help find common answers to common problems. Monnet never defended a merely national and therefore of necessity a partial view, but tried to define the general interest of the community the negotiations were establishing together. Some of the delegates, formed in the tug-of-war of economic negotiations of the "Schachtian" decade, at first believed that they were simply being tricked when, during meetings, they saw the little group of Frenchmen around Monnet disagreeing among themselves just as much as with other delegations. How could one negotiate one nation's special interest in orderly fashion against another's, if the inviting delegation seemed to have no clear view of the national interests it wanted to defend? But Monnet's method was so contagious, the attempt to find solutions for common problems instead of defending simply one's own national interests was so liberating and exhilerating, that none of the chief delegates resisted this new approach for very long. Monnet thus succeeded in creating out of these hard-boiled negotiators a group of ardent Europeans, many of whom later came to Luxemburg to make the community work.'[27]

THE HIGH AUTHORITY AND ITS INFLUENCE

In Luxemburg, the High Authority that the Schuman treaty ultimately set up was itself the embodiment of this new method of together seeking and identifying the common interest. Originally, the Schuman declaration had proposed no Council of Ministers: during

[26] In a lecture given in 1953 at the College of Europe in Bruges.
[27] Max Kohnstamm, 'The European Tide', in Stephen R. Graubard (ed.), *A New Europe?* Boston, 1964, pp. 140–73 (pp. 151–2).

the negotiations, the Dutch delegation put the idea forward, and
it was accepted – not as a 'concession' to the Dutch in exchange for
some *quid pro quo*, but as a good idea which at length appealed to
everyone. Together, the High Authority and the Council of Ministers established what Monnet was later to call 'a permanent dialogue
between a European body responsible for proposing solutions to
common problems and the national Governments, which express
the national point of view' – while 'the Parliament and the Court of
Justice underline the Community character of the whole'.[28] As first
president of the High Authority Monnet was largely responsible
– after one or two false starts – for setting the tone of this dialogue;
and the method continues in the institutions of the European
Economic Community.

Monnet's first role in Luxemburg was essentially that of a pace-
setter. When he took up his duties he was sixty-three years old, but
he exhausted many who were half his age.[29] He called the first,
ceremonial meeting of the High Authority for 10 August 1952 – a
Sunday, and ten days after the vast majority of Frenchmen and
others would normally have left for their summer holidays. The
first working session took place on the following afternoon; and
from then on the pace never slackened. Lights burned until all
hours of the night in the High Authority's offices, ultimately established in the former headquarters of the Luxemburg national
railways; officials' weekends were invaded by urgent meetings; on
at least one occasion, Monnet summoned an assistant from the
woods, where he was having a Sunday picnic with his family. Some
newcomers complained that Luxemburg was far from the gayest
of capital cities: '*L'Europe ne se fera pas dans les boîtes de nuit*', is said
to have been Monnet's reply. How did he wring such hard work and
such loyalty from his multinational team? Partly by working just
as hard as his staff. One evening, he was due to leave on a long-
awaited family holiday: hotel rooms had been booked, seats reserved, and baggage packed; but the High Authority was meeting,
and Monnet insisted on staying until its business was dispatched.
One by one, urgent messages were passed to him: there were only
a few minutes to go before the train left – it had gone – so had the

[28] On the Council of Ministers, *ibid.*, p. 152n; quotation from Action Committee for the United States of Europe, *Déclaration commune du 26 juin 1962*, in
Recueil des Déclarations et Communiqués, Lausanne, 1965 (cf. Note 5, above),
pp. 111–17 (p. 114).
[29] He himself took an enforced rest in the summer of 1954.

one after that; but one by one, he brushed them aside. Work came first, recreation second. It was a difficult time for officials' families: but to the officials themselves it was a time of great exhilaration if sometimes of exasperation too.[30]

Monnet's way of working, moreover, was as exhilarating as the pace he set. He drove the members of his staff hard, almost autocratically: but at work together they enjoyed – as they still enjoy – a sense of intellectual equality with him. Part of Monnet's strength derives from his unpretentiousness. It would be misleading to call him modest, as one of his assistants has pointed out;[31] but he has no intellectual vanity. He has no scruples about putting the simplest and most naïve of questions: 'why do we need tariffs?' is one example that comes to mind. The endless discussion which is his method of tackling problems is therefore able to get to the root of most questions, to accept no answers ready-made; and one of its by-products is the inclusion in the debate, on equal terms, of anyone who thinks he may be able to contribute, or from whom Monnet himself hopes for a fresh view. At the Paris headquarters of the French Plan, several of whose officials accompanied Monnet to Luxemburg, one secret of Monnet's success had been to bring round the table all those involved and affected – officials, employers, trade unionists producers, consumers.

For once, there was no sense of exclusion or of *fait accompli*: participants were treated as equals, and everyone had the right to his say. This method Monnet transplanted to Luxemburg; and one of its most striking results was to win over to the 'European' cause a number of people who had been initially hostile. Paramount among these had been the German Socialist Party, led by Kurt Schumacher, until his death in 1952. His successor was Erich Ollenhauer; and he and Herbert Wehner regularly attended meetings of both the ECSC Common Assembly in Strasbourg and its parliamentary committees in Luxemburg. In the words of Max Kohnstamm, at that time secretary of the High Authority, 'their trade union friends told them that they got more information in Luxemburg about what was going on in German heavy industry than they ever had obtained at home. Monnet never tired of explaining the need for and the way towards European unity. On closer acquaintance there seemed to be nothing sinister about either

[30] Private information.
[31] François Duchêne, quoted in John Brooks, *The European Common Market*, Buffalo, N.Y., 1963, p. 67.

the man or his concept. Very few of the leading politicians and trade
unionists failed during those years in Luxemburg to discuss privately
and at length the problems of the day and of Europe with Monnet.
They never found him seeking power, or keeping secret from one
the thoughts which he had exposed to another. They also found,
him open to their own questions and problems, not brushing these
aside but trying to relate them to the common task and problem [of]
uniting Europe. The grapevine, the secret telegraph which later
seemed to link "good Europeans" in every one of the six countries
and which contributed so much to the success of European integration, owed its origin to these conversations. . . .'[32]

During his years in Luxemburg, Monnet faced a number of
'European' tasks. One, obvious enough – and overwhelming enough
in its novelty and magnitude, was to set the Coal and Steel Community on its feet. At the same time, he sought in particular to
achieve the closest possible relations with Britain, partly in the
hope that by doing so he might induce her to join. As it was, he
secured her 'association' with the Community; but it soon became
clear that the British regarded this as a *terminus ad quem* rather than
a half-way house on the road to membership.[33] But beyond these
particular tasks, Monnet continued to pursue the more general
purpose of uniting Europe outside the field of coal and steel. It
was he, as René Pleven has revealed, who had originally proposed
what became known as the 'Pleven Plan' for a European Defence
Community when Pleven made it public on 24 October 1950;[34] a
year later, Monnet had joined Averell Harriman and Sir Edwin
Plowden as executive members (the so-called 'Three Wise Men') of
the Temporary Committee of the NATO Council appointed to
report on the external security needs and the political and economic
capabilities of the member countries.[35] It was natural, therefore,
that he should follow very closely the gradually darkening fate of
EDC. When it finally came to grief in the French National Assembly
on 30 August 1954, many 'Europeans' in Luxemburg and elsewhere
feared that the whole process of unifying Europe had come to an
end; but Monnet has never been easily discouraged. On a similar
occasion some years later, when one of his assistants described a

[32] Kohnstamm, *op. cit.* (cf. Note 27 above), p. 155.

[33] Cf. Gilles Anouil, *La Grande-Bretagne et la Communauté Européenne du Charbon
et de l'Acier*, Issoudun, 1960, esp. pp. 107 ff.

[34] Georgette Elgey, *La République des Illusions 1945–1951*, Paris, 1965, p. 462.

[35] NATO Information Service, *Facts about NATO*, Paris, n.d., p. A3 1, 1.

disastrous political setback as *'déprimant'*, he looked up, blinked, and said *'Non: mais c'est attristant.'*[36] Almost as soon as EDC failed, in fact, he began a fresh series of talks with his network of friends throughout the Community of the Six, debating with them what could be done.

By November 1954, these talks had reached a point at which Monnet felt that his continued presidency of the High Authority was a hindrance rather than a help to him in promoting further steps towards European unity. On 11 November, he announced that he would not seek re-election when his term of office expired in the following February – 'in order', he said, 'to be able to take part with complete freedom of action and speech in the construction of European unity'.[37] What form this 'action and speech' might take was still unclear: one of his advisers even suggested that he might stand for the French Assembly – a suggestion he quickly rejected.[38] The full record of his journeyings, his meetings, and his innumerable telephone calls during the autumn of 1954 and the spring of 1955 has yet to be published; but as one historian has put it, 'it was . . . an open secret that he was in very close touch with the Benelux Governments and with others within the Six who were working on plans for the *relance* – the "relaunching" of Europe'.[39]

As his discussions continued, the focus of attention shifted from the idea of 'action and speech' by Monnet himself towards the idea of collective action by 'Europeans' in the Six; and in February, 1955, when a more 'European' French government led by Edgar Faure succeeded that of Pierre Mendès-France, which had left EDC to its fate, there began to be some prospect of governments, as well as private citizens, fostering a *relance*. Its precise scope remained a matter of some controversy. Paul-Henri Spaak, then Belgian Foreign Minister, was said to favour extending the Coal and Steel Community's powers to other related sectors of the economy, such as transport, and the other forms of conventional energy; J. W. Beyen, the Netherlands Foreign Minister, preferred to abandon the 'sector' approach to integration, and embark on a general common market such as had been mooted by the 'Ad hoc Assembly' set up at the time of EDC to prepare a European Political

[36] Personal knowledge.
[37] Richard Mayne, *The Community of Europe*, London, 1962, p. 107 and n. 1.
[38] *Ibid.*, p. 109; private information.
[39] Miriam Camps, *Britain and the European Community 1955–1963*, Princeton/London, 1964, p. 21.

Community; and Monnet's own foremost pre-occupation was with
the idea of a Community organization for the peaceful uses of
atomic energy.[40] Edgar Faure, for his part, rather more guardedly
called on 13 April 1955, for 'certain formulae of European co-
operation (sic) for atomic energy', and stressed that while there
might be some European organization for other forms of conventional energy and transport, it would not necessarily be the ECSC.[41]

RALLYING THE POLITICAL FORCES OF EUROPE

The scene was now being set for what was to become the crucial
meeting of the Six. The new French Foreign Minister, Antoine
Pinay, was due to meet Adenauer in Bonn at the end of April to
discuss a number of bilateral problems, including the Saar, the
canalization of the Moselle, and the strengthening of economic and
cultural ties. The Benelux governments, which had mistrusted the
apparent bilateralism of Mendès-France's policies, were anxious that
such Franco-German contacts should as far as possible take place
within a multilateral European context; they therefore proposed
that Adenauer and Pinay hold their talks in the margin of a special
meeting of the six foreign ministers during the last ten days of the
month. As it turned out, this would have been inconvenient for
Adenauer, and it was finally agreed that a meeting of the Six be held
later. Meanwhile, however, anxious to put his own ideas on record,
Beyen made a speech to the Netherlands Council of the European
Movement, meeting in The Hague on 21 April, calling for a study
to be made of general economic integration, on supranational lines.[42]
When Pinay and Adenauer met as arranged on 29 and 30 April,
their final joint communiqué stated that they 'were agreed in thinking that the time has come to give a new impulse to European co-
operation' (sic): but they singled out, as possible fields for action,
transport, air navigation, aeronautical construction and research on
atomic energy and its peaceful use.[43]

Spaak and Beyen seemed thus to have forced the pace: but there
appeared to be still disagreement both about objectives and about
methods. Presenting the High Authority's annual report to the

[40] Miriam Camps, *Britain and the European Community 1955–1963*, Princeton/
London, 1964, p. 21.
[41] *L'Année Politique 1955*, Paris, 1956, p. 381.
[42] *Ibid.*, p. 382.
[43] *Ibid.*, pp. 375–6.

Common Assembly on 9 May 1955, Monnet argued that there was
no essential contradiction between extending integration to new sectors and pursuing general economic integration. In response, on
the following Saturday, 14 May, the Assembly voted a unanimous
Resolution calling on the six foreign ministers – whose meeting
had now been set for 1 June 1955, in Messina – to 'charge an inter-
governmental conference or conferences to work out, with the
appropriate aid of the Community's institutions, the necessary draft
treaties for the achievement of the next steps in European integration, of which the establishment of the European Coal and Steel
Community was the beginning'. On the previous day, moreover, the Assembly had asked Monnet to 'intervene' with the
six governments to ensure that its views on social policy were
heard.[44] The *relance* was thus firmly linked with the High Authority
and its interim president, Jean Monnet. Meanwhile, moreover,
on 18 May, the three Benelux governments sent to their partners
in the Six the memorandum on European economic integration
which Spaak and Beyen, in particular, had drawn up in its final
form.[45]

It was in these circumstances that Monnet now took what seemed
to some an extraordinary step. One purpose of the Messina meeting
was to be the choice of his successor as president of the High Authority; the name of René Mayer was already being canvassed in Paris.
But on 21 May 1955, Monnet wrote a letter to the six governments
which he gave to the press three days later – just before the French
cabinet met to agree on its proposed candidate. In his letter Monnet
stated that 'in the face of the relaunching of policy undertaken by
the governments, it would not be understood if I were not to
declare myself ready once again to participate directly in the development of the task undertaken, should the governments wish to
confirm the desire that several of them have insistently expressed to
me'.[46]

This has generally been interpreted as a bid for re-appointment
to the presidency of the High Authority. If so, there were arguments
in its favour. The 'anti-Europeans' in Edgar Faure's cabinet – chiefly
the social republicans, represented in particular by Gaston Palewski,
General Koenig and General Corniglion-Molinier – may well have
had doubts about the candidature of so strong a 'European' as

René Mayer. But if Monnet's name were also in the running, Mayer might be presented as a 'compromise' nominee. Similarly, a 'concession' of this sort on the part of the 'Europeans' might in compensation give them greater freedom on the matters of substance to be discussed at Messina. The unaccustomed ambiguity of Monnet's letter, moreover, left it unclear whether he was in fact offering his services as president of the High Authority or for some other task in the working-out of the *relance*: at this stage, it remained uncertain whether the two roles would be separate or not.

In the event, Monnet's offer was not accepted: René Mayer was adopted as official French candidate, and was shortly appointed by the Six. But on the day after the French cabinet meeting which refused Monnet's last-minute candidature, Edgar Faure was constrained to address a press conference in unusually 'European' terms. 'A true organization', he said, 'cannot be given too loose a formula, cannot become a mere club or a conference of ambassadors; if the term "supranationality" is alarming, let us say that nevertheless it must be given powers of decision.'[47] At Messina, the French government endorsed the constructive line of the Six. The task of working out the implications of the Messina Resolution, based largely on the Benelux Memorandum, but with echoes of the papers submitted by Germany and Italy, was entrusted to an inter-governmental committee presided over by Paul-Henri Spaak. The committee was assisted, moreover, by several of Monnet's closest associates from the High Authority – one of whom, Pierre Uri, became principal co-author of the eventual 'Spaak Report'.[48] The resultant Rome Treaties, establishing the European Economic Community and Euratom, were thus very clearly the offspring of Monnet and his friends. It was not merely that Monnet had played an important role behind the scenes of the *relance*, nor even that the treaties themselves embodied some of his essential ideas. It was also that even after Messina he continued – this time more publicly – to work for their realization.

THE ACTION COMMITTEE

The instrument he forged for this purpose resembled nothing so much as an institutionalization of his 'grapevine' or network of

[47] *L'Année Politique 1955*, Paris, 1956, p. 416.
[48] Mayne, *op. cit.* (cf. Note 27, above), pp. 108, 117–18.

European friends. Already, during the months preceding Messina, he had been travelling constantly between Luxemburg and Paris, Luxemburg and Brussels, Luxemburg and Bonn. He was always, it seemed, on the train or on the telephone; and even now, in the first days after his leaving the High Authority, the round of talks did not stop. By now, the idea of some kind of 'European' Action Committee had begun to crystallize. Throughout the summer, with only brief respite, Monnet continued his visits to the capitals of the Six, talking incessantly and persuasively with political leaders and trade unionists. It had become a veritable recruiting campaign. At last, on Thursday, 13 October 1955, Monnet was able to announce to the press that thirty-one political and trade union leaders from all six countries, representing all shades of opinion except the extreme Right and the communists, 'have agreed . . . to take part in the establishment of an Action Committee for the United States of Europe'.[49]

Together with the announcement, Monnet made public the letter of invitation that he had sent to the committee's prospective members. This made clear that they would request their respective organizations to adhere, so that they themselves might be those organizations' delegates on the committee. It also described the committee's aims – 'to arrive by concrete achievements at the United States of Europe'. 'Its action will consist first of all, through its own intervention and that of its constituent organizations, of demonstrating to Governments, to Parliaments and to public opinion, their determination to see the Messina Resolution of 2 June made into a veritable landmark on the way to the United States of Europe. . . . It is indispensable that states should delegate some of their powers to European federal institutions representing the participating countries as a whole.'[50]

Among those who accepted these aims were Guy Mollet and Erich Ollenhauer for the socialists; Amintore Fanfani and Kurt Kiesinger for the christian democrats; Maurice Faure for the liberals; and Robert Bothereau, Auguste Cool, Walter Freitag, Heinrich Imig, Giulio Pastore and André Renard for the trade unionists. Other well-known figures who have since sat on the committee include Herbert Wehner, Willy Brandt, Fritz Erler, Léo Collard, Giuseppe Saragat, Heinrich von Brentano, Rainer Barzel, Paul vanden Boeynants, Pierre Pflimlin, Aldo Moro, Erich Mende,

---

[49] *Recueil* (cf. Note 18, above), p. 11.
[50] *Ibid.*, pp. 11–12.

Roger Motz, Giovanni Malagodi, Antoine Pinay, René Pleven, Ugo
La Malfa, Ludwig Rosenberg and Enzo Dalla Chiesa – to quote a
handful of names at random from an array that includes well over
half a dozen prime ministers, and one Chief of State.[51] It was and
still is the world's most illustrious and influential action group, and
has been described as 'something like the collective democratic
conscience of the European Community'.[52]

Since its creation, the Action Committee has held twelve meetings
and issued fifteen public statements: one meeting produced no
statement, and three statements (a press communiqué, a resolution,
and a joint declaration) were issued without a meeting being held,
while the most recent meeting produced both a joint declaration
and a resolution.[53] To the outside observer, the distinction between
'resolutions' and 'declarations' seems inevitably academic: what is
more pertinent is the manner of their drafting. Each normally begins
with a series of rough outlines produced by Monnet and his staff
on the basis of talks with the committee. These are discussed
repeatedly both within Monnet's small secretariat, and between
Monnet and the committee's members: a text may well go through
more than a hundred versions over a period of months. At length
a draft emerges which is fit for distribution to the committee:
Monnet and Max Kohnstamm, its vice-president, then intensify
the round of talks that has been proceeding on their travels round
the capitals; committee members meanwhile send their written
comments on the text. By the time the committee meets – usually
for a two-day session – there is normally a broad consensus on what
is to be said: but this by no means precludes very searching and
sometimes heated debate, which may lead to a thorough overhaul,
or even the replacement, of the proposed draft. During the night,
if agreement has been reached on the first day, the final text is
stencilled, translated and duplicated by Monnet's staff – eight people
in all, including four secretaries and encompassing between them
four nationalities and five languages. The committee holds its
final meeting on the following morning, and then presents its

---

[51] *Recueil*, pp. 13–14, 167–75.

[52] 'Setting the Pace for Unity', *Common Market*, Vol. IV, No. 6, The Hague,
June 1964, pp. 104–6 (p. 106); for an analysis of the committee's membership and
operations, cf. Walter Yondorf, 'Monnet and the Action Committee: the Forma-
tive Period of the European Communities', *International Organization*, Vol.
XIX, No. 4, 1965, pp. 885–912.

[53] Cf. *Recueil* (Note 78, above), *passim*.

statement in full to the press: by then, it is the official policy of the member organizations. Throughout this whole process, Monnet's role is crucial. Arguing, cajoling, intervening with suggestions, gently cutting short a fruitless debate or dissolving some apparently insuperable difficulty, he gives a remarkable and partly unwitting display of 'committee technique'. What impresses and persuades his hearers is his persistence, his patience, his seriousness, his good humour and the quickness of his reactions. He always seems willing to return to a point of detail if it involves a principle – or to accept a major change at a moment's notice if he thinks he has been wrong. Coupled with his painstaking preparations over the preceding months, it is this presidential skill that helps to explain how the committee is normally able to agree unanimously on its policy, despite its diversity of nationality and language, and despite the fact that its members in each country, on matters of domestic politics, may well be each others' bitterest opponents.[54]

It is largely through the Action Committee, then, that Monnet has played his most recent role in the unification of Europe. One of its first achievements was to help secure, from among some parties that had opposed or been divided over previous 'European' ventures, the conclusion and ratification of the Treaties of Rome.[55] It scored a spectacular success in this process when on 16 November 1956 the six Community governments followed the advice it had given on the previous 20 September, and appointed 'three wise men' to report on 'A Target for Euratom'. Although this nuclear power production programme was later scaled down, its publication undoubtedly encouraged the Parliaments of the Six to accept the Euratom Treaty.[56]

During the next phase of the committee's work, much of its attention was focused on the implementation of the Community Treaties. It pressed, to some effect, for the beginnings of a European energy policy, for firmer action against cartels, for steps towards monetary integration and for greater aid to developing countries. It called, unsuccessfully, for all the Community institutions to be centred in the same place. Its further proposal, made in November 1959, for the merger of the three separate Executives of the Coal

---

[54] Personal knowledge.

[55] The German socialists had voted against the ECSC, and the French Socialist Party had been split over EDC.

[56] Cf. Mayne, *op. cit.* (Note 27, above), p. 113.

and Steel Community, the Common Market and Euratom, was still
in practice pending at the time of writing – largely owing to disputes about persons between General de Gaulle and his Community
partners: but a detailed agreement on the subject was concluded
among the Six on 8 April 1965. Similarly, the Action Committee's
long-standing pressure for greater powers to be accorded to the
European Parliament has since been officially endorsed by the
Italian, Dutch and German governments; and this was one bone
of contention between France and the other members of the Community in the crisis of June 1965.[57]

The nature, as well as the apparent 'success', of the committee's
work has clearly been affected by the political difficulties within the
Community that first broke into the open when General de Gaulle
closed the door to British membership on 14 January 1963. During
the previous years, Monnet and the committee had gradually swung
round from a general endorsement of British 'association' with the
Community to active pressure for her membership, once they saw
that this was seriously envisaged in London. The full story of
Monnet's continuing efforts in this direction cannot yet be told:
nor is it ended. But in the confusion which followed the breaking-
off of negotiations, and which was increased by the death of
President Kennedy and the growing political tension within the
Community itself, the role of the Action Committee became perhaps
even more important, if very much harder to document. Essentially,
its task was to 'hold the line'. Already in June 1962 it had preceded
by one week President Kennedy's Independence Day call for an
'equal partnership' between united Europe and the United States;
and one of its main preoccupations now was to make this concept
more concrete, laying down thereby a general line of foreign policy
for the Community whose shape and extent it was at the same time
trying to define. Partly as a result of the committee's and Monnet's
efforts, the issues at stake within the Community, and the path that
a united Europe will one day pursue in international relations, are
now very much clearer: many of the committee's formulations, indeed, have passed into the everyday language of European politics.
How this has happened, and what precisely is the secret of Monnet's
ever pervasive influence, are matters that will need much deeper

---

[57] Cf. Miriam Camps, *European Unification in the Sixties*, New York, 1966,
pp. 62 ff.; John Newhouse, unpublished paper in the 'Tocqueville Series',
passim. For German, Dutch, and Italian positions, cf. *Recueil* (Note 28, above),
p. 136.

investigation; and here too the future historian may find himself at a loss. He would do well, however, to remember that if historiography is a matter of evidence and the written record, history – in Monnet's case at least – has often been made in ways that leave no trace.

Etienne Hirsch

Relations between the Officials of the European Communities and the Governments of the Member-States*

THE SETTING UP OF COMMUNITIES, ACTING THROUGH THEIR OWN powers and with competences of which the national governments have divested themselves by treaty, clearly needs an appropriate institutional framework. The development of the European Communities, their day-to-day existence raise problems in human relations which are particularly complex and delicate because of the fact that the actual means of coercion: army, police, fiscal and customs authorities, remain in the hands of the national states, accustomed, through centuries of tradition, to enjoy absolute and unrestricted sovereignty.

These difficulties are increased by the addition of novelty: the impossibility of referring to precedent or to well-established practices, as national administrations or traditional diplomacy can do. Thus a new style of relations has had to be invented and applied, which would both help to foster the dialogue indispensable for the mutual understanding of the needs and legitimate aspirations of each of the national partners, and assist in bringing about solutions of common interest and in accordance with the letter and the spirit of the treaty.

For this reason it is useful to have some concrete understanding of current practices and to search for the improvements by which a smooth functioning of the community could be achieved. This article cannot provide more than a summary exploration, with the hope of drawing attention to an important problem, worthy of more profound study. We will consider successively problems concerning members of the High Authority and of the commissions

* Vol. 2, No. 3, April–July 1967. The author wishes to underline that this article refers to the situation in 1967.

(to be called here, for reasons of simplification, the members of the executives, including, of course, the presidents and vice-presidents) and those concerning the directors of the administrations of the communities.

THE MEMBERSHIP OF THE EXECUTIVES

The first thing to take into consideration is the very special character of the status of these members, which can be said to have a dual nature. By the method of his appointment, through a common agreement between the governments, the member concerned can be said to be an international official. But once he has been appointed, he is responsible during his term of office, only to the European Parliament; thus it is clear that he also has a political status. This is strengthened by the terms of the treaty which stipulates that:

> The members of the Commission fulfil their function quite independently. In the carrying out of their duties, they will neither ask for nor accept instructions from any government or outside organ. They will refrain from any act incompatible with their office. Each member-state undertakes to respect this character and undertakes not to try to influence the members of the Commission in the course of their duties.

In order to understand and to appreciate the nature and the object of relations between the membership of the executives and the national governments, one must have some idea of the mechanism by which the main decisions are taken in the Communities.

This mechanism can be described essentially as a dialogue between the executive concerned and the Council. The executive is responsible for the expression and defence of the general interests of the Community and must express and defend the interests of the Community and watch over the application of the treaty. The Council, made up of representatives of the member-states, is the defender of the particular interests of the various states. The executive is responsible for preparing proposals which it alone, except when there is unanimity in the Council, can amend. The Council debates the proposals in the presence of the executives and decides, according to the subject, by a simple majority, a qualified majority or unanimously. (There are appreciable differences in procedure in the

case of the Coal and Steel Community, but current practice has
tended to reduce them.)

The preparation of proposals is not a purely technical operation.
A solution which is perfect in theory is worthless if it has no hope
of being accepted. Thus the members must not only have an objective knowledge of the problems and of the concrete difficulties
which must be overcome in the different countries, but should also
be able to assess the subjective reactions of the governments. Hence
the need for frequent contacts with the political authorities in order
to understand their reactions, to explain to the governments the
solutions under consideration and the positions which have been
taken, and to defend them.

It is here that, according to temperament, the members can, without actually betraying their promise to remain independent, allow
themselves to be, to a greater or less degree, influenced by the objections which they encounter and be led to practice a kind of self-
censorship. In order to fulfil their mission properly, they must
constantly fight against the natural tendency on the part of any
authority in power to resist changes which are themselves always
a source of political difficulties. They must, like great seducers 'know
just how to go too far' and must not hesitate, when the stake is
important, to use the whole weight of their authority to force a
favourable decision. Thus President Hallstein made several representations in Bonn in order to obtain a positive attitude in the
establishment of a single price for wheat, a first stage in the agricultural common market.

The Council has a built-in tendency to postpone a decision, even
when unanimity is not mandatory, unless such unanimity can be
achieved by compromises and bargaining which rarely serve the
common interest. I remember how difficult it was to obtain the
first majority decision in the framework of the Treaties of Rome.
The question was not an important one, but the fact that it had not
been solved blocked for many months the adoption of the statute
on the officials of the community. Finally, when the decision was
taken, even the member of the Council who was in a minority was
pleased with the result, because he could go home without having
given way. This precedent later led to the present procedure of
approval of the budget by a qualified majority.

From time to time, serious difficulties have arisen from the fact
that governments had agreed beforehand to oppose an executive.
During an official visit to Bonn of the Commission of Euratom,

Adenauer asked us if we had any complaints against his government. I replied that we had and explained that the Commission was treated as though it were the Soviet government, in the sense that whenever the question of meeting it arose, the governments undertook mutual consultations as though they were preparing a reply to a note from Moscow. Upon which the Chancellor proposed that in case of any serious difference with his government, the German member and one other member of the Commission should take part in the meeting of the federal cabinet. Such a meeting did take place, with very satisfactory results, but the practice has not been continued and has not been extended to other governments.

Now let us come to the problems of the persons involved. The application of the treaties establishing the Community is, strictly speaking, the setting in motion by peaceful means of a genuine revolution. Without dwelling here on the more remote purposes of the 'ever closer union between the European peoples' conjured up by the preambles to the treaties, the daily problem was and remains how to surmount the resistance to change of all the governments. This resistance is particularly fierce when the problems discussed involve sovereign rights and entail the transfer of some of these rights.

Only men endowed at the same time with competence, independence, conviction and strength of character are equal to such a task. But it must be admitted that the selection of members of the executive has gradually strayed far away from the spirit, if not the letter, of the treaties. Appointment by common agreement among the governments has become simply a rhetorical formula. In fact, each government proposes a member or members of its own nationality and the proposal is approved, not so much in the light of its intrinsic merits but provided there is a *quid pro quo*.

Such a deterioration is extremely dangerous. The setting up of a single Commission to replace the High Authority and the two Commissions has come to grief precisely on the question of the appointment of its members and of its president. Meanwhile the mandates of all the members of the Commissions have expired in January 1966. If this has not led to the paralysis of the institutions through the dissolution of the Commissions, it was thanks to a provision of the treaties themselves whereby a member remains in office as long as he is not replaced.

A corrective then must be found to the actual way in which

members are appointed. The allied problem of the procedure by which mandates are renewed must also be examined.

Mandates are renewed in the same conditions in which the initial appointments are made, that is to say by means of a common agreement between the governments. This clearly creates an obstacle to the genuine independence of the members. If a member, as is natural, wishes his mandate to be renewed, he is bound to behave in such a way as to earn the goodwill, or at least not provoke the hostility of any of the governments, above all of his own. But even so his situation remains precarious, for considerations of internal policy, which have nothing to do with his behaviour, can always result in the fact that, no matter what services he has rendered, another candidate will be preferred to him.

In the search for solutions, it is premature to envisage those which could only come from a far reaching evolution of the Communities towards a federal state, and which would entail either the direct election of the executives or their appointment by an assembly chosen by universal suffrage. But very considerable improvements of a more immediate and more realistic kind could be expected from the intervention of the European Parliament.

Taking American constitutional procedures as an example, the appointment of officials could be submitted to the approval of the European Parliament which would decide by a two-thirds majority on the appointment of new members. This procedure would have a salutary preventive effect. Simply by existing it would correct the deviation which has occurred in the appointments procedure. It would also prevent the nomination of people who clearly do not have the necessary qualifications.

As for the renewal of the mandate, one could go even further because in this case the European Parliament would have been able to see the people concerned at work and thus to form its own opinion of them. It would thus seem possible and normal to refer back to the European Parliament decisions on the renewal of mandates without the intervention of the governments. Thus the independence of the members could be genuinely assured in relation to the governments.

THE OFFICIALS OF THE COMMUNITIES

European public administrations have had to be created from scratch. The task was all the more difficult because the qualifications required of a European civil servant are far greater than those expected of a national civil servant and no training exists to enable him to acquire them.

The requisite administrative or technical knowledge should comprise familiarity with the legislation, practices and problems of all the member states. A European civil servant should also have some understanding of differences in attitude, outlook and tradition and be able to adapt himself to them, otherwise the dialogue and co-operation with national officials may lead to difficulties and give rise to constant misunderstandings.

Another difficulty is that of language. The four languages: German, French, Italian and Dutch are officially on an equal footing. A high-ranking European official, if he is not to be handicapped in his daily tasks, must be fluent in at least two, as well as English which is indispensable in many cases. This greatly reduces the choice of candidates.

Lastly, the officials must give unquestioning loyalty to Europe. They must have no national bias, while at the same time they must not fall into the opposite error, of being moved by prejudice against their own country in order to guard against any such bias.

Contrary to the pessimistic warnings of those who believed that the creation of a genuinely European civil service was impossible, an undeniably European idealism was born from the first and has survived. Men of different nationalities, outlooks and customs have been welded into homogeneous and efficient teams, devoted to the common good.

This has been rendered easier by the methods of recruitment adopted during the setting up of the first community, the Coal and Steel Community. Most of the directors were chosen from among those who had taken part in the negotiations for the treaty of Paris. For a year they had the opportunity to familiarize themselves with the problems and above all to get to know one another and to weigh each other up. They worked together on something of which they were proud. During the creation of EEC and of Euratom, the same method was adopted, although to a less degree, but it was possible to benefit from the transfer of a considerable number of officials at every level, who had been employed by the first community.

The recruitment of highly qualified officials has been facilitated by the existence of a strong current of European idealism. It has been helped by the fixing of salaries which, although considerably lower than those paid by international organizations were, all things considered, higher than those paid by the national administrations. On this last point, however, the situation has gravely deteriorated in the last few years, since the rise in prices has not been adequately offset by adjustments in remuneration, which now clearly lag behind those given by the national administrations.

In spite of their youth and the brevity of their experience, the European administrators in general measure up to their duties. They are able to fulfil their role both in the frequent exchanges of views which they have with their opposite numbers in the national administrations, and in the framing of policies for the Communities and the preparation and implementation of directives. This is largely due to the fact that the multinational teams benefit from the continuous emulation within them and from the way in which the professional qualities and mental attitudes of their members complement each other.

But there are two problems which, if they are not solved, may gravely affect the working of the administration of the Community.

In order to fill a certain number of important posts, it was necessary at the beginning to rely on national officials who were seconded from their own civil services and who, after several years spent with the Communities, return to them. This practice has been maintained although internal promotion should often have supplied replacements. Moreover, it is the governments themselves which put forward the replacements for the officials whom they are recalling. This is obviously dangerous for the independence of the administration of the Communities and discourages those officials who wish to make their career within them. To be sure, it is all to the good that national civil servants should spend some years in a European administration, and should learn to know it, to understand it, to become familiar with its problems and should thus tend to smooth relations between it and the national governments. It would also be extremely useful if, reciprocally, European officials were to be called upon to spend several years in a national administration, if possible in a country other than their own. But in order to avoid further inconveniences, it would be advisable if acceptance by the Community of officials drawn from the national administrations were restricted to the lower ranks.

The other danger threatening the European administration results from the problem of the balance between nations. It is right that a balance should be sought in the composition of the body of officials, except for those in the lower ranks who are mostly recruited on the spot. This balance should be observed both in the numbers and the sharing out of high level posts.

But this has crystallized into such a rigid form that every post of director general or of director has become the fief of a particular nation. It needs an incredible effort to replace a German by a Dutch director general. Things even threaten to go further. I came up against very strong objections when a Flemish Catholic Belgian was replaced in the post of director general by another Belgian, but who was a socialist and a Walloon.

Clearly in these conditions one cannot make the most suitable choice. What is more serious, however, is that within each service, the opportunities for promotion are limited by considerations of nationality, which hamper the advance of those who could hope by reason of their deserts, to make careers in the service, and discourage the best.

What is the remedy? Above all the executives must be protected against the pressure brought to bear by the governments. Somehow the executives must be forced to overcome the internal difficulties facing them. Here again, the best answer may well be to have recourse to the European Parliament and, as in the United States, to submit appointments to important posts to the endorsement of a representative organ.

Democratic structures and practices are the only safeguard for the building of Europe. Only the searchlight of public explanations and discussions will free it from secret pressures and overcome the inevitable internal difficulties.

(Translated from the French)

Stephen Holt

British Attitudes to the Political Aspects of Membership of the European Communities*

ONE DOES NOT NEED TO BE A PARTICULARLY CLOSE OBSERVER OF THE political scene to be aware that politicians do not always mean what they say. It has always been true that those who excercise political power, or who aspire to do so, have to consider the feelings of the people or groups on whom they are dependent. This consideration governs the choice of the words, the emphasis and the timing of the statements made by the actors on the political stage. In this kind of play, moreover, the script itself is liable to change according to the mood of the audience and only by studying the audience can one make any sense of the plot. For an absolute ruler the audience is usually a small, tightly knit group with whom he can conduct his dialogue in private. In the mass liberal democracies of the 20th century the audience is huge, consisting of a large number of groups of varying importance, and much of the dialogue has to take place in public. The long British debate about the advisability of going into the Common Market has been conducted in front of an interested audience of unprecedented size – i.e. not just Britain but the whole of the Commonwealth, the countries of the EFTA, the United States and the prospective partner countries of the Common Market. The latter, in their turn, have differed among themselves. Even though English is the world's richest language, no skill in the choice of words could hide the conflicts in this myriad of interests. When making a speech to the Labour Party or to Parliament, Harold Wilson could never prevent President de Gaulle from listening and collecting useful quotations. At the Press conference in the Elysée in May 1967 which effectively vetoed our second application, de Gaulle said :

> There are many reasons for thinking that there are formidable
> obstacles to overcome, as, for that matter, the British Prime

* Vol. 6, No. 4, Autumn 1971.

Minister himself has stated with his deep experience and great foresight.[1]

All these complications would have been quite enough on their own, but the whole debate has been attended by a further and equally unhelpful factor. Not only has Britain's relative position in the world been changing in the last 25 years, but the attitude of different groups in the country to what this role should properly be has also been changing. Unfortunately, these two sets of changes have been going on at a different rate. This helps to explain the confusing picture of whether the debate since 1961 has really been about the price of butter or about a major change of political direction for Britain. Those in both Conservative and Labour Parties who have thought the former have been joined by others who for one reason or another did not want to commit themselves. Mr Jo Grimond articulated the feelings of those who take the latter view in a speech in 1962 : 'Is one of the great political decisions in history to be reduced to a question of 5% more or less on the tariff on canned peaches? It is as if at the Reformation someone had said they were unable to make up their mind until they knew what price the monasteries were likely to fetch.'[2]

HISTORY OF BRITAIN AND EUROPE

In facing the challenge of the Common Market Britain has not only had to contemplate changes in long established trading relationships, but a break eventually with her political traditions as well. The latter prospect has hit a particularly sensitive nerve ; foreign observers often see more clearly than the British how much this country is a prisoner of her history. In historical terms, it is hard to dispute the conclusion of Friedrich Heer when he wrote :

England does not belong to Europe. Since the eighth century England has considered itself another world, *alter orbis*, circling the Continent like the comet on the Bayeux tapestry which was regarded as an omen of the Norman conquest in 1066. It was the same comet that Newton's friend, Halley, calculated in 1692. According to popular belief comets appear in times of crisis. Thus England has always intervened in the history of Europe when a

[1] *The Times*, 17 May 1967.

[2] Press release of speech to Liberal Assembly, 22 September 1962 (Liberal Party Press Office).

religious, spiritual or political balance was disturbed. . . . This
reaching out to Europe has usually ended with lightning retreats.[3]

A strong sense of history is taken utterly for granted in Britain.
Few Englishmen, for example, would think it particularly odd or
inappropriate that the Queen still gives a dinner every year at
Windsor Castle to celebrate our victory at the battle of Waterloo. A
Belgian acquaintance of the writer found it unbelievable after Britain
and France have been allies in two world wars that this ceremony
should be continued.

In literature on European integration since the second world war,
one frequently finds expressions of regret that Britain did not take
the lead in building a united Europe when the leadership was hers
for the asking. Many people on the continent felt that the statements
of some British leaders gave encouragement to the idea that such a
lead would be forthcoming. There was Churchill's Zürich speech
in 1946 and Clement Attlee said in *Labour's Peace Aims* 'Europe
must federate or perish'. But the statements of both men are only
really misleading if they are taken out of context. Referring to
the latter quotation in his autobiography Attlee explained that he
did not think such a proposition was immediately practical.[4] Similarly, any careful reading of Churchill's Zürich speech makes it
clear that Britain should be one of the 'friends and sponsors' of a
United States of Europe, not its leader, as the following passage
shows:

> In all this urgent work, France and Germany must take the lead
> together. Great Britain, the British Commonwealth of Nations,
> mighty America, and I trust Soviet Russia – for then indeed all
> would be well – must be the friends and sponsors of the new
> Europe and must champion its right to live and shine.[5]

However much in later years, with the benefit of hindsight,
British ministers may regret that the opportunity of giving a lead in
Europe was not taken, it would clearly have been psychologically
unthinkable straight after the war. While Britain was in a very

[3] F. Heer, *The Intellectual History of Europe* (translated by Jonathan Steinberg),
Weidenfeld & Nicolson, London, 1966, p. 348.
[4] See extract from *As it Happened* quoted in R. W. G. Mackay, *Towards a
United States of Europe*, Hutchinson, London, 1961, p. 108.
[5] See extract from Zürich speech in U. Kitzinger, *The European Common
Market and Community*, Routledge & Kegan Paul, London, 1967, p. 37.

serious economic and financial situation she attributed this to the perfectly respectable reason that she had made great sacrifices. Indeed, it is probably fair to say that rightly or wrongly, Britain regarded herself, along with the Commonwealth, as the principal moral victor of the second world war. All the other allies had skeletons in the cupboard somewhere. The Americans came in late, some of the French had given in and the Russians had to explain away the Hitler–Stalin pact. The opposition of Churchill to Munich allowed anyone to forget Britain's own skeleton if they wished. In this climate it is hardly surprising that the forging of new close relationships with a series of defeated nations was regarded in Britain as an entanglement to be avoided. It is true, of course, that even if these sentiments had not been present, the conflicting loyalties outside Europe – to the Commonwealth and the United States – would have taken priority. In placing Britain in the centre of three overlapping rings[6] – Commonwealth, Europe and the special relationship with the United States, Churchill articulated the feelings of most people in this country throughout the 1950s and for many into the 1960s and 1970s as well.

THE BRITISH CHANGE OF MIND

Why, then, was Britain prepared even to contemplate a change of political direction by 1961 when the first application to the Common Market was made? I suggest there are basically two answers to this question : (a) the government saw the economic facts of life in a different perspective compared to the 1940s and early 1950s ; and (b) most supporters of entry still believed that the political aspects of membership could be confined to such modest proportions that ties with the other two 'rings' need not be jeopardized. Some still believe this today and in the rest of this article we shall be considering this in more detail. But before doing so a point should be made about changes in the economic facts of life. While the facts themselves have changed, there has been an even bigger change in Britain in attitudes towards the facts. Technological advances, particularly in the fields of communications and computer science, have greatly extended the economies to be reaped from large scale commercial operations. On the other hand, even without these advances there was still a strong case for saying in the late 1940s that the nation states of Western Europe would not, in the long run,

[6] Speech to Conservative Party Conference, Llandudno, 1948.

be economically viable on their own. However, this was not the main argument used in support of European integration even in the early 1950s. The principal impetus behind the Schuman plan was political – to 'neutralize' the principal war industries of Germany and France and of any other European countries who cared to join. By the late 1950s, even countries like Sweeden and Switzerland with healthy economic records were recognizing the need to get into some larger grouping. The only disagreement between European states has been about how far reaching, economically and politically, these larger groupings should be.

The task of examining British attitudes to the political aspects of membership of the Common Market is complicated by the conspicuous desire of opinion leaders to avoid the subject whenever possible. The Common Market issue has been sensitive enough as a whole, but the political aspects of membership have been the most sensitive of all. In treading carefully, politicians have been mindful not only of the traditional outlook of public opinion, but of the fact that both major parties have been deeply split on the whole subject of entry. This partly explains why the issue has played such a small part in general elections. The British voter is always very unfavourably impressed with a party which appears to be split and to ignore this is a sure recipe for defeat. Divisions in both major parties have prevented each one from effectively exposing the divisions in the other. The absence of clear terms until June 1971 has also enabled forms of words to be drawn up which have kept together people who really disagree. It is also true, however, that the dates of the last four general elections have mostly coincided with 'off peak' periods as far as our European policy is concerned.

In the general election of 1959 the Common Market was not referred to in the manifestos of any of the three parties and it does not receive a mention in the index of the Nuffield study of the campaign. During the following Parliament, all three parties adopted some kind of a position on the subject but the French veto in 1963 removed it from the agenda. Brief and vague references appeared in the 1964 manifestos of all three parties, but Sir Alec Douglas-Home said that as an election issue the Common Market was dead.[7] In 1966 the Labour government's new European initiative had not yet been launched and as there was no evidence that the French veto had been lifted it is not surprising that our relations with Europe played hardly

[7] D. E. Butler and Anthony King, *The British General Election of 1964*, Macmillan, London, 1965, p. 132.

any part in the campaign. By 1970, however, the French veto had been removed and both parties had supported the opening of negotiations in the near future. Even in these circumstances, however, differences of opinion within the two major parties effectively ensured that discussion of British entry was kept in a low key. Two out of three of the major party candidates made no mention of the subject in their election addresses at all.[8] Tactics must have been the governing factor here because there is evidence that the voters were very interested. According to the 1970 Nuffield study, candidates who responded to a survey of issues most often raised on the doorstep listed the Common Market as second only to high prices.[9]

In view of the fact that election campaigns tell us so little about the European policy of the parties, we are confined to their party conferences and statements in the House of Commons. It would be simplest if we now take each party in turn and see how they have handled the political aspects of membership.

THE LIBERAL PARTY

The Liberals were not only the first party to support entry to the European Communities but have also gone much further in advocating the political advantages of membership. They also played some part, although probably not a decisive one, in pushing the Conservatives towards a change of European policy in 1961. They constantly put questions down in Parliament, divided the House on the subject in 1960 and began to emerge as a serious challenger at by-elections.

For the Liberals to embrace the idea of a customs union was for them an important change of policy. It represented a *de facto* abandonment of the party's traditional policy of free trade. The changeover was smooth because the leadership had the sense never to put the party through the traumatic experience of actually voting *against* free trade. Having accomplished the change of economic policy, however, the party accepted as early as 1960 the political implications. In a conference resolution supporting entry into EEC it was affirmed that the assembly 'accepts that the Common Market is a step towards the political integration of its member nations, and

[8] D. E. Butler and Michael Pinto-Duschinsky, *The British General Election of 1970*, Macmillan, London 1971, p. 440.
[9] *Ibid.*, p. 326.

urges Great Britain to take the lead in establishing common political institutions for Western Europe of which it is a part.'[10]

It was at the Liberal assembly in 1962 that the political aspects of membership of the Communities received most prominence. There were two major debates but in neither of the resolutions passed did the party go as far as supporting outright federalism for Europe even though such a step was clearly favoured by many of the delegates. Francis Boyd, reporting for the *Guardian*, records an incident in the first debate :

> Mrs Elma Dangerfield, the prospective candidate for Hitchin, asked a series of rhetorical questions expecting answers hostile to federalism. 'Do we accept that we want this country to go into federation', she asked – and was given a loud 'yes' for an answer.[11]

Sensing perhaps that the party was letting itself be carried away the president-elect, Lord Ogmore, made a special plea during the second debate that there should be no commitment to federalism, at any rate for the time being. In the event, the final resolution called for early and close political unity in Europe with a directly elected European Parliament. This was said to be an 'integrationist', not federalist approach.[12]

In 1965 the party went a little further in officially calling for 'supra-national institutions' and for defence and foreign policy to be subjected to the kind of institutional system developed within the Common Market.[13] In 1967 the party decided that the common European defence policy should be non-nuclear and voted down a contrary amendment.[14] This policy was given a topical shift of emphasis in 1969 in a resolution which called for an independent European foreign and non-nuclear defence policy aimed at reconciliation with Eastern Europe.[15]

While the Liberal Party has officially adopted the policy of federalism for the internal governments of the United Kingdom, it has not yet done so for Europe. There are undoubtedly, however,

[10] Resolutions adopted at Eastbourne 29–30 September–1 October, published by the Liberal Party Organization, London, 1960

[11] The *Guardian* Report, Liberal Assembly 1962, published by *The Manchester Guardian* and *Evening News*, p. 13.

[12] *Ibid.*, p. 45.

[13] The *Guardian* Report, The Liberal Assembly, 1965, p. 24.

[14] *Ibid.*, 1967, p. 31.

[15] *Ibid.*, 1969, p. 30.

a large number of European federalists among its active
members.

THE CONSERVATIVE PARTY

The Conservatives were the second party to change course for the
EEC. The initial reasons were economic as the party came to realize
that unless some positive steps were taken following the formation
of EFTA, Europe might consolidate into two rival economic blocs.
A resolution along these lines was passed at the party conference in
1960 but by the time the following conference came round the
government had decided to apply for full membership of the Common Market. The motives behind this change of policy were undoubtedly a mixture of economic, political and tactical. Besides
accepting the economic arguments, Macmillan and some of his
senior colleagues had also become convinced that there was evidently
insufficient buoyancy in the 'three rings' to which Churchill had
referred to keep Britain afloat as an influential world power and that
exclusion from the Common Market would ensure that her decline
in influence would continue. On the tactical side, after having won
three elections in succession, there were signs at by-elections and in
opinion polls that the party was losing its hold on the electorate
and some imaginative new policy would be needed to win another
election. The problem for Mr Macmillan was how, having seen this
far ahead himself, he could sell the whole idea to his party. The two
most sensitive areas, as events were to prove, were the effect on
British sovereignty if the Community realized the ambitions of
some of its founders and the damage that might be caused to the
Commonwealth by interfering with the trading privileges of its
members. It is perfectly clear by the way the Conservative Party
speaks about the Commonwealth in its debates that the organization's primary importance is seen to be *political*. Britain's leadership of it continues to give some credibility to the belief that she is
still a major world power with far reaching influence. This important belief is by no means confined to the Conservative Party and in
this difficult period of adjustment, the willingness of the Commonwealth countries to continue to work with Britain has greatly
softened the blow of losing an empire. The anxieties about the
damage to the Commonwealth were not to the forefront at the
beginning because government policy was quite explicit that
essential Commonwealth interests would have to be safeguarded if

Britain were to contemplate joining the Communities. When this proved much more difficult to achieve than anticipated and the negotiations dragged on, the pressure from the Commonwealth increased and reached embarrassing proportions by the time of the Commonwealth Prime Ministers' Conference in 1962.

It has been said that the Commonwealth is a product of British genius. The strength of the organization certainly lies in its great flexibility; member countries can see in it what they wish and can hold differing views about what it is for. The Conservative Party values it primarily as a vehicle for British leadership, but most of the member states are mainly interested in the economic relationships involved. The Economist Intelligence Unit carried out a survey which was published in 1960 about the effect on the Commonwealth of British participation, either in a common market or a free trade area. Those conducting the survey spoke to a great many responsible people in Commonwealth countries and learned that the great majority were ready to accept whatever the UK might find the best solution, so long as their exports would not be damaged.[16] Probably the most accurate description of the Commonwealth has been produced by J. D. B. Miller. After insisting that it is indeed a going concern, he has called it 'a concert of convenience'.[17]

When the Conservative government fixed their first party conference after applying for membership, anxieties were expressed not only about the Commonwealth but also about the possible surrender of British sovereignty. Mr Edward Heath made the now familiar analogy with other international organizations in which we had given up a degree of sovereignty in return for wider benefits. He went on to reassure the conference that there was no commitment to federation at this stage, although his words do not actually close the door:

> From the point of view of federation it would be a bold man who would say what the future of Europe would be in 15, 30 or 50 years' time. There are a wide variety of views in Europe about this today, but this much is clear: that no step can be taken towards any constitutional development without a further amendment to the Treaty of Rome and on both of these things each member country has a full right of veto, so that situation is fully

[16] *The Commonwealth and Europe*, The Economist Intelligence Unit, London, 1960, p. 474.

[17] *The Commonwealth in the World*, Duckworth, London, 1965, p. 271.

safeguarded and we should not frighten ourselves by false appre-
hensions about these matters.[18]

As we have seen, even the liberals have shrunk from advocating
outright federation for Europe in the near future. Both Conservative
and Labour governments have been repeatedly asked for assurances
on this point both in Parliament and at their party conferences.
They have invariably given them and in ten years their policies on
federation have not undergone any substantial change. There are
certain minor nuances about the way the question is answered.
Mr Heath has generally been more relaxed about the whole issue
and when returning to the same theme at the party conference of
1962 he took a similar line to the one in the above quotation, urging
his audience to take a pragmatic view.[19]

For the most part, however Conservative spokesmen have taken
a more obviously negative line as did Harold Macmillan in his
closing address at the 1962 conference. After reassuring his audience
about the need for unanimous consent before any moves towards
political union were made, he referred to the Treaty of Rome in the
following terms : 'It has its political implications ; but while close
cooperation is involved there is no question of our being asked or
expected to accept any system of a federal character involving the
sovereignty, in the true sense of the word of the Crown and Government and people of these islands.'[20]

Eight years later at the 1970 conference Geoffrey Rippon underlined precisely the same policy. He said 'There is no question of the
imposition of theoretical solutions from above; no threat of instant
federation.'[21] The use of the word 'threat' makes unmistakably
clear the attitude to the whole idea and it seems unlikely to change in
the near future.

While the opponents of entry in the Conservative Party will
doubtless continue to try and tie their leaders down to a rigid
position on the political aspects of membership, developments
inside the Common Market itself have set a good many fears at rest.
Majority voting in the Council of Ministers which Britain formally
accepted, both in the 1961-3 and 1970-1 negotiations, has never
been used on any issue of vital interest to a member state. For

[18] 80th Annual Conference, Brighton 11-14 October 1961, National Union
of Conservative and Unionist Associations, p. 54.
[19] 81st Annual Conference, Llandudno, 10-13 October 1962, p. 65.
[20] *Ibid.*, p. 149.
[21] 88th Annual Conservative Conference, 1970 – Verbatim Report, p. 60.

some time to come, the British can rely on the French to keep it that way. With regard to the alignment of foreign and defence policies, the slow progress that the Community itself has made in this sector has once again removed anxieties that we shall lose control over our own foreign policy. The first serious attempt at political union was under the auspices of the Fouchet Committee during 1961 and 1962. The Conservative government was in the awkward position of negotiating on the basis of the Treaty of Rome at the time and yet was unable, formally, to take part in the Fouchet Committee meetings. Nevertheless, the government supported the Bonn Declaration of July 1961 in which the Fouchet Committee was instructed by the Six to submit concrete proposals for political union. The mandate of the Fouchet Committee was not renewed in April 1962 for a variety of reasons. The Dutch and Belgians in particular had shown themselves unwilling to go too far until the question of British entry had been settled.[22]

The veto on the second British application in 1967 was followed by a series of plans by which foreign policy and possibly defence could be brought into some new political community including Britain. French opposition prevented these proposals getting very far and accordingly Britain did not reach the point of taking any very firm decisions.

The first serious steps towards political union since the Fouchet negotiations were taken following the Davignon Report of October 1970. This report did not make such ambitious proposals as the first Fouchet Plan of 1961 and its principal suggestion was that the foreign ministers of the Six should hold regular meetings at least every six months. It further proposed that an additional meeting should be held together with the four applicant states so that the latter could be kept informed. Once again, it was a Conservative government that had to react to these proposals. Referring to them at the Conservative conference of 1970 Geoffrey Rippon said 'The recommendations of the report of the six foreign Ministers on ways of coordinating foreign policy are quite modest; more modest, in fact, than what we have been trying to do in the Western European Union.'[23] The proposals have been implemented and the meetings of the Ten take place on convenient dates close to the meetings of the

[22] For an excellent account of the respective positions on political union of the Community countries themselves see Susanne J. Bodenheimer, *Political Union: A Microcosm of European Politics 1960–66*, Sijthoff-Leyden, 1967.

[23] 88th Annual Conservative Conference, 1970, Verbatim Report, p. 60.

Six. Now that the representatives of these countries have actually begun to face concrete foreign policy issues together it is more clear than ever that Britain is not going to find herself suddenly isolated and dragged off in some unwelcome direction in the conduct of foreign affairs. The pace is being taken very gently indeed. The realities of the situation seem to have given the government sufficient guarantees for Sir Alec Douglas-Home to say that Britain would go 'as far and as fast' as the rest of the European Community along the path of closer political union.[24]

The only remaining interesting question about Conservative policy on this subject concerns the possibility at some future time of Anglo-French co-operation in the manufacture of nuclear weapons. Edward Heath seemed to be in favour of this when delivering the Godkin Lectures in 1967. This was more important than it seemed because of the special responsibility which devolves upon the leader in the Conservative Party in determining policy. However, it is not being talked about at the present time because there are obvious problems about letting the issue complicate the Common Market negotiations. It is impossible to predict whether the issue will be revived later and if so, in what form.

THE LABOUR PARTY

Those responsible for maintaining the unity and cohesion of the Labour Party must often have wished that the Common Market would go away. The European challenge has touched the party at a number of sensitive points, some of them the same, others different from those that have worried the Conservatives.

Like the Conservatives, the Labour Party has expressed anxiety both about the *internal* effects of too great a measure of political integration between member states *and* about the effect on Britain's relations with the outside world of a common foreign and defence policy. The party has shown the same outright opposition to federation in Europe but for slightly different reasons. The Labour Party conference debates on the Common Market show quite clearly that fears about loss of sovereignty stem from the belief that future Labour governments might be prevented from implementing social-ist policies after other community governments had overruled them. At Conservative conferences, while delegates have also been con-cerned about this in relation to limitations on our freedom to trade

[24] *The Times*, 12 February 1971.

with the Commonwealth, they have seemed more interested in sovereignty *as an end in itself*. In the foreign affairs field, Labour has shown the same anxiety, but again on slightly different grounds. The Conservatives have wanted Britain to be free to exercise leadership in foreign affairs whereas the Labour Party have been more concerned about 'independence' in foreign policy. In other words, many Labour members would be happier if they could see Britain pursuing a genuinely *socialist* foreign policy even if other countries were *not* also following it.

Hugh Gaitskell's death at a very early stage in the common market debate prevents us from being very sure about which of his anxieties really had priority. But his objections to federation were clearly not just concerned with the obstacle to socialism. He faced the issue squarely in his now famous speech at the Labour Party conference of 1962 when he asked the delegates to consider what federation means. After suggesting that Britain might be relegated to the status of Texas and California he went on to say 'it does mean the end of Britain as an independent nation state'. It would, he said, mean 'the end of a thousand years of history'.

Freedom to pursue an independent foreign policy was the fourth of the 'Five Conditions' laid down in the NEC document which Gaitskell introduced. While neither the document nor Gaitskell's speech formally ruled out British membership of the Communities, the conditions laid down prescribed terms of entry which could never have been negotiated. This caused some embarrassment later when the Wilson government put in a new application in 1967. It was then necessary to show how the situation had changed since the five conditions were laid down. On foreign policy the approved policy statement had this to say : 'Our earlier fears about the drive for Federalism in the fields of foreign policy and defence have been allayed. There can today be no doubt that freedom to decide a nation's foreign policy is entirely compatible with Common Market membership.'[25]

The possibility that Europe might become a separate nuclear power has always been opposed by the Labour Party. In a resolution carried overwhelmingly at the 1969 Conference the party committed itself quite specifically on this point : 'Conference further rejects the proposal for a nuclear armed Federal European State,

[25] Report of the 66th Annual Conference of the Labour Party, published by the Labour Party, London, 1967.

including Britain.'[26] On several occasions while he was Prime
Minister, Harold Wilson specially underlined the continuity of
Labour thinking since Gaitskell's time on the question of supra-
nationality in relation to defence and foreign policy.[27]

PUBLIC OPINION

Politicians are not the only 'opinion leaders' in a liberal democracy
but they are of course the main ones in political affairs. The divisions
within the main parties to which we have referred have meant that
the lead given to public opinion on the Common Market issue has
been decidedly muted. The political aspects of membership have
been deliberately played down by most supporters of entry. When
they see their leaders prevaricating, British voters have not surprisingly developed erratic and sometimes negative reactions. Social
Surveys (Gallup Poll) Ltd. undertook a series of polls on Common
Market questions between 1961 and 1969.[28] Most questions do not
touch on the political aspects of entry but respondents were asked if
they thought it would be a good thing or a bad thing for Britain to
agree to have as the goal achieving closer political relationships
with members of the European Common Market. The answers
were :

	1961	1969
	%	%
Good	63	55
Bad	11	13
Don't know	26	32

In February 1969 people were asked 'Which of these three – Europe,
the Commonwealth or America – is the most important to Britain?'
The answers throw interesting light on the question of whether the
British are yet 'good Europeans' :

	%
Europe	21
Commonwealth	34
America	34
Don't know	13

[26] Report of the 68th Annual Conference of the Labour Party, p. 309.

[27] See *Hansard*, Vol. 717 (1272), Vol. 746 (326) and Vol. 746 (1093).

[28] Following figures taken from material supplied by Social Surveys (Gallup
Poll) Ltd., London, W.1. These questions last asked in 1969.

The questions were less general when Gallup International conducted a very detailed survey of public opinion in the countries of
the Common Market in early 1962. Even at that early stage, sixty
per cent of those asked favoured a common foreign policy for the
Six and only nine per cent were against.[29]

In conclusion, it would seem that the difficulties the British people
have had in feeling much enthusiasm for the political aspects of
membership of the Communities stem mainly from history. For
substantial periods in the past, Britain has been accustomed to
playing a leading role in world affairs. All peoples want their
countries to exercise a *special* role in the world – nowadays few can
and do want to exercise a *leading* role. But it is the prospect of leading
that arouses Britain's interest in the game. This is frequently evident
from speeches made by members of all parties and from the reaction
of ordinary voters on European or general foreign affairs questions.
Speaking in the House of Commons on 16 November 1966, George
Brown said: 'The issue today is not do we join Europe – we have
always been there. The issue is can we play such a role that from here
on the Continent shall be unified and we shall be effectively a leader of
it ?'[30] John Biggs-Davison in an earlier debate in 1961 had remarked
'as I move around among my constituents I find them hungry for a
British lead in world affairs'.[31] Anyone involved in active politics
during the last ten years and who has done much canvassing on the
doorstep will confirm how often these kinds of sentiments are
expressed. Even after the crises of Suez and Southern Rhodesia many
can be found who still take the view that 'it is time that Britain
went it alone'.

Finally, it is unfortunately true that one cannot lead others any-
where unless one is also going somewhere oneself. The long struggle
to secure access to the Common Market has delayed any firm decision
about a choice of direction for Britain in international affairs.
Whether it is still possible for her to exercise any kind of leading role
in or out of the Community is impossible to say. Those who hope
she can will take comfort from the fact that we live in a century
of rapid change. Who, after all, could have foreseen in the last
year of de Gaulle's presidency that by June 1971 a new French

[29] L'Opinion Publique et l'Europe des Six, 1962. Gallup International
(representé par l'Institut Français d'Opinion Publique, 20 rue d'Aumale, Paris
9e) p. 23.
[30] *Hansard*, Vol. 736 (446).
[31] *Hansard*, Vol. 643 (571).

president would be addressing his people on television and commending his policy of enlarging the Common Market. Who, also, would have believed that in the same evening a Gaullist deputy would be on British television having an argument with Douglas Jay?

Michael A. Wheaton

The Labour Party and Europe 1950–71

ON 3 OCTOBER 1971 AT ITS ANNUAL CONFERENCE AT BRIGHTON, the Labour Party committed itself, by a predictably large majority of 5,073,000 votes to 1,032,000, to a policy of opposition to Britain's entry into the EEC on the terms negotiated by the Conservative government. This Conference decision was the culmination of a shift in opinion in the party, which had taken place throughout the year. The opening of 1971, however, saw the Labour Party still formally committed to a policy favouring entry, provided adequate terms could be negotiated.

By early 1971 anti-Common Market groups within the Labour Party, organized by John Silkin and Brian O'Malley (the former Chief Whip and Deputy Chief Whip in the previous Labour government) began to campaign for support of a policy of opposition to British entry into the EEC. This group, which found the basis of its support among the *Tribune* group of Labour MPs, soon achieved a degree of success when in February a motion inspired by Silkin calling for opposition to the EEC attracted the signatures of 108 members of the Parliamentary Labour Party. This figure clearly illustrates the extent to which the anti-Common-Marketeers were able to find support beyond the confines of the left of the party. On the pro-Market side, 'The Labour Committee for Europe', included 80 members of the Parliamentary Labour Party. This group actively engaged in organizing meetings throughout the country, but never really extended its influence beyond the Parliamentary Party into the party as a whole. Equally, the 'Trade Union Committee for Europe', organised by Alan L. Williams a former Labour MP, singularly failed in its attempt to enlist support for entry from the trade union leadership. Opinion in the party as a whole and in the trade union movement was largely opposed to entry, and as the year progressed, the anti-Common Market groups found it considerably easier to gather support for their position than did those groups favouring entry.

Despite the operation of these anti-Common Market groups, Wilson's position throughout the first half of the year was a simple restatement of his support for Labour's official policy of approving entry provided the terms negotiated were acceptable. The degree of controversy generated within the Labour Party on the Common Market issue, however, made it clear that Wilson would soon have to make a declaration of support or opposition to entry if the party was to have a definable policy on the issue. The first indication that Wilson may have been having doubts about the EEC enterprise came at the end of May 1971 when, speaking at a gathering of European socialists in Helsinki, he was particularly critical of the terms so far negotiated on New Zealand and Commonwealth sugar. But whatever doubts Wilson felt about supporting entry, the party as a whole, as represented by the National Executive Committee, had reached the view that the Labour Party should adopt a policy of total opposition to the EEC on the terms negotiated by the government. At its meeting at the end of June the NEC agreed to a motion supported by James Callaghan, Barbara Castle and Ian Mikardo, which called for a special conference of the Labour Party on the Common Market issue once the government's White Paper setting out the terms of entry had been published. This move to hold a special conference was opposed by Wilson, who still appeared to wish to keep his options open at this stage of the EEC debate. But once this decision had been taken by the NEC, there could be little doubt that the anti-Common-Marketeers in the party would be successful in achieving their objectives, given that the block votes of the trade unions would be cast almost exclusively in their favour. Faced with the almost certain event that a special conference would vote overwhelmingly against entry it was clear that Wilson could not maintain his existing policy if he was to avoid a serious split within the Labour movement.

From early July, then, an increasing number of Labour MPs had come to believe that Wilson would soon declare himself against entry, and in a number of speeches in Parliament and elsewhere Wilson became noticeably more critical of the agreements so far reached on the EEC by Geoffrey Rippon. But Wilson still hoped to delay any final decision by the Labour Party on the EEC issue in the hope that his decision to oppose entry would appear as a considered political judgement and not as a policy stance dictated by the block votes of the trade union movement. To achieve such an appearance it was necessary that the final decision by the Labour

Party on entry be delayed until the October Conference at Brighton. Wilson was successful in persuading the NEC to accept such a policy and it was agreed that the special conference should be consultative, the final decision being delayed until the full Conference in October.

In the period between the NEC meeting and the special conference on 17 July Wilson clearly began to move against entry into the EEC. At a speech at Montgomery on 4 July[1] Wilson spoke negatively about the EEC and was particularly critical about the terms negotiated for New Zealand and the West Indian sugar-producing countries, and the effects of entry on Britain's balance of payments. But the essential theme of his speech was a call for party unity, and Wilson maintained that the Parliamentary Party had responsibilities to the movement as a whole. In emphasizing this theme of party unity, Wilson was clearly indicating that only by adopting a policy of opposition to the EEC could the Parliamentary Party avoid an open split with the national party as represented at Conference.

The publication of the government's White Paper on the EEC on 7 July further enhanced the anti-market trend in the Labour Party, but more important was the fact that it showed clearly that Wilson himself was moving in that direction. In particular, Wilson's criticisms of the government White Paper's failure to forecast the effects of entry on Britain's balance of payments was taken by many in the PLP as an indication of Wilson's forthcoming opposition. This critical stance taken by Wilson on the publication of the government's entry terms, may have accounted for the fact that the number of Labour MPs who had signed Silkin's anti-EEC motion had now risen to 128, a few short of an outright majority of the Parliamentary Party.

But whatever the shifts of opinion that were taking place within the Parliamentary Party, it was clear that a decision on the EEC at Conference would depend entirely on the block votes of a few large trade unions. It was already clear that the majority of trade union leaders were opposed to the EEC, and this position was confirmed when throughout July a number of unions meeting in conference formally declared their opposition to entry. In early July, both the ETU and the NUM voted against entry, thereby committing over one million votes at the Labour Party Conference to the anti-Common Market position. When the TGWU also voted overwhelmingly against entry on 15 July, committing another one million votes to the anti-EEC cause, it was clear that no Labour Party Conference would support a pro-Market policy.

[1] *The Times*, 5 June 1971.

Given the certainty that the special conference would vote against entry, Wilson had little option but to move clearly against the EEC. In taking this line, Wilson was supported by Healey and Crosland (both pro-Marketeers), thus leaving only 5 or 6 members of the Shadow Cabinet in favour of entry and virtually isolating Roy Jenkins at the top levels of the party.

It still remained unclear, however, whether the special conference, which was due to meet in London on 17 July, would agree to Wilson's request, accepted by the NEC, to delay the final decision on the Common Market until October. In the period immediately preceding the conference many trade union leaders expressed the view that the special conference should take the final decision, and, given the votes at their disposal, they could overrule the NEC's policy of delay. When the special conference finally met at the Central Hall, Westminster, delegates were asked to approve a motion from the NEC which stated, '. . . the National Executive Committee will at its meeting of July 28th agree in the light of the Special Conference on a definitive resolution on British entry into the EEC'.[2] In other words, the special conference was being asked to perform a consultative role. Immediately the conference began, however, a motion was proposed by Alf Morris, a long time anti-Marketeer, which called for the rejection of the NECs motion, thus allowing the conference to take a final vote on the issue. This motion of Morris's was defeated by 3,155,000 votes to 2,624,000 votes, and its rejection surprised many observers who had felt that it would receive the support of most of the trade union leadership. It was clear that the defeat of the motion was only achieved through negotiation between Wilson, Callaghan and a number of trade union leaders. It was common knowledge immediately after the conference that the text of Wilson's speech had been communicated to a number of trade union leaders who, seeing that Wilson was about to declare himself against entry, decided not to support Morris's motion. In particular, the switching of votes by such anti-Common Market unions as the Post Office Workers, the Agricultural Workers and the NUM, were decisive in the defeat of the motion and the success of the NECs policy of delay.

In his speech to the conference Wilson maintained that the policy of the Labour Party since its defeat at the general election had been consistent: the party would support entry provided adequate terms

[2] *Labour and the Common Market*. Report of the Special Conference of the Labour Party, 17 July 1971.

could be negotiated. With regard to the negotiated terms set out in the government's White Paper, however, Wilson stated that the agreements reached on New Zealand, Commonwealth sugar, capital movements and the budgetary contribution were all unsatisfactory. As he put it in his speech, 'The terms which were set out in detail in the White Paper of July 1967 and indeed made clear to Europe, are not the terms now before Parliament. It is irresponsible for anyone who knows the facts to assert otherwise.'[3] Wilson finally declared that he would not have recommended these terms for acceptance to a Labour cabinet.

There could be little doubt from the tone and content of Wilson's speech that he had now adopted a policy of opposition to British entry into the EEC, and that the entire Parliamentary Labour Party could be expected to follow Wilson's lead. Despite Wilson's move to opposition, however, at a meeting of the PLP held on the Monday following the special conference, Roy Jenkins spoke enthusiastically about his support for the Common Market. Jenkins's speech, which delighted the pro-Marketeers within the party, was taken by many to be an attack on Wilson's position, and there were demands from the left of the party that he resign from his deputy leadership. In the days following this meeting there were definite moves by Wilson, Callaghan and others attempting to achieve unity on the issue within the Parliamentary Party and avoid an open split. But despite Wilson's obvious desire for party unity, it was clear that a number of senior members of the party, including Jenkins, Houghton, Mason and Shirley Williams, were all prepared to maintain their pro-Common Market positions.

On 28 July a meeting of the NEC was called to finalize the Labour Party's position on the EEC. At this meeting it was agreed to present a resolution to the October Conference which called for total opposition to the Conservative government's EEC policy. The resolution itself, and a background document setting out the NEC's position, argued that the government's economic policies had so weakened the country that entry into the EEC would have disastrous consequences for Britain's future economic development. But the document emphasized that the Labour Party was only opposed to the terms negotiated by the government and not to the principle of entry itself.[4]

[3] *Op. cit.*, pp. 43–9.
[4] *The UK and the European Communities.* Labour Party Background Document, September 1971.

Given this decision by the NEC and opinion within the party expressed at the special conference, there could be no doubt that the pro-Market forces within the party would find themselves largely isolated at the Annual Conference. The mood of the party was clearly reflected in the fact that of the 24 resolutions on the Common Market presented for consideration at the Annual Conference, only 2 were in favour of entry.

Since the decision of the Annual Conference was a foregone conclusion, the debate on the Common Market lacked the drama that one would normally have expected on an issue of this kind. The NEC's case was put by Denis Healey, who, arguing mainly on economic grounds, stated that entry into the EEC would lead to an end to Britain's cheap-food policy and would place an intolerable burden on her balance-of-payments position. For both these reasons the Labour Party could not support entry. James Callaghan, following a similar line of attack on the EEC, accused Heath of selling out Britain's vital interests in the hope of reaching some closer association with Pompidou. Moreover, he promised that when a Labour government was returned to power it would seek to renegotiate the terms of entry.[5]

The huge majority in favour of the NEC resolution was thus predictable. Only four trade unions of any size voted against, the Clerical Workers, the Bleachers, the Iron and Steel Trades and the General and Municipal Workers, while the constituency parties voted approximately 3–1 in favour of the motion. This clearly reflected the strong anti-EEC mood of the party, and indeed a motion calling for total opposition to the EEC on any terms and the withdrawal of the government's application, although it was defeated, none the less attracted over two million votes.

Although Conference itself had voted overwhelmingly in support of the NEC's policy of opposition to the EEC, it still remained doubtful whether the entire Parliamentary Party would agree to this policy. It was this problem of party unity which clearly dominated Wilson's speech to the Conference on 5 October when he called on all Labour MPs to unite behind the Conference decision. As he put it, 'I call for a united party – what has divided us is an important policy issue, not an article of faith. The whole of the PLP will fight against the mass of consequential legislation. I cannot imagine a single member of the PLP who will not be in the lobbies against the Government.' The emphasis in Wilson's speech

[5] *The Times, Daily Telegraph*, 5 October 1971.

on the consequential legislation was widely interpreted by a number of commentators as meaning that the pro-Common-marketeers would be allowed to vote for the Common Market on 28 October in the vote in the Commons, provided that they voted with the Labour Party against all the subsequent legislation.[6] Such an interpretation was denied by Wilson, who personally assured Mikardo and Foot that the entire PLP would be expected to follow the party line and vote against entry.

The October Conference, then, had seen the Labour Party commit itself to policy of opposition to entry of the EEC. But this decision must be examined in the light of Labour Party's earlier responses to European initiatives. Such an examination will show, that apart from the European commitment by the Wilson government, the Labour Party has consistently in the post-war period been opposed to any involvement with Europe.

THE ATTLEE GOVERNMENT AND EUROPE

The Attlee government's attitude towards the development of an integrated Europe was one of suspicion. While this government was prepared to join in defence agreements with the European continent and to cooperate in a programme of economic recovery, it was only prepared to pursue such a policy on the basis of intergovernmental cooperation, and not, as some were proposing, on the basis of an integrated or federal Europe. Indeed, the NEC of the Labour Party actively discouraged its members from participating in The Hague Congress of May 1948, which attempted to galvanize support amongst European governments for a federal Europe. None the less, despite the Labour government's reluctance to participate in any European institutions, it was prepared to join the Council of Europe, although it was only prepared to accept the Council as '. . . a body for the formation of European opinion, and not as an executive authority which imposes its will upon governments'.[7] The British delegation to the Council of Europe, led by Hugh Dalton, negotiated to prevent the Council from ever becoming more than a mere consultative assembly. At no point was the Labour government prepared to see the Council develop real political powers.

[6] *The Times, Financial Times,* 6 October 1971.
[7] Quoted in Ulrich Sahm, 'Britain and Europe 1950', *International Affairs,* January 1967, p. 13.

The Labour government's attitude to the Council of Europe had clearly illustrated the suspicions harboured by it towards European institutions organized on federal or pre-federal lines. It was this underlying suspicion, and above all a concern for national sovereignty, which dominated the Labour government's attitude to the proposals put forward by Jean Monnet for the establishemnt of a European Coal and Steel Community. The details of the plan for the Coal and Steel Community were communicated to the British government on 9 May 1950 by Robert Schuman, the French Foreign Minister, and called for, '. . . the placing of the whole of the Franco-German production of coal and steel under a common high authority in an organization open to other countries of Europe.' The initial reaction to the plan by the British government, while not enthusiastic, was not wholly unfavourable. As Attlee said in the Commons on 11 May 1950, '. . . the government will approach the problem in a sympathetic spirit and desires to make it clear at the outset that they welcome the French initiative.'[8] But this apparently favourable response to the Schuman proposals masked a basic difference of view between the British and French governments. It became clear, after Monnet visited London between 14 and 19 May 1950, that the two governments disagreed as to the nature of the negotiations that were to take place on the basis of the Schuman proposals. The French insisted that the British government should accept in advance the substance of the plan, and that any negotiations should only be concerned with the practical application of these proposals.

This essential problem of the nature of the negotiations was dealt with in a series of notes exchanged between the two governments from 25 to 31 May 1950. There was little chance of agreement, given the British position contained in a note of 27 May, which stated that '. . . if the French Government intend to insist on a commitment to pool resources and set up an authority with certain powers as a prior condition to joining talks, the government would be unable to accept such a condition'.[9] On 3 June discussions between the British and French governments were broken off, and negotiations between the six European states for the establishment of a Coal and Steel Community began without British participation.

[8] *Hansard*, May 1950, Col. 515.
[9] *Anglo–French Discussions regarding the French Proposals for West European Coal, Iron and Steel Industries*, Cmd. Paper 7920, 1950.

At no time during this exchange of notes was the Labour government prepared to accept the Monnet notion of Europe. Indeed in Whitehall, the proposals were largely dealt with by a group of civil servants under the leadership of Sir Edwin Plowden, and the full cabinet does not appear to have given much serious consideration to the plan. As Kenneth Younger, who was Minister of State in the Foreign Office at the time, has written, '. . . a more serious impression made was that this was not really a serious proposal, but one more desperate manoeuvre by the French to make up for their failure either to split Germany up, or get the Ruhr industries placed under international control'.[10]

The rejection of the Schuman Plan reflected the Labour Party's deep-rooted mistrust of European institutions and this attitude is clearly illustrated in a document on European unity issued by the NEC in May 1950.[11] This lengthy statement of the Labour Party's position on Europe strongly opposed the establishment of any European institutions as proposed by Monnet, and even went as far as to oppose any further extension of the powers of the Assembly of the Council of Europe. As the document points out, 'No socialist party could accept a system by which important fields of national policy were surrendered to a European representative authority'. It goes on to argue that any Labour government must be free to pursue its own foreign and domestic policies without the possibility of any supranational controls, and also expresses fears that any European organization would be dominated by a permanently anti-socialist majority. The latter point was an important one, for many felt that the Labour government's programme of nationalization of the coal and steel industries would be placed in jeopardy if Britain joined the Coal and Steel Community.

The Attlee administration, then, paid little serious attention to the ideas of the European federalists. The Labour government saw the Monnet plan as a radical reshaping of national sovereignty, which would prevent the government from carrying out its economic and social policies. And the policies and priorities of the Attlee government in relation to the possibility of an integrated Europe established the framework within which the Labour Party was to approach the problem in future years.

[10] K. Younger, 'Comment on Sahm's Article', *International Affairs*, January 1967.

[11] *European Unity*. A statement issued by the NEC of the Labour Party, May 1950.

Throughout the 1950s little difference of view could be detected between the Labour and Conservative parties in their approach to Europe. Because the Maudling proposals for a Free Trade Area and the later EFTA project were simply inter-governmental trading arrangements and involved no commitment to a supranational Europe, the Labour Party was content to question the detailed application and not the substance of the policy.

THE LABOUR PARTY AND MACMILLAN

By the summer of 1960, it was clear that the Macmillan government was moving to a position which would allow it to apply for membership of the EEC. The Labour Party as a whole, however, remained sceptical about the whole EEC enterprise and in its report to the 1960 Labour Party Conference the NEC emphasised that if Britain entered the EEC the government's ability to pursue appropriate economic and social policies would be severely limited. It called upon the government to establish some form of trading arrangement between EFTA and the EEC as the only appropriate policy to be pursued.[12] Throughout the latter part of 1960 and early 1961, it became clear that there were considerable divisions within the Labour Party as to its attitude to the Macmillan negotiations, and given this division, it was equally clear that Gaitskell would have to adopt a policy stance which would prevent a split in the party, such as that which had recently occurred on the disarmament issue.

The first major debate within the Labour Party on the Common Market since the Macmillan government committed itself to entry took place at the Labour Party Conference held at Scarborough in 1961. Here the Labour Party rejected a motion calling for support for British entry into the EEC although it did at the same time reject a motion of outright opposition proposed by Clive Jenkins's union, ASSET. Instead the Conference adopted a resolution put forward by John Stonehouse, which called upon the Labour Party to oppose entry into the EEC unless, 'guarantees protecting the position of British agriculture and the EFTA countries are obtained, and Britain retains the power of public ownership and planning as a means to ensure social progress in the United Kingdom'. This motion could be seen as a positive one, simply as a demand by the Labour Party for adequate safeguards if Britain was to enter the

[12] Labour Party Conference Report 1960, p. 75.

EEC. But it was clear from Stonehouse's speech proposing the motion that it was intended to be negative and opposed to entry. As Stonehouse put it, 'I see no great value in being stampeded into an association with capitalist regimes, which would in fact give more power to international cartels than to elected parliaments'. This first major debate within the Labour Party had demonstrated that there would be little enthusiasm for any policy other than one opposed to the principle of entry.[13]

The year 1962 witnessed a hardening of positions within the Labour Party, although the position Gaitskell himself was to adopt remained uncertain. Indeed in January 1962, the Victory for Socialism Group on the left of the party criticized Gaitskell's neutrality on the issue and demanded that he should declare himself against entry. As the year advanced, in response to growing anti-Market feeling, Gaitskell appeared to be moving in a direction which would allow him to come out against entry. In a speech at Fulham on 16 April he attacked the government's handling of the negotiations; speaking on television on 8 May, he stated that he was generally in favour of entry, but added that, to go in on bad terms would really mean an end to the Commonwealth, it would be 'a step we would regret all our lives'. Further, in a debate in the Commons on 6 and 7 June on the current state of the negotiations, although the Labour Party abstained from voting, Gaitskell's contribution to the debate was decidedly negative in tone. He demanded that the government should only agree to entry provided that the negotiations were acceptable to the forthcoming Commonwealth Prime Ministers' conference, and dismissed the possibility of the Commonwealth existing in parallel with the EEC, should Britain enter.[14] Only George Brown and Roy Jenkins on the Labour front bench expressed themselves in favour of entry, and in general Labour Party contributions to the debate were critical. It was clear that a sizeable majority of the Parliamentary Party was opposed to entry.

Gaitskell's concern for the fate of the Commonwealth, highlighted in a number of speeches, appears to have been reinforced by a meeting of European socialist leaders which took place in Brussels on 16 July. Here Gaitskell clashed with Spaak, the Belgian socialist leader, on the problem of protection of the Commonwealth should Britain enter the EEC. Gaitskell seems to have reached the conclusion

[13] Labour Party Conference Report 1961, pp. 213–27.
[14] *Hansard*, June 1962, cols. 507–14.

that the federal Europe which Spaak was proposing was incompatible with the continued existence of the Commonwealth.

But one of the most important influences on Gaitskell's position was a meeting of Commonwealth Labour leaders, which took place in London, immediately prior to the Commonwealth Prime Ministers' Conference in September 1962. Here the delegates had before them the government's White Paper of August 1962, which set out the agreements so far reached on the EEC. At this meeting B. K. Lall, the Indian ambassador to Brussels, appears to have had a considerable impact on Gaitskell and convinced him that many countries such as India would suffer greatly through loss of trade if Britain entered the EEC. In a communiqué issued at the end of this meeting the participants stated that they did not believe that the agreements outlined in the White Paper were sufficient to safeguard the relationship between Britain and the Commonwealth. It was this meeting which finally brought Gaitskell down firmly on the side of those opposed to the government's policy.[15] In taking this line he was largely following the line supported by the majority of the members of the party, although there were still a large number of MPs not committed either way, who were prepared simply to follow the party leader's view.

The official position of the Labour Party with regard to British entry into the EEC was spelled out in detail in a statement issued by the National Executive of the Party on 29 September 1962. Here it was argued that Britain could probably play a greater world role within the EEC than it could do alone, and that it was this potential political advantage which constituted the real case for entry and not an uncertain economic advantage. The document listed the possible advantages and disadvantages of entry into the EEC, but in its conclusions it accused the Conservative government of causing a major crisis in Commonwealth relations, and of being prepared to make any concessions to the Six in a desperate bid for entry. The document set out five broad conditions which would have to be satisfied if the Labour Party were to support entry. These were:

(1) Strong and binding safeguards for trade and other interests of our friends and partners in the Commonwealth.
(2) Freedom to pursue our own foreign policy.
(3) Fulfilment of the government's pledge to our associates in EFTA.

[15] See R. L. Pfaltzgraff, 'The Common Market Debate in Britain', *Orbis*, Vol. 17, No. 3, Autumn, 1963 p. 293.

(4) The right to plan our own economy.
(5) Guarantees to safeguard the position of British agriculture.

These five conditions put forward by the Labour Party could be interpreted either as reasonable demands designed to protect certain vital areas of British interest or as an anti-Common Market statement. As Richard Crossman wrote '. . . the five conditions were not a piece of anti-Common Market propaganda, but a considered expression of the attitude adopted by the leadership of the Labour Party',[16] though it is hardly likely that agreement could have been reached on these points in any negotiations with the Six.

But whatever interpretation is placed on these conditions there could be no doubt of the Labour Party's position following Gaitskell's speech to the 1962 Labour Party Conference held at Brighton. In his speech Gaitskell attacked the government's handling of the negotiations and the case they had so far made out for entry. He opposed the notion of Europe organized on a federal basis, and saw British entry into the EEC as the end of the Commonwealth. As he put it in a now famous quotation, 'We must be clear about this, I make no apology for repeating it. It means the end of a thousand years of British history. You may say let it end, but my goodness it is a decision that needs a little care and thought'.[17] Gaitskell received a standing ovation for his speech attacking the Common Market, and the Transport and General Workers Union agreed to pay for one million copies to be distributed free of charge to party members. The speech delighted opponents of entry and dismayed its supporters, but it had the effect of pulling the uncommitted members of the party behind their leader in opposition to entry into the EEC. As Crossman put it, '. . . Gaitskell's declaration of outright opposition to entry on Macmillan's terms won him unprecedented popularity within his own party and for the first time compelled the general public to accept him as a genuine alternative to Macmillan'.[18]

Gaitskell's move to outright opposition was largely conditioned by his attitude to the interests of the Commonwealth, but it was also determined by a desire to avoid a major split within the party. Wilson's move to opposition in 1971 to a large degree parallels Gaitskell's in its concern for party unity. Unlike Wilson, however,

[16] R. H. S. Crossman, British Labour Looks at Europe', *Foreign Affairs*, Vol. 41, No. 4 July 1963, p. 740.
[17] Labour Party Conference Report 1962, p. 159.
[18] R. H. S. Crossman, *op. cit.*, p. 736.

Gaitskell was not faced in 1962 with a trade union movement largely opposed to British entry. Indeed, in 1962, apart from Cousins and Hill, all the other members of the General Council of the TUC favoured entry and, at the 1962 TUC Conference, a resolution calling for the adoption of a policy similar to that of the Labour Party failed to be accepted.

THE WILSON GOVERNMENT AND THE EEC

Considering what the Labour Party's attitude to the Common Market was in 1962, it is remarkable that, like the previous Macmillan government, the Labour government should have changed its policy by 1966 and decided to seek entry into the EEC. The 1964 general election campaign saw little public debate on the Common Market, whereas only two years previously it had been a highly contentious issue. The Labour Party's election manifesto condemned the Conservative government's humiliating attempt to gain entry into the EEC, and stated that while a Labour government would seek a closer relationship with Europe, its main concern in the field of foreign policy was the maintenance of existing Commonwealth relationships.

The early period of the Labour government's term of office was largely taken up by concern with domestic economic problems. But 1965 saw a revival of interest in the EEC by the Conservative and Liberal Parties, and there were signs that a number of leading members of the Labour Party were beginning to believe that membership of the EEC did offer a solution to many of Britain's economic difficulties. In a debate on foreign affairs in December 1965, the Foreign Secretary, Michael Stewart, stated that Britain was ready to join the Common Market if the right conditions could be found, and went on to say, that the Labour Party's five conditions were now easier to meet than they had been in 1962.[19] But whatever Stewart had to say about the five conditions, Wilson publicly at least was sticking to the traditional policy of non-involvement with Europe. As he said in reply to a question in Parliament, 'There is no question whatever of Britain either seeking or being asked to seek entry into the Common Market in the immediately foreseeable future'.[20]

During the 1966 general election campaign, the Common Market was more of an issue. The Conservative Party, now led by Edward

[19] *Hansard*, December 1965, col. 1724.
[20] *Hansard*, April 1965, col. 623.

Heath, pledged that it would attempt to enter the EEC at the earliest opportunity, while the Labour Party manifesto simply talked of establishing closer contacts with the European continent. In his one major speech on the Common Market at Bristol,[21] Wilson did not totally condemn the EEC although he did say that he was opposed to Britain entering any entity organized on a supranational basis. By the autumn of 1966, however, it became clear from a number of statements by members of the government, that the 1962 five conditions were no longer regarded as entirely relevant and that the government would soon announce a new attempt to negotiate entry into the EEC.

After much press speculation, the government made its announcement on 10 November 1966. In his statement to the Commons, Wilson announced that, after a careful review by the cabinet of Britain's relations with Europe, the government had decided to embark on a series of discussions with the governments in the EEC to explore whether negotiations for entry were possible. It was clear from his statement that Wilson was serious in this attempt, for as he said, 'I want this House to know that the Government are approaching the discussions with the clear intention and determination to enter the EEC if essential British and Commonwealth interests are safeguarded. We mean business.'[22] Indeed, a number of Labour MPs were clearly disturbed by this announcement and regarded it as a declaration of intent by the Prime Minister, rather than the announcement of a fact finding mission. Anti-Common-marketeers were even more disturbed when a few days later at the Lord Mayor's banquet, Wilson spoke with obvious enthusiasm about the EEC and likened the forthcoming discussions to the exploits of the old merchant adventurers of the City of London.

Early in 1967 Wilson and Brown visited each of the Six governments in the hope of gauging whether the climate was right to make an application. Taking into account the discussions, the cabinet met to discuss the issue and, on 2 May, an official announcement was made stating that the government intended to begin negotiations on entry into the EEC. This new initiative by the Labour government was debated in the Commons between 8 and 10 May and all matters relating to the EEC were discussed. In particular the Labour left were sharply critical of the government's new-found

[21] For the full text of Wilson's Bristol speech see U. W. Kitzinger, *The Second Try, the Labour Party and the EEC*, Pergamon Press, 1968, pp. 95–7.

[22] *Hansard*, 10 November 1966. col. 1540.

enthusiasm for Europe; the arguments used by Michael Foot against entry during the debate were typical of those used by others on the left of the party. Foot criticized the Common Market agricultural policy and its effect on domestic food prices, and further argued that Britain's relationship with the Commonwealth was more important than membership of the EEC. But the core of his attack related to the political implications of membership, and here Foot argued that the EEC was a narrow and inward-looking organization, which prevented any *détente* with the Eastern block. Clearly the left of the party had no intention of supporting the government's policy, and on 8 May, 74 Labour MPs signed a manifesto in *Tribune* opposing entry.

The final vote at the end of the debate to approve the government's policy was carried by 488 votes to 62 with 80 abstentions. In this vote 36 Labour MPs voted against their party, defying a three-line whip, while 51 abstained. The following day, seven Parliamentary private secretaries were dismissed from the government for abstaining.

Given the Labour Party's position on the EEC in 1962, we may consider at this point some of the reasons which may have accounted for this fundamental change of policy. With regard to the Commonwealth, which Gaitskell saw as the central issue in the debate, much had changed by 1966. The Indo-Pakistani war had clearly demonstrated the British government's impotence in dealing with inter-governmental disputes within the Commonwealth, while the declaration of independence by the Smith regime in Rhodesia had severely weakened the unity of the Commonwealth and lessened its appeal in the eyes of the British government. Moreover, on the economic front, the period 1962–6 had seen a considerable increase in trade with the EEC, and the Commonwealth no longer remained such a vital trading area. On the European front, the government had already demonstrated its disregard for the EFTA partnership, when it introduced a 15 per cent surcharge on British imports without prior consultation. But perhaps the most important explanation was to be found in the continued economic difficulties faced by the government at home. In a number of speeches Wilson constantly stressed the technological contribution Britain could make to Europe, and saw the EEC as providing a stimulus to Britain's flagging rate of industrial production. It is noteworthy that the decision to negotiate was taken at a time when the popularity of the Wilson government had reached a particularly low ebb, and it seems clear that Wilson hoped that the conclusion of successful negotiations would restore credibility to his government.

A certain degree of controversy now surrounds the extent of the Wilson government's commitment to entry in May 1967. Richard Crossman has argued, in an article in the *New Statesman* in February 1971, that there was no commitment by the Wilson government to enter the EEC, and that the government sought merely to negotiate in order to discover what precise terms could be obtained. Crossman declared that at no time did the cabinet make a collective decision to approve entry and added that 'it was clearly appreciated that the application had been made on the understanding that while entry into the Common Market was an objective of policy if the terms proved reasonable, it was just as much an objective to stay out if they proved too high'.[23] Crossman's view has been supported by Brian O'Mally, who was deputy-chief whip at the time. O'Mally states that the instructions given by the Whips Office to Labour MPs voting in May 1967 were that the government was simply committed to testing the price of entry and was not approving the principle of entry itself. George Brown, however, in a letter to *The Times* has contradicted this argument and stressed that the Labour cabinet was agreed on the desirability of British entry, and on this point he wrote, '. . . no body of people was ever more clearly committed in intention and in principle as the last Labour cabinet on this issue'.[24] Considering Wilson's statements at the time, it is difficult to believe that his policy was based on anything less than the desirability of British entry into the Common Market. Moreover, in the period following de Gaulle's veto of Britain's attempt to negotiate her entry in November 1967, the Labour government made it clear that it was still its policy to negotiate at the earliest opportunity. Indeed, in February 1970, Michael Stewart said in the Commons, '. . . the government's policy towards the EEC has been steadily based since 1967, we have made our application, it stands, we press it, we desire that negotiations should be opened, we are anxious that they should succeed'.[25] The Labour government's policy then from 1967 to 1970 remained basically unchanged, and undoubtedly had not the general election of June 1970 intervened, George Thompson would have begun substantive negotiations in the summer of that year.

[23] R. H. S. Crossman, 'The Price of Europe', *New Statesman*, 12 February 1971.
[24] *The Times*, 16 February 1971.
[25] *Hansard*, 24 February 1970, col. 997.

CONCLUSIONS

This cursory examination of the Labour Party's attitude to Europe since 1950 reveals a deep-rooted prejudice against participating in any European organizations. A considerable proportion of the Labour Party both within and without Parliament has consistently held the view that for Britain to participate in any supranationally controlled organization would seriously impair the Labour Party's ability to pursue socialist policies and priorities. This body of opinion has opposed any surrender of British national sovereignty. The Wilson government's decision to seek entry into the EEC appears to have marked a break in a fairly consistent policy, but it was a decision clearly taken for short-term political advantage. Released from the constraints and pressures of government by its defeat at the general election in 1970, the Labour Party rapidly returned to its traditional policy of non-involvement with Europe. However, it is more than likely that whatever may have been said in the current debate, had the Labour Party been returned to power in 1970, had it been subjected to the pressures of government, it would have negotiated with the Six, and accepted conditions of entry not substantially different from those agreed to by the Conservative government.

Emile Noel and Henri Étienne

The Permanent Representatives Committee and the 'Deepening' of the Communities *

THE NINETEEN YEARS DURING WHICH THE TREATY OF PARIS HAS been in force and the thirteen years of the Treaties of Rome have led to a development in the Communities which, in its extent, variety and depth, exceeds anything the signatories could have hoped for. The volume of derived Community legislation has increased considerably and it now governs important sectors of economic activity. The enlargement of the Communities provides the best confirmation of this success.

Furthermore, the dynamic force of the Community system has been such that the deepening of the Communities has extended far further than the areas delimited by the Treaty. More and more action has been undertaken in sectors at or beyond the limit of the Communities' responsibilities – not to speak of decisions taken on 'foreign policy', which, since 1970, have led to the introduction of procedures for political co-operation. Although the Europe of the Six has never been able – or wished – to give an institutional content to these 'extensions', they were to be sanctioned by the communiqué issued at The Hague, which noted that 'the Communities remain the original nucleus from which European unity sprang and developed'.

It is no longer possible to distinguish today in the deepening of the Communities between what comes strictly under the Treaties and what is situated in the sidelines or even outside, but is being tackled in the Community framework. It seemed interesting to follow the role of the Permanent Representatives Committee in the Communities as the action of the latter goes deeper and covers ever-expanding areas of European life. What have been the consequences of this twofold tendency on the Committee's power of decision and

* Vol. 6, No. 4, Autumn 1971.

on its relationships with the other institutions? What assessment can be made from an institutional point of view of this development?

THE COMMUNITY 'NUCLEUS'

The big 'first generation' of Community decisions consisted chiefly in the opening of frontiers between the Six and in the definition of the Community's stance vis-à-vis the outside world.

The opening of the internal frontiers was first aimed at the removal of obstacles to trade – customs duties, quotas and technical requirements. It necessitated the development of the first common policies – agricultural policy and policy on competition and economic and social co-ordination – and led to (limited) institutional development – the allocation of 'own resources' to the Community and reinforcement of the European Parliament's budgetary powers.

The establishment of a common system of protection facing the outside world was to be the first manifestation of the Community personality vis-à-vis non-member countries. Subsequently, the Community came to establish special links with a number of countries and to play a role of its own in the organization of world economic relations.

During this twofold development – internal and towards the outside world – Community procedure took shape and affirmed itself. The main decisions are taken by the Council, which is composed of members of the governments of the Six, on proposals from the Commission. The final responsibility for a decision therefore belongs to the representatives of the governments, but they must adopt a position in relation to a proposal drawn up by an institution whose task is to seek the interest of the Community itself. The Community process of decision therefore comprises an element of proposal and one of acceptance – and the system of the Treaties is designed to keep these components independent of each other and place them on a near-equal footing. It is here that the Community procedure differs profoundly from diplomatic procedure and likewise from that of the traditional intergovernmental organizations, whose secretariats more often than not have only a limited power of independence and political initiative.

The system developed in the Treaties of Rome, in particular the Treaty establishing the European Economic Community, has proved moreover to be in line with the latest ideas on business administration, in which the tasks of conception and invention are separate from those of decision-making, with the 'pole' of preparation having equal importance with the 'pole' of decision-making.

Finally, the Communities have become an important administrative reality and a vast system of confrontation. The central departments of the Commission alone comprise over 5000 officials and their administrative ramifications extend far beyond the activity of the Community's offices, since Community decisions are executed by administrations in the member states. The inventory of decisions taken in 1970 gives an idea of the size of this decision-making machinery.[1]

Being based on dialogue, the Community system bears little resemblance to the concept of government in the traditional sense of the word. The Community does not have a single head or a single leader. Decisions are collective and taken only after much confrontation of viewpoints.

The Communities have in fact been transformed into a vast convention. They are a meeting place for experts, ambassadors and ministers at hundreds and even thousands of meetings. The figures in the appendix are more eloquent on this point than any description.

It may be wondered whether this development has not sometimes had the effect of weakening the dialectical character of the Community system, causing it to glide in the direction of co-operation. It may also be wondered whether this system, well adapted to the nature and need of economic discussions, will function equally well when, for instance, the institutions have to administer a European monetary union.

[1] Community measures adopted in 1970

COUNCIL:	Regulations	249
	Decisions	71
	Directives	25
COMMISSION:	Regulations	2426
	Decisions	435
	Directives	3
	Recommendations	7

In 1970 the Council took 599 decisions in the form of 'A' items as against 497 in 1969.

The number of measures adopted by the Commission by written procedure was approximately 4000 in 1969 and in 1970 (including internal administration measures).

THE EXTENSION OF COMMUNITY RESPONSIBILITIES

The extension of Community responsibilities to problems which did not really come under the Treaties has in the main been the consequence of the execution of the Treaties themselves or of the more far-reaching exploitation of the possibilities they offer. As it became more complete, the implementation of the measures required by the Treaty for individual sectors – dismantling of customs tariffs, ban on certain aids, common agricultural policy and so on – had ever-wider repercussions on other sectors of economic activity. Consequently, the Commission has come to adopt a global view of problems and has taken to setting out its broad ideas no longer in 'proposals' as understood in the Treaty, but in vast memoranda which are veritable statements of policy: preparation of a medium-term economic policy, definition of an industrial or a monetary policy, survey of a stage-by-stage plan for economic and monetary union.

It was inevitably felt, when the practical consequences of these general guidelines were drawn, that the legal instruments provided by the Treaty were sometimes incomplete or insufficiently effective. In some cases recourse to Article 235 of the EEC Treaty – which allows the institutions to take measures not specified in the Treaty but essential for the setting-up of the Common Market – has permitted a purely Community solution. In many other cases it was necessary, to overcome opposition or differences of interpretation between institutions or between member states, either to accept mixed formulae or solutions whose Community nature was attenuated – for example a decision by the Council and governments of the member states or a decision by the governments of the member states meeting in the Council – or to resort to special procedures – for example the establishment of committees *sui generis* in which the representatives of the governments and of the Commission sit as equals under a neutral chairman as if there were seven delegations (this is the case of the Medium-Term Economic Policy Committee and other committees generally modelled on the Monetary Committee).

The results achieved by these means are considerable. Even if the conclusions at which it has been possible to arrive have only rarely been of a normative nature, the value of the marriage of minds must not be underestimated. The political decision taken in 1969 at The Hague summit to embark on the road to economic and monetary union was the spectacular result of a long process of 'ripening'

which began as far back as 1962 with the Commission's first proposals on the co-ordination of economic and monetary policies.

Co-ordination of economic and monetary policies was laid down
in the EEC Treaty. As, however, this Treaty affords the institutions
only limited opportunities for action, the Council and the Commission have had to set up a complex system of co-operation between
member states and institutions. It works through a number of
committees, already referred to in the preceding paragraph, modelled
on the Monetary Committee, established under the EEC Treaty.

The monetary difficulties of the last few years have made these
procedures more and more important, while at the same time revealing the limits of their possible effects. In the Commission's view
these are transitional procedures until revision of the Treaties makes
it possible to supplement the Community's powers and give the
institutions new responsibilities. The resolution adopted by the
Council on 22 March 1971 on the stage-by-stage introduction of
economic and monetary union largely confirms this line of thought
by laying down that the measures leading to the full union can be
adopted before the end of the first stage, i.e. in 1973, on the basis, for
example, of Article 236 of the EEC Treaty (which deals with revision
of that instrument). What is done in this sphere will have a decisive
influence on the future of other extensions of Community action,
which are reviewed rapidly below.

In the matter of scientific and technological research – in all sectors not covered by the Euratom Treaty – despite a political agreement on the utility of Community-type developments, expressly
mentioned in The Hague communiqué, divergences on procedures
and responsibilities have up to now more or less paralysed any action. Indeed, the resolution adopted by the ministers on 31 October
1967, which constitutes in some way the charter for this field, does
not settle the question whether it is a matter of a Council measure or
of an agreement between governments, for both terms have been
inserted in brackets in the text.

A procedure for studying the matter has been established on the
pattern of the committees already described for economic and monetary policies. But after four years' work no substantial decision has
yet been taken.

The concepts of Community regional policy and industrial policy
were put forward at a later stage, the basic memoranda being submitted by the Commission in 1969 and 1970 respectively. What is
needed is to combine in one package decisions to be taken on the one

hand by the Community's institutions – some by the Commission itself as in the matter of aids and agreements, others by the Council on a Commission proposal – and on the other hand by the central or local public authorities, without prejudice to support to private initiatives by the two sides of industry or occupational groupings. Hence the novelty and complexity of the problems.

Talks in the institutions are directed at present to finding a flexible framework for co-ordinated and concerted action comparable to those used in the economic and monetary sphere, it being understood that such concerted action should not stand in the way of adoption of rules that the institutions may already take, or even an extension of strictly Community action on the basis of the already-quoted Article 235.

A radically different process has been chosen for employment, for here the Treaties stipulate only relatively lightweight procedures. A Standing Employment Committee was set up in 1970 under the chairmanship of the President of the Council, which is a kind of round table of national ministers, the Commission and both sides of industry. The Committee is called in before the institutions, that is the Commission and the Council, take decisions which may have a direct or indirect influence on employment policy in the Community. While this new force of Community-concerted action at the highest level between those with political responsibility and employers and employees has been developing, the Community has provided itself with an improved instrument for taking practical action in this field by reforming the European Social Fund.

Lastly, the holding of joint meetings – meeting of the Council and Conference of Representatives of the Member States – on matters of justice (June 1971) and education (held in the autumn of 1971) points to the interpenetration of matters dependent on the Community nucleus and its extensions. These steps are, however, too recent for as assessment to be made of the probable results.

AMENDMENTS TO THE TREATY

One of the most striking discoveries, which arises from an examination of this remarkable evolution of the integration process, is how few amendments have been made to the basic texts which determine the structure and the powers of the institutions. However, there has been no lack of opportunities since 1958. The institutional crisis which the EEC went through in 1965–66 did not cause any change in the texts or in their uniform interpretation. The merger of the institutions, which took effect in July 1967, led to a simplification of the structures but did not affect in the slightest the powers of each institution and their mutual relationships (with the exception of a special provision concerning the Permanent Representatives Committee). The merger of the Treaties, planned in connection with that of the institutions, was put off *sine die*. Finally, the institutional adjustments which have been agreed on should the Communities be enlarged, involve merely a transposition of the rules and procedures which are applicable to the Six.

Since 1958 only two changes have been made in the institutional system of the Rome Treaty. These two changes differ greatly in their scope.

As was pointed out above, the Merger Treaty (Article 4) officially integrated the Permanent Representatives Committee in this system; in the Treaties of Rome it had only been mentioned as a future possibility, to be created under the rules of procedure of the Council.

No change was made in the tasks and powers of the Permanent Representatives Committee, as Article 4 ('a Committee consisting of the Permanent Representatives of the Member States shall be responsible for preparing the work of the Council and for carrying out the tasks assigned to it by the Council') merely repeated what had already been laid down in the rules of procedure.

The establishment of the Permanent Representatives Committee as an institution – justified by the amount of work which it does – sets the seal on its main, or even exclusive, role, in preparing·the work of the Council. However, there are some notable exceptions to this rule.[2] Furthermore, the former practice has been continued whereby all groups depending on the Council are set up directly by the Permanent Representatives Committee which is responsible for their organization and watches over their functioning. However, the committees which have a special status (such as those responsible both to the Council and the Commission) have maintained their autonomy.

Despite the limits to which it is subject the strengthening of the powers of the European Parliament, which took effect on 1 January 1971, at the same time as the system of 'own resources' was introduced, has a much wider political significance. This is, however, the

---

[2] Particularly as regards agriculture (preparation by the Special Committee on Agriculture).

beginning of far-reaching transformations and not, at the present stage, of any substantial modification in the balance of power within the Community. When the Treaty introducing these measures was signed, the Commission officially announced its intention of submitting, by 1973, further plans on increased budgetary (and legislative) powers for the Parliament, and the Council took note of this intention, stating that it 'will examine these proposals in the light of discussions which are to take place in the Parliaments of the Member States, the development of the European situation and the institutional problems to which the enlargement of the Community would give rise'. This examination could take place at about the same time as that of the institutional changes which economic and monetary union would render necessary (cf. page 102).

Arrangements have therefore already been made for the position of the institutions to be examined when the enlargement of the Community has become a fact.

Without wishing to underestimate the value of these changes in the Treaties, it is clear that, as far as the Permanent Representatives Committee is concerned, they basically do no more than put the official stamp on positions which already existed, and with regard to the European Parliament, represent the immediate consequence of the achievement of a plan contained in the Treaties (i.e. the introduction of the system of own resources). New elements should therefore be sought not in the texts but in the role and daily functioning of the institutions. Here, we shall deal only with those which concern the decision-making process and especially the respective positions of the Commission, Council and Permanent Representatives Committee. Moreover, as regards the role of the Commission as guardian of the Treaty, as the source of decisions (exclusive right to make proposals) and as the administrative basis of the Community – a role which, along with the procedure and the power of decision, is one of the major elements of the Community system – has never been contested or hindered in any matter which is of Community competence.

To make the analysis easier we shall look in turn at four possible kinds of decisions:

(i) Decisions on the daily running of the Community and the common policies;

(ii) Important decisions concerning economic policy which do not raise any major political problems;

(iii) Major decisions on political or economic matters;
(iv) Decisions or acts which affect the 'extensions' of the Community.

This classification is of course based on a qualitative appraisal of acts adopted and not on their legal nature. For this reason it is completely subjective. It might, however, help us to get at the real situation by showing where the power of decision actually lies in each case.

THE PROCEDURE FOR TAKING DECISIONS ON THE DAILY RUNNING OF THE COMMUNITIES

By vesting the Commission from the outset with the power to adopt a number of measures to implement rules set out in the Treaty, especially in giving it exclusive rights on most of the decisions of an individual nature, the Treaties laid down a clear guideline. This was confirmed in Article 155 of the EEC Treaty which states that the Commission 'shall exercise the powers conferred on it by the Council for the implementation of the rules laid down by the latter' especially as this is the only possibility which the Treaties give the Council of delegating its power.

The Council has made wide use of these possibilities, with the result that the Commission now enjoys extensive powers over the daily running of the agricultural policy, customs union, commercial policy, animal and plant health matters, etc. In general all current implementing measures are adopted by the Commission after consultation with various committees.

Decisions of this kind are taken on a majority vote. Depending on the case, the committees consulted must either give a favourable opinion by qualified majority or not give a contrary opinion by qualified majority, whereas the Commission's own decisions are taken by simple majority.

Under these procedures the possibility exists of returning a matter to the Council (depending on the case, when a contrary opinion is given by qualified majority or when there is no positive opinion). However, resort to these procedures has been exceptional. Only a few examples exist out of the thousands of decisions taken during the last ten years.

The result is that the Permanent Representatives Committee and the other subordinate organs of the Council have very little if any influence on this important sector of Community activity. When the Commission's action in these fields is under discussion (sometimes in Council sessions on agriculture or in meetings of the special committee which prepares these sessions), the discussions are of a general nature, with the Commission explaining the policy it is pursuing in its running of matters and listening to the observations of the members of the Council or of their collaborators.

Another comment must also be made. Although all the management decisions which the Commission adopts are taken under the full responsibility of the institution, the fact cannot be blinked that the nine members of the Commission are physically not capable of discussing and deciding everything. Even if they attempted to do so they would be failing to measure up to their real task, as they would be abandoning their responsibilities in policy matters and limiting themselves to pure administration.

For these management measures, the Commission itself merely lays down a few general guidelines. These are filled out in greater detail by the Commission member with special responsibility for the sector in question, in the form of general directives or specific instructions when special cases arise. The written procedure system (proposals drawn up by one Commission member are communicated in writing to the others who then have a certain time in which to make known any reservations they have) enables all the members of the Commission to be kept regularly informed and to express their point of view at any time they feel it necessary. Each year three to four thousand acts of all kinds including acts of internal administration are adopted by this method.

For really current matters (e.g. daily fixing of levies or refunds on exports), the Commission has delegated its powers to its members and even to senior officials on the basis of strict guidelines and on condition that regular reports are made on how these powers are exercised.

Subject to the directives which it must implement, the administration of the Commission is thus called upon to play an extremely important and even a predominant role in the daily running of the Communities. This is not surprising. It corresponds to the situation existing in every modern state where the political authority has had to vest very broad powers in its body of officials while continuing to accept full political responsibility for the exercise of the powers thus delegated.

THE DECISION-MAKING PROCEDURE FOR MATTERS WHICH DO NOT RAISE ANY MAJOR POLITICAL PROBLEMS

Although the Council has made wide use of the possibility of delegating powers to the Commission, it has nevertheless retained responsibility for a number of implementing decisions of derived law. In most cases the measures involved are of great economic or political significance (e.g. the annual fixing of agricultural prices). At times, however, the contingencies of discussion and compromise in drawing up a basic regulation have swung the balance towards the Council rather than the Commission in matters which should have fallen within the province of administration.

Similarly, it is written into the Treaties themselves that the Council is to handle not only all major decisions but also quite a number of less important matters for which experience now indicates that more flexible arrangements could usefully have been employed. Thus, for instance, all measures relating to the harmonization of technical standards – on points like the size of driving mirrors, or the characteristics of cut glass – can be adopted only by the Council acting unanimously (Article 100 EEC).

The Council has thus, on proposal by the Commission, to take a great many decisions which can be fairly important or very important, and of economic or political significance. The preparation of these decisions is the business of the Permanent Representatives Committee and its sub-committees and working parties.

Just how extensive is this preparation? The ambassadors being both called upon and wishful to go into the subject really thoroughly, it is frequently the case, in matters both of moderate and of top importance, that full agreement is reached at Permanent Representative level, between the six ambassadors and the Commission representative.

To cover this kind of eventuality, the Council in 1962, with the Commission's entire agreement, instituted the so-called 'A Point' procedure. 'A points' are adopted by the Council without debate at the beginning of each session. Thus the rule is observed that acts falling within the Council's purview must be adopted by the Council and the Council only (unless it should have opted to delegate powers to the Commission only). However, the substance of the decision has in fact been settled in the Permanent Representatives Committee.

The number of 'A point' decisions by the Council has grown

steadily with the building-up of Community policies (there were, for instance, 599 of them in 1970). In addition, the 'A point' procedure is being used more and more even where there is disagreement on the substance. When an 'A point' is put forward in these circumstances, it means that all concerned are willing to forgo ministerial-level debate because the matter at issue is of limited importance: thus an 'A point' document may mention that the Commission has expressly maintained its proposal against the unanimous feeling of all the member states, or that one member state has abstained or even dissented, and the decision has in fact been taken by a majority on proposal by the Commission.

'Part One' of the Permanent Representatives Committee (consisting of the deputy Permanent Representatives) is a fertile source of 'A points': it deals with the bulk of the mainly technical or economic matters, while the ambassadors themselves handle the more political issues.

The Commission, generally speaking, has encouraged recourse to the 'A point' procedure, so that the ministers' meetings can be devoted to cases rating personal commitment by a member of a government, and the ministers have the time to consider these cases fully. This deconcentration of the Council's proceedings is, incidentally, in line with the steps of various kinds which the Commission has itself had to take to enable its own deliberations to be devoted to questions of policy (see page 106).

In any event no one has ever disputed the Commission's right to request that a point on which it does not agree should be discussed in Council. Admittedly, if the Commission is alone in its view, it will be politely but firmly pressed to withdraw its request to argue a case before the Council, but so too will the representative of a member state similarly in a position of total isolation and wanting to place a 'hopeless' case on the ministers' agenda. In fact, it has happened a good deal less rarely that the Commission in such circumstances has won its point, or part of its point, in Council, than that one minister has managed to convince the rest against a solid front of the other five Permanent Representatives, and sometimes the Commission as well.

While only the Council can adopt the acts listed in Article 189 EEC (regulations, directives, decisions and recommendations), the Permanent Representatives Committee has gradually taken to adopting itself a number of acts which are decisions in the sense of the German *Beschluss* (as opposed to *Entscheidung*, which is a decision within the meaning of Article 189) – merely implementing decisions, not the normative instruments referred to in the Treaty.

This is the case for a number of administrative 'decisions', for instance in preparing replies for the President of the Council or fixing specific details or procedures after the Council has adopted a decision of principle, the idea being usually that *de minimis non curat praetor*. Sometimes, also, the ministers realize that a ticklish but technically complex problem can be more easily dealt with in the Committee, with the ambassadors bringing to bear their knowledge of the supporting material, their patience and their negotiating skills.

The Commission has always made sure that these 'decisions' really are no more than administrative acts in no way encroaching on the prerogatives of the institutions, and it has never had any difficulty, in the few cases where dispute arose, in convincing the Committee that the matter had better go before the Council. The only field in which real problems have arisen has been external relations.

The Permanent Representatives have always attached great importance to these, and have come in course of time to play an appreciably larger part in them.

The EEC Treaty provides that agreements between the Community and any state or states, or any international organization, must be negotiated by the Commission and concluded by the Council[3] (see in particular Articles 113 and 228 of the EEC Treaty). Article 113 which deals specifically with trade and tariff agreements, also provides that the Council may issue negotiating directives to the Commission; Article 228, which covers all other agreements, does not actually say this in so many words, but in practice the Council has acted in the same way there too, which is reasonable enough since it is the Council that has to conclude the agreement, that is, to approve the outcome of the negotiations.

These Council directives are as a rule prepared by the Permanent Representatives Committee, from a Commission recommendation or communication to the Council. Very often they are adopted by the Council without debate as to substance (though for convenience sake they are not treated as 'A points'). It may be added that as time has gone on they have become steadily more precise and detailed, sometimes leaving very little to the discretion of the negotiators.

---

[3] The Commission does in some cases have wider powers under Article 101 of the Euratom Treaty, but the number and importance of the matters for negotiation in the EEC field are such that EEC practice is the more typical of the two.

Article 113, on trade agreements, provides that the Commission is to negotiate these in consultation with a 'special committee' appointed by the Council. For negotiations on other matters the Commission has accepted an arrangement whereby observers from member states sit in at the plenary sessions, and the Commission representatives consult with them during the talks.

In certain cases where difficulties arise at these levels as to the interpretation, and if necessary clarification or amplification, of Council directives they are referred to the Permanent Representatives Committee, which gives the necessary particulars without asking the Council. This arrangement, which gives the Committee a key position in all negotiations, is abundantly justified in practical respects by its convenience and speed. It is the upshot, on the external relations side, of the need for deconcentration already mentioned.

The system I have outlined is employed also, and indeed in still larger measure, in negotiations on matters where there is division of powers between the Community and the member states. Here the negotiations are conducted by a joint Commission/member states delegation, and the Permanent Representatives Committee may intervene both to clarify the Council directives and, also, to co-ordinate, at high policy level, the position of the member states' representatives.

The various associations between the Community and non-Community countries have likewise brought a considerable extension of the functions of the Permanent Representatives. The six present associations each consist – with minor variants – of an Association Council, which may sit either at ministerial or at ambassadorial level, and below it an Association Committee.

The Association Council sitting at ambassadorial level has powers of decision. Accordingly, it is the Permanent Representatives Committee, in co-operation with the Commission – but not necessarily working via the Council of Ministers – which settles the Community position to be taken at such Association Council meetings, and it is usually the chairman of the Committee who states that position and leads in debate for the Community. The Commission can take a line only on internal aspects during the prior hammering out of the Community position.

Similarly, the Permanent Representatives Committee, acting alone if necessary, draws up the general directives to determine the Community position in the Association Committees.

Under the institutional rules embodied in the Yaoundé Convention (the Association with the African States and Madagascar) and the Ankara Agreement (the Association with Turkey), negotiations for the renewal of the convention, and for the conclusion of a supplementary protocol to the agreement, had also to be conducted, according to the level concerned, by the Council and by the Permanent Representatives Committee, with the co-operation of the Commission. The President of the Council and the chairman of the Permanent Representatives Committee were as a rule the spokesmen for the Community in these negotiations.

In the negotiations for Community enlargement, in which, by the terms of the Treaty, responsibility rests mainly with the member states, it was likewise the President of the Council and the chairman of the Permanent Representatives Committee who conducted the talks at ministerial and deputy level respectively. It was understood that the positions to be taken at deputy level were to be settled by the Permanent Representatives Committee – here acting as the assembled representatives of the member states – without need of clearance with the Council. It was also part of the arrangement that there were to be special mandates to the Commission on particular points: this procedure was frequently used and to good purpose.

More recently, a further extension of the role of the Permanent Representatives Committee has taken place with respect to 'contacts' – a legally rather vague concept not explicitly covered by any Treaty provision. Thus, following the Buenos Aires Declaration of 29 July 1970 by the ministerial meeting of the Latin American Special Co-ordinating Committee, the Council of the European Communities decided, on 14 December 1970, to institute contacts with the Latin American countries. A first meeting was duly held between the Latin American heads of missions to the Community and a Community team consisting of the Permanent Representatives and the Commission representative, with the chairman of the Permanent Representatives Committee and the Commission representative acting as its spokesmen.

It seems very possible that a similar procedure will be followed for other 'contacts' in the future.

There does not appear to be anything in these arrangements that infringes the letter of the Treaties. In point of fact, the Council, and still more the Permanent Representatives Committee, have, in consequence of the somewhat vague wording of the Treaties where they concern external relations, made substantial inroads on the role and scope of the Commission as sole negotiator – a tendency aided and intensified by the special procedures in the Association Agreements and the many joint negotiations on matters simultaneously within the purview of both the member states and the Commission. As a result, the changes which were due to come at the end of the transitional period – more particularly the implementation of Article 113 and the first paragraph of Article 116 – have had only a limited impact.

This is not without its political implications. It will be recalled that certain procedures in connection with relations with non-member countries and international organizations figured prominently in the discussions which ended the institutional crisis of 1965–66, and in particular in the resolution adopted on the subject by the Council on 29 January 1966 when the crisis was settled.

Two persons play a special part in the working out of the conclusions of the Permanent Representatives Committee, the Commission representative and the chairman of the Committee.

The Commission's representative sits as of right at the meetings of the Permanent Representatives Committee, except on the rare occasions known as 'internal meetings', held to discuss the few matters in which the Commission is not involved, such as the budget estimates of the Council itself. The Commission's General Secretariat, which is responsible for this regular representation on the Committee, also maintains continuous liaison with the Commission itself, which, at each of its weekly meetings, is given a detailed report on the proceedings of the Permanent Representatives Committee, and decides on new instructions for its own representative as and when necessary.

Although a number of the Council's decisions each year are taken by qualified majority on proposal by the Commission, generally speaking the ministers, and still more the Permanent Representatives, try hard to reach unanimity, whatever the particular matter at issue. This has considerably enhanced the importance of the chair – very greatly so in the case of the Permanent Representatives Committee. (The chair is taken, it will be remembered, by each of the member states in turn for six months at a time.)

With majority voting, delegations in 'way-out' positions have to draw closer to the Commission's proposal if they are not to be isolated when the question is put to the vote. The Commission for its part can help to bring about a majority by amending its proposal; it is able to combine its initiating and its conciliating functions.

With de facto unanimity, the Commission representative is more

obliged to uphold, even practically on his own, the Simon-pure position which the Commission has decided is most in accordance with
the Community interest. The delegations generally want the Commission to adopt this kind of line, even if they do not support it, in
order to keep the element of Community give and take in the debate;
delegations which do favour the Commission's line would be taken
aback if the Commission were to abandon it and submit compromise
formulas departing appreciably from the principles it had been maintaining.

So it is the chair that has the most scope for quietly taking sound-
ings, putting out feelers, and coming forward at the right moment
with compromise suggestions – particularly suggestions some distance away from the Commission's original proposal. In this it is
assisted with tact and efficiency by the General Secretariat of the
Council.

All commentators must agree that the successive Presidents of the
Council and chairmen of the Committee have always been out to
forward the work of the Community, even where they did not see
eye to eye with the Commission. The 'Community' character of the
structure and operation of the Council's General Secretariat has
certainly had much to do with the continuity and consistency which
has prevailed in this.

The chair has thus a moral authority which it can bring to bear in
seeking to break up any log-jam that has developed. By management
of the agenda (having the same item included time after time), by
teaming up, and getting the Commission to team up, with the delegations that are in the majority, on occasion by availing itself of other,
more political arguments – such as the linking of two or more
issues – an active chair possesses the means to get quite a number of
proposals through during the six months available, provided they
present sufficient political interest both for the chair itself and for
several of the delegations.

The standard-bearer of Community orthodoxy, the Commission
representative, though he has less freedom of action than the chair,
nevertheless does have means of his own to resort to. Above all, in
many cases he has managed to gain for his position, or the great part
of it, the support of a majority of the delegations, with the result that
the compromise put forward by the chair is not far removed from
the Commission's original proposal. Even where he is in the minority,
the chair is usually reluctant to come out in flat opposition to the
Commission's view; really determined opposition by the Commis-

.sion representative can result in a compromise failing to secure acceptance.

The calibre of the Commission representatives and the merits of their case play a very great part in all this. It hardly ever happens that the Commission, taking its stand on a carefully prepared and well-argued case, nevertheless finds itself facing the unpleasant spectacle of all six delegations agreeing on a text it considers unacceptable. Even then, it can refer the matter to the ministers.

There remain those instances in which, despite repeated deliberations in the Permanent Representatives Committee and all sorts of efforts by the chair, it still remains impossible to reach general agreement in the Committee. This is the weakest point in the system I have been describing. In the first place, even if anyone wanted to, it would be difficult – in fact institutionally impossible – to call a vote in the Permanent Representatives Committee; in the second place, the custom has gradually grown up of regarding some classes of cases as not 'worth' discussion at ministerial level. As a result there is the undeniable risk of some cases bogging down.

The fact that these cases are isolated and unconnected is often a further complication. They are seldom sufficiently important to justify bringing six specialist ministers to Brussels for a whole day, while it is not possible to lump several of them together because they fall within the provinces of different ministers. As for the Foreign Ministers, who could discuss all these matters at a 'general' Council session, the political questions the Community has been grappling with for the last few years have been much too important to leave any space available on the agendas for dealing with this kind of thing.

The problem remains open, and will have to wait for a solution until the Community settles down again to a normal rhythm of operation after its enlargement. That the specialist ministers responsible for the various fields within the Communities' jurisdiction should meet regularly at least once in each half-year is felt to be essential if there is not to be stagnation or sanding-up in some of the spheres covered by the Treaty. The fact that the ministers do actually go to Brussels has always been, as we shall see, one of the things that makes the Community really work. The practical possibility of referring a matter to the judgement of the ministers is not merely an ultimate means of leverage for extracting a decision at Permanent Representative level: it is a means of investing – or reinvesting – that matter with its due political importance, and so making it possible

to overcome the opposition of vested interests or to jog governments and government departments into taking action.

DECISION-MAKING ON MAJOR POLITICAL AND ECONO-MIC ISSUES

The preparatory work that is done in the Permanent Representatives
Committee rarely culminates, where matters of major political or
economic importance are concerned, in general agreement among
the ambassadors or their alternates. After all, the ministers respo-
sible come themselves to Brussels in the ordinary course of events,
and so, when the matter in question is in that class, the Permanent
Representatives are neither willing nor able to go too far in the way
of concessions and compromises: they leave it to their ministers to
assess how far they can commit themselves politically and to shoulder
the responsibility of accepting or rejecting.

The accompanying table shows the frequency of ministerial meetings. As well as the Ministers of Agriculture, who sometimes meet as
often as twice a month, the Foreign Ministers meet regularly for two
days every month, the Finance Ministers are in Brussels at least three
times a year, and in practice much oftener, and the Transport Ministers and Ministers for science and research also come regularly,
though at rather longer intervals.

The fact that ever since EEC was first set up the leading ministers
in each government have been directly and personally associated
with its work has had very considerable effects on the Community's
development. It has meant that proposals radically affecting the policies of each of the member states could be submitted to the Council
without the risk of their being simply pigeonholed at administrative
level: instead, they would be considered by the respective governments and discussed multilaterally in the Council with the Commission by the ministers themselves. It meant that opinion could be
alerted to the prospect of policy decisions, and a political will arrived
at to enable technical and administrative obstacles to be overcome.

Whatever procedures might be thought up for improving the
functioning of the Communities, their effectiveness and development will continue to depend on the presence in person in Brussels
or Luxemburg of the principal members of each government concerned with Community affairs.

In important matters the role of the Permanent Representatives
Committee is firstly to single out the politically touchy questions on

which there will have to be some political give and take. If the question allows, they will go further and propose the options from which the ministers can choose. The other aspects will, of course, have been settled by the Permanent Representatives Committee or will be settled later, after the decisions of principle have been taken by the ministers.

This explains the importance of the contribution of the Permanent Representatives Committee, whose report is the starting point for the discussion on the question at issue. It would, however, be incorrect to conclude that the Commission's initial proposal no longer has any importance or influence. All the preparatory work will have been carried out on the basis of this proposal, and the Commission's representatives, acting on its strict instructions, will have been in a position to take full part in the choice of the options submitted to the ministers and in presenting these options. The importance of the introductory report of the Permanent Representatives should neither be underestimated nor exaggerated, for it is essentially an objective presentation of the diverging points of view which are expressed in the preparatory work.

In the Council the members of the Commission speak directly with the ministers themselves. Admittedly, in the absence of the minister or state secretary, the delegation is led by the Permanent Representative, but, quite apart from the requirements of the quorum (i.e. three of the six members of the Council must be present at the session) on an important question or one which directly concerns his government, the minister is always present.

For the most touchy political questions, preparation by the Committee of Permanent Representatives is almost always very brief. The minister prefers to set out his position himself and to compare it with that of his colleagues and of the Commission before the senior officials come together to discuss the question.

In the most important matters in recent years, all the discussions have been held at ministerial level until a common position has been reached, without the Committee of Permanent Representatives intervening as a body. This has not, of course, prevented each permanent representative from playing a role and sometimes an important role in drawing up the position of his own delegation and in any later changes.

By way of example it is possible to mention the work on the system of the Communities' own resources and the granting of budgetary powers to the European Parliament. In December 1969, immediately after The Hague summit, three long, all-night sessions of the Foreign Affairs Ministers (8/9–15/16–18/22 December) laid down the bases of agreements on which the Permanent Representatives were later to build the final structure. In the preceding months it had been impossible for the Committee in its preparatory work to do more than simply list the points on which there was disagreement.

Likewise, during the negotiations on enlargement, only at ministerial level were the compromise proposals discussed, adjusted and finally accepted. In this way agreements have been reached on such very delicate problems as the United Kingdom's financial contribution and the system of imports of sugar from the Commonwealth developing countries and of dairy products from New Zealand.

Many other examples could be given at various stages in the Community's existence, and in particular whenever it has reached a major crossroads.

These meetings are often tailor-made occasions for the Commission to take initiatives. In direct contact with the ministers, the Commission is in a better position than anybody to assess the political implications of the situation, to clear up misunderstandings and to propose compromises. Its duty is either to propose new solutions which will break the log-jam or present package deals to bring long sessions to an end. Even the President of the Council would rarely take it upon himself to propose a compromise without the backing or the assistance of the Commission.

These political debates in the Council and this direct dialogue between the Commission and the ministers are nothing other than the full implementation of the Communities' institutional rules. It is significant that they are employed for the most important matters and those in which the political aspect is strongest. This is proof of the validity and effectiveness of these rules; it confirms that they maintain all their force despite the adjustments which have had to be made to accommodate the practical necessities of coping with the mass of day-to-day affairs.

THE DECISION-MAKING PROCEDURE IN THE 'EXTENSIONS' OF THE COMMUNITY

The variety of fields where it has seemed justified to exceed the powers fixed by the Treaty and the extreme differences in the nature of the progress achieved make it difficult to reach general conclusions on the way in which decisions on these questions are taken.

In general the Commission has taken the initiative in putting in hand study of these extensions of the Community. The Committee of Permanent Representatives has thus had an important role to play in fixing the procedures to be used and in choosing the organs for preparing the work. It has never sought to keep these new powers for itself by transforming itself into a group of representatives of member states called upon in this capacity to discuss the problems which go beyond the limits of the Treaty. On the other hand considerations of a political or institutional nature seem to have been behind the different attitudes which have so far been adopted in the various fields.

On economic and monetary questions, as we have already seen, the Council, the Commission and the member states have agreed on the creation of organs of concertation, which are largely independent, along the lines of the Monetary Committee (Medium-Term Economic Policy Committee, Short-Term Economic Policy Committee, Budget Policy Committee, etc.). These Committees often bring together the most senior officials in the administrations concerned. They may even be chaired by a state-secretary (as in the case of the Medium-Term Economic Policy Committee). They report directly to the Council. They are responsible for almost all the preparations of ministerial meetings where problems of economic and monetary co-operation are on the agenda, the contribution of the Permanent Representatives Committee remaining marginal or being limited to questions of procedure.

In this process of concertation the Commission remains in a position to play an active role by its participation in the work of the Committees, by the possibilities offered by the activities of its officials who assist these Committees and, finally, by its presence as an active participant in ministerial meetings. Although this process does not offer the same possibilities for discussion as exist in the Community system, it does go beyond simple co-operation, in particular as a result of the openings it creates at political level.

Several member states and the Permanent Representatives Committee itself have, on the other hand, shown a certain apprehension about purely and simply applying these possibilities of concertation to other cases. For what are clearly political reasons, work on scientific and technical research in the non-nuclear field is dealt with under the close supervision of the Permanent Representatives Committee, although it has been prepared by a group made up of senior administrative and scientific officials (Working Group on Scientific and

Technical Research Policy); these same political reasons on the part of several member states have led to the issue being practically put on ice, as was mentioned above.

In industrial and regional policy the decisions on the procedure to be adopted will be significant for the other work to be undertaken in fields which are marginal to the Treaties. The Commission would like (and its point of view is fairly widely shared) to see a flexible system of concertation introduced in which senior officials with very broad responsibilities would be able to examine, with the Commission, a vast range of problems in fields which are or are not covered by the Treaties and then report (or render opinions) to the Commission and to the Council, without prejudice to any later measures adopted by the Community itself. However, other approaches are also under consideration which would make of the new committees to be created organs depending directly on the Permanent Representatives Committee and whose activities would be contained in a much tighter political framework.

Institutional concerns are among the decisive factors in any discussion about exceeding the strict provisions of the Treaty, and it is in the Permanent Representatives Committee that these concerns can be expressed with most ease and defended with a maximum of effectiveness. This institutional obstacle has been removed (as far as concertation is concerned) on the question of economic and monetary union by successive political discussions, the most prestigious of which was The Hague Conference. As long as this obstacle continues to exist in other fields, they will probably remain under the strict supervision of the Permanent Representatives Committee.

CONCLUSIONS

This rapid survey of Community activities shows clearly that the role and influence of the Permanent Representatives Committee has increased considerably as the Communities have been deepened and the strict powers accorded by the Treaties exceeded, and that this increase has been more than proportionate with the growth of Community activities. It would seem that the principal factors in this development are the notable mass of questions which belong to the 'intermediate level', the rapid development of the Community's external relations (questions to which the Committee has always paid great attention) and the need to extend further and further outside the Community framework, with the institutional problems which this entails. The (too) systematic search for unanimity, even on minor issues, has also helped, indirectly perhaps, but nevertheless undeniably.

Some of the responsibilities the Permanent Representatives Committee discharges today might well have been assigned to the Commission if the policy line of the Council and the member states had been different: the Commission might have been allotted still wider administrative jurisdiction, its role as negotiator might have been made a more prominent one, there might have been less reluctance to explore the 'fringe areas' of the Communities and extend the Community institutional system to apply to them too. But there was nothing in the Treaties that required such courses to be taken, and if they had been they would have meant changes in degree rather than in kind.

For the rise of the Permanent Representatives Committee, striking though it has been, has not impaired the institutional balance designed by the Treaties. The political dialogue of Council and Commission is still there, the more genuine and the more thoroughgoing in character the more important and political the subject at issue. It is there too at ambassadorial and at expert level, where it works very well indeed, the Commission being so ably and authoritatively represented. Besides, the Permanent Representatives Committee obviously could not perform on its own both halves of the double process of initiation and decision which is the distinguishing feature of the Community dialectic, and it has made no attempt to do so.

And then again, the quality of the Committee's work, its members' selfless acceptance of a truly exhausting workload – take a look at that table! – and their devotion to the Communities make the Permanent Representatives' contribution, past, present and to come, a particularly outstanding one.

And yet, given all this, is it desirable that in the years ahead things should simply continue developing on the lines I have been describing? In my account of the decision-making process one great institution has been conspicuous by its absence – the European Parliament. For the Parliament's role is still, under the present organization, a marginal one, and I have been able to go at some length into the workings of the system without once mentioning its name.

This is an unsound state of affairs, and will become more so. While the huge administrative machine of the Communities, with its departmental staff and its pyramid of expert panels and working parties and committees, is growing and growing, the area in which those with political responsibility play a direct part is becoming relatively smaller (leaving aside the importance of the matters dealt with there). And how can we not be struck at the same time by the fact that the legislative process is unaccompanied by public debate, that there are directly elected law-makers, and hence that Parliament has so little say in affairs?

Nor is it right that uncertainty should persist as to the way in which the 'extensions' of the Communities are to be handled. As things now stand, larger and larger sectors, which look like ultimately becoming the most important ones of all, are treated as matters more for Community concertation than for Community dialectic. This is all very well in an exploratory period. But if that period goes on too long, the institutional balance will be noticeably affected.

The enlarged Community of the future will have to face up to these problems, and will have, inescapably, to produce an answer. We must trust that the new members, who are not tied to the past but are the possessors of the most ancient traditions of representative democracy, will bring to these problems a fresh mind, and will not recoil before the solutions to be entertained.

APPENDIX

STATISTICAL ANALYSIS OF MEETINGS ORGANIZED BY THE COUNCIL AND THE COMMISSION

	Number of days	
	1969	*1970*
I. COUNCIL		
A. MINISTERIAL SESSIONS		
Council; Councils of Association; negotiating conferences	80½	91
including		
(a) Council sessions other than agriculture	40½	44½
(b) Council sessions on agriculture	31½	31½
(c) Councils of Association	8½	4½
(d) Negotiating conferences		10½
B. SESSIONS OF THE PERMANENT REPRESENTATIVES COMMITTEE		
Total	129	153
including		
(a) Ambassadors		78
Deputies		9
(b) Assistants		76
Actual presence of Ambassadors		
Aa, c, d; Ba		146½
C. MEETINGS OF EXPERTS AND OTHER COMMITTEES		
Total days of meetings organized by the Council (other than meetings of the Council and Permanent Representative Committee)	1417½	1632½
including (Experts)		
(i) External relations	347 (24%)	484 (29%)
(ii) Internal development	1070½ (76%)	1048½ (71%)
II. COMMISSION		
A. DAYS OF MEETINGS OF THE COMMISSION	64½	51½
B. TOTAL NUMBER OF MEETINGS OF EXPERTS ORGANIZED BY THE COMMISSION (including meetings with private experts)	1527	1793

H. Vredeling

The Common Market
of Political Parties *

A CURIOUS PHENOMENON MAY BE NOTED WITHIN THE EUROPEAN Community, and also in the negotiations on the entry of other European countries into it. This is the *absence* of any move towards European integration among the political parties in the member states. Rather surprisingly, an obstinate silence prevails in Europe and within the national political parties regarding this deficiency. One cannot help wondering what is the reason for this and what can be done to break this silence.

Outwardly the process of European integration presents in the main an *economic* aspect. The EEC Treaty is a classic example of this. The goal striven for is a customs union with a common policy in the economic sphere. Thus the first steps are being taken in the Community towards a common policy in a number of sectors (agriculture, transport, energy, external trade). Recently attempts have been made to link this sector-by-sector policy through the inauguration of a common economic and monetary policy.

In the social sphere, however, far less progress has been made. A common social policy is not one of the aims of the EEC Treaty. Consequently what there is in common in the social sector is of a secondary nature. Efforts are made through the European Social Fund to hold in check any adverse effects of the process of economic integration. The Community, however, lacks a social policy as such (that is, one actively concerned with full employment, a fair distribution of income, and a bigger say for the citizen in macro-economic and micro-economic affairs). In education, cultural affairs, housing, town and country planning, control of the environment, local government, the administration of justice and other important sectors of every national policy the European Community lacks even the rudiments of common aims and of a common policy.

In so far as one can speak of a common approach by member states to external and defence policy, this is governed mainly by factors

* Vol. 6, No. 4, Autumn 1971.

unrelated to the existence of the European Community. It should no doubt be noted that the first signs of co-operation in external policy can be detected, for example, in the Davignon Committee.

The only conclusion that can be drawn from this is that the member states of the EEC are obstinately bent on confining co-operation to the economic sector and are not as yet inclined to extend such co-operation to other sectors.

EUROPEAN PARTIES AND PARLIAMENT

Now how do the national political parties of the Six feel about all this? First it should be noted that these parties leave it mainly to their respective political groups in the national parliaments to follow up the European integration process. These groups are brought in touch with EEC affairs only through their governments. They themselves are not, apparently, directly involved. That in fact was the intention of the authors of the European Treaties. These make provision for the setting up of a European Parliament com-posed of national representatives appointed to sit there by their national parliaments. In addition one of the aims laid down in the Treaties is the holding of direct European elections. Unfortunately they fix no time-limit within which these elections must be organized. Nor, in fact, have they ever been held. Although most of the national political parties have included European elections in their programmes, they have never made a real issue of them. As a result of all this the national political parties are brought only indirectly in touch with European questions – that is, through their governments and members of national groups sitting in the European Parliament.

The European Parliament, however, has only an advisory role. Decisions are taken in the Council of Ministers of the European Communities. In the eyes of the national groups, members who sit in the European Parliament are of only limited importance. They are certainly of great help in shedding light on the obscure process of European integration. But they have no real say in policy-making. The result is that members of national political groups who play an important part in shaping domestic policy are practically never members of the European Parliament. The selection of representa-tives to the European Parliament is a negative process for two reasons. On the one hand national groups tend to put forward only second line politicians as candidates; and on the other, if influential national parliamentarians become members of the European

Parliament or if lesser known figures – as often happens – discharge their European parliamentary duties with devotion and zeal and in so doing acquire national recognition, the time inevitably comes when they are called upon to assume a responsible post in national politics, either in the national government or in opposition. This may be beneficial to the national groups but the overall effect on the European Parliament is adverse. This phenomenon is due to the fact that the European Parliament has no political power.

Meanwhile the process of European economic integration is moving ahead. It is accompanied by the growth of trans-national economic power groupings. The EEC is a paradise for industrialists. The creation of a huge market of 200 million consumers (close on 275 million after the accession of the four applicant countries) at a time of buoyant business activity is a political act by the governments but it is also a 'give-away' with an unusually high goodwill value for business interests. (The British government is having to pay a substantial price for a benefit it could have obtained for nothing in the early 1950s). The governments of the Six are working on the completion of this paradise. Almost all the measures taken in the Community are designed to eliminate obstacles to trade and distortions of competition. Even the free movement of workers helps to create a source of cheap labour. The governments seem to have only one concern: to stem the influx of American capital. European capital is their ally. But does anyone believe there could ever be a real conflict between American and European capital?

The consolidation of political power is lagging far behind. The Council of Ministers is the only institution to embody real political power, but this merely serves the economic Common Market because economic strength seems to be the only objective of political power. Significantly the political power of the six governments, culminating in the Council of Ministers of the European Community, stems from the domestic political power of each government which only exists by the grace of the national balance of political power. In the West European democracies, national political power rests with the governing political parties which are to some extent held in check by the opposition. In the parliamentary democracies this national process of checks and balances is dependent on the system of free elections, i.e. on the fact that citizens are allowed to have their say.

There is, however, a real risk that the derived power of the EEC Council may become an independent factor on which the national political parties can exercise little influence even indirectly. The Council is the cuckoo in the nest of European integration. The national political parties are like the sorcerer's apprentice in their dealings with the Council. They have waved their magic wand in the national parliaments to set the process in motion but they do not know the spell to control the Council's policy.

Against this background, we propose to examine the role of the social-democratic and other left-wing progressive parties in the European Communities. Not only because we are best acquainted with these parties from our own political conviction and experience but also because they have, or should have, a much more ambivalent attitude to the neo-liberal phenomenon known as the Common Market. The right-wing parties have always identified themselves to a greater extent with the interests of commerce and industry. Their problems are therefore minimal if these business interests, and above all the large corporations, find the Common Market to their liking.

THE ATTITUDE OF THE SOCIALIST PARTIES

The socialist parties, which are affiliated to the Socialist International, have established a Liaison Office for the European Communities in which they co-operate. This is, however, a completely free form of co-operation and the Office has no power to take or implement decisions unless there is unanimous agreement between all concerned. In this respect it does not differ from the Council; the difference lies in the fact that the Council decides and does a great deal whereas the Liaison Office does nothing whatsoever. The Liaison Office held its last congress of affiliated parties in Berlin in November 1966. There have been no further meetings, even though the major decisions affecting the EEC have been taken since 1966. The process of economic integration has therefore completely by-passed the socialist parties which have shown themselves more Gaullist than de Gaulle. And within the parties there has never been any significant criticism of this state of affairs.

The Socialist Group in the European Parliament is also leading a shadowy existence. In all these years it has been answerable to nobody for its policy. The present author has been a member of the Socialist Group for thirteen years and has never been called to account for his actions (many of which must surely have appeared curious to others). What kind of democracy is that?

Because of this highly unsatisfactory state of affairs a number of members of the socialist parties in the European Community have decided to set up an action group with the ultimate aim of founding a Progressive European Party. Many Dutch members helped to prepare the project for this action group. They wanted to align themselves not only with the 'traditional' social-democratic parties but also with related left-wing democratic groups in the European context.

This initiative aroused interest in certain quarters. Reactions were favourable in the Netherlands but in the other countries – with a few exceptions – the project was greeted with indifference. The Progressive European Movement or PEP (as the movement is known) met with a highly negative response from the West German SPD which suggested, quite wrongly, that the PEP must be a transnational political party side by side with the existing national parties. However, that was never the aim or intention. The main purpose in launching the PEP idea was to create a shock effect in the national parties. And then it was hoped to form the nucleus of a group which could establish European links between national progressive parties. The PEP has always tried to be a movement in which existing parties could in the first instance recognize their own image and in which they could ultimately be absorbed.

This unorthodox and matter-of-fact solution was chosen simply because of the inertia of the national political parties. Curiously enough our English friends in the Labour Party, who always adopt a rather more pragmatic approach, showed a far more understanding and sympathetic attitude to our movement than the SPD.

In the light of their experience the Dutch backers of the PEP have now moved back into line with the existing organizational arrangements. They followed the normal channels by submitting a proposal to the National Congress of the Dutch Labour Party through its local branches. They encountered considerable support because the publicity given to the PEP helped greatly to crystallize opinion in the Labour Party on the need to found a European party. At the National Congress in February of this year a resolution was passed by an overwhelming majority; the text of the resolution is annexed to this article.

Work is now progressing again in the Liaison Office of the social democratic parties in the European Community with a view to establishing the PEP. Resistance, particularly from the SPD, is still unusually strong.

THE CAUSES OF RELUCTANCE

What are the principal causes of this internal resistance by the national parties to the formation of European political parties? Such resistance is not confined to the SPD. It is particularly strong in the SPD because of the national character, adverse political experience in the past and the special political situation of the Federal Republic in Europe, but all political parties will show the same opposition when it comes to the point, and everyone realizes that the formation of European political parties means that national party congresses will no longer have the last word. Perhaps this factor will not seem so very important to the ordinary party member who attends congresses, but it may appear vital to the party executive which often uses the decision-making process at the party congress to force through its own opinions and override its opponents. As but one component of a democratic European party, the national party executive would never have the last word, because a European party congress might come out against the decisions which the national party executive has been able to force through at a national congress.

The exercise of power will therefore be an important problem for European political parties. Power can be directly embodied in a national party when it is in government and indirectly when it is in opposition. But this is only possible at national level.

What is to be done when power is taken out of the hands of national authorities? This is already the case in the economic sphere in the European Community, and the same transfer of authority will soon be made in the monetary sector too. Power then shifts to the European decision-making machinery in the Council of Ministers. The national party still remains very close to the centre of power through its national government representation; but the power it wields is less absolute. The opposition is in an even worse position because attacks on a national minister after difficult secret negotiations in the Council – in which he will always claim to have defended national interests particularly successfully – are seldom popular.

The supervisory powers of parties in government and opposition over the process of national government are being eroded while the powers of the Council of Ministers are increasing. But since in a parliamentary democracy the national parties are the mouthpiece of public opinion and the channel of democracy in an elected parliament, this is a dubious anti-democratic process, especially as the Council of Ministers wields its increasing power without any form of supervision.

This process ought to give rise to serious concern among the leaders of the social democratic parties in the EEC member states. Unfortunately this is not the case. If the leaders of the national parties recognized the facts, they would surely be more willing to reach agreement on the creation of a political counterbalance to the concentrated power of the Council. However, they seem satisfied with their attempts to maintain power at national level. In general election campaigns they make all kinds of promises to the voters which they cannot implement once they are in government. This generally unintentional deception of the electorate is most apparent in small countries.

The average voter is not so clearly aware of the facts. He is not told the truth but when he reads the newspaper he gains a vague impression that the general election campaign is not really as momentous as his political party would have him believe. The result is a waning interest in national politics. Responsible people (especially in the younger age groups) are therefore adopting an increasingly reticent attitude to the supranational decision-making process in important areas of EEC activity.

THE ATTITUDE OF THE CONTINENTAL TRADE UNIONS

One group which has close links with the socialist movement has sized up the shift in power in Europe particularly well. This is the trade union movement. An extract from a speech made by drs Harry Ter Heide, the chairman of the Dutch General Trade Unions Movement, last April in London, to a meeting of the British TUC is particularly revealing: 'Actually, the trade unions' influence works through the national parliament and is based on the fact that no political party is eager to risk an open conflict with the trade unions. At European level this influence can only be achieved if here too a directly elected European Parliament, equipped with the usual parliamentary powers, is present. At the same time the position of the European Commission must be strengthened. It is therefore not only out of sympathy with democracy, but also out of well-understood self interest that the trade union movement figures amongst the most ardent advocates of a democratic federal Europe.'

The trade union movement knows that European co-operation is the only way of reinforcing its position in face of the increasing strength of trans-national economic power groupings in Europe. But influence cannot be brought to bear without an appropriate institutional framework. The trade union movement has only been able to achieve substantial social progress in our countries through the legislative work of national parliaments. The position will be the same in Europe. The trade union movement has no direct influence on the European Council. It can only achieve its aims through the European Parliament, provided that this Parliament itself has effective parliamentary powers.

EUROPEAN ELECTIONS

The organization of direct European elections in accordance with Article 138 of the EEC Treaty is being officially blocked by France. The governments of other countries have acquiesced in this obstruction. They have never made direct elections an important negotiating issue. It is true that the Council has set up an official working party to examine how these elections should be organized. In 1960 the European Parliament tabled a plan setting out procedures for holding these elections. Since then the Parliament has been able to do no more than stress repeatedly the political importance it attaches to these elections, but to no avail.

The national political parties have been content to include this item in their election programmes and do nothing more. Not a single party has made its participation in government conditional on the holding of European elections by a specific date. What is more, the national political parties would be highly embarrassed if the governments took a positive decision. No political group – not even the Socialist Party – is ready for this step. Meanwhile we have an abnormal situation in which government officials are considering technical aspects of European elections while the political parties are kept in the dark. And they do not even seem to mind.

The failure to organize direct European elections has resulted in steps being taken in some Community countries to arrange the direct election of their own national delegation to the European Parliament. This would be done by nominating for election members of the national parliament whom the national parties would like to see appointed to the European Parliament from their own group in the national parliament. This is the only possible course since the European Treaties stipulate that the national parliaments must nominate representatives to the European Parliament from among their own members, by a procedure which they are free to determine individually.

The Dutch Parliament has made the most progress with this problem. A bill tabled by the christian democrat Mr Westerterp is due to be debated in the next few months in the Second Chamber. This development raises certain problems. On what political programme are these national elections to be based? A European programme drawn up by a national party remains by definition a national political programme for a European policy of the kind which the individual national party would like to see implemented.

In preparing this bill for submission to the Dutch Parliament it has been stressed that as long as direct European elections are blocked by one country, i.e. France, the organization of direct national elections for the national delegation to the European Parliament can only be accepted if several countries follow suit. As far as possible national elections should be held in the various countries on the same date. One possible criterion for the national transition to European elections would be agreement between a combination of countries representing about half the members of the European Parliament. In practice this would mean that one of the large countries, e.g. Italy or the Federal Republic of Germany and the three Benelux countries, could organize national European elections. After the accession of the four applicant countries a combination of two large countries and several smaller countries or alternatively three large countries would be necessary. However, the whole procedure seems rather unwieldy. Admittedly there is one advantage: if national European elections were arranged jointly, there would be a strong incentive for like-minded national parties to form trans-national parties. Because national members of parliament nominated in different countries as candidates for the European Parliament would co-operate in a single political group, it would be necessary to draft a European programme with broader implications than any European policy programme which any national party would like to see implemented.

Citizens will only feel directly involved in European affairs if they are allowed to vote in direct elections to the European Parliament. One crucial problem remains, however: can direct elections be held for a parliament which has no real powers? Of course the same question can be formulated differently: can real powers ever be given to a parliament which is not directly elected?

Theoretically the remedy is obvious. The European Parliament should be given effective powers and at the same time direct elections should be organized for a fully-fledged parliament. But looking at the matter more realistically, the attribution of genuine parliamentary powers to the European Parliament does not seem feasible as a short-term proposition because the majority of governments do not want this and the national political parties refuse to force their hand. The governments object to direct European elections on the ground that citizens cannot be called to the polling booths to elect a mock parliament. This vicious circle can only be broken at its weakest point, i.e. by organizing direct elections in the countries in which a political majority is in favour of them. Real powers cannot be granted to the European Parliament without co-operation between all the governments. Similarly, direct European elections cannot be held without such co-operation. The direct election of national delegations to the European Parliament in countries which are willing to adopt this course seems to be the only way left of making a start on the much-needed democratization of the European Community.

In addition, resistance to the organization at national level of elections for the European Parliament is felt to be considerable. Under a system of this kind the national political parties would still be faced with the problem of power. By adhering to the basic principle that national members of parliament are elected for European groups, the national parties will be compelled for the first time to take up genuine European positions. As an example the election programme of the Dutch Labour Party includes recognition of the German Democratic Republic. What must the socialist group do about this point if European elections for the European Parliament are held, say, in a combination of the three Benelux countries and the Federal Republic? Could the SPD agree to such recognition? Or could the Dutch Labour Party claim that it is being overruled on this point by the SPD if a common election programme is drawn up with the latter?

What procedure should be followed to draw up this common programme? Even the combination of national elections for the national delegations to the European Parliament encroaches on the power of national parties. Resistance will therefore be considerable. At the same time the European approach is definitely worth a try.

A POSSIBLE CO-OPERATION

Finally I should like to outline the possible forms of co-operation between political parties. The following observations are based on a working document submitted by the Dutch Labour Party to the Liaison Office of social democratic parties in the European Community for discussion at the congress which the Liaison Office held in Brussels at the end of June 1971. I have, however, departed from the working document in some respects. The proposed organizational structure could easily serve as a model for other political parties wishing to co-operate in the European Community.

The structure of the Liaison Office and of the congresses it organizes is purely 'intergovernmental'. Decisions can only be taken unanimously. There is no common executive machinery. In addition, none of the affiliated parties has an official delegation either to the executive or congress of the Liaison Office. Decisions can therefore only be binding at the very most on the individual party executives and not on the parties themselves whose highest representative body is their own national party congress.

These organizational arrangements lag far behind the institutional structure of the European Communities which have bodies such as the Commission, Council, Parliament and Court of Justice. There is no organizational equivalent of these institutions in the European parties which co-operate in the Liaison Office. It would seem highly desirable to base organizational co-operation between the democratic left-wing progressive parties in the European Community countries on the structure of the Community institutions.

The parties concerned in the member countries of the (enlarged) European Community would have to set up a *European Union of Socialist and Allied Parties*. This Union could be joined by the European parties which co-operate in and are accepted by the Socialist Group in the European Parliament. The socialist parties of the six EEC countries which are members of the Socialist International already co-operate in this political group. The Italian Republican Party is also represented in it. It is an open secret that if Monsieur Servan-Schreiber's French Radical Party could appoint one or more members to the European Parliament they would join the Socialist Group. In the Netherlands there is the new progressive political party 'D'66'. This year it is entitled to nominate a representative to the European Parliament for the first time, and it is not improbable that he will join the Socialist Group in Parliament.

This proposed Union of Socialist and Allied Parties should have the following representative bodies:

- a European Congress;
- a European Union Board;
- a European Executive.

The *European Congress* would consist of representatives of the national parties nominated by the national party congresses. Decisions would be taken in this congress by a qualified majority.

The Union Board and the Executive would be answerable to this Congress for the policy followed by them. The Congress would draft a programme of action based on a proposal of the Union Board. When direct European elections are organized or co-ordinated national European elections held (see above), the Congress would prepare an election programme. In addition, it could give binding instructions to the Executive and Union Board in the form or resolutions.

At a later stage, parallel with further development of European political integration, delegates to the European Congress could be nominated by regional branches of the national parties. At the same time a transition could be made from qualified majority voting to simple majority decisions.

The *European Union Board* would be elected by the European Congress on a proposal of the political parties concerned, with a special weighting for the number of members in each party. Members of the Union Board would also have to be members of the national party executive. They must be empowered to take decisions binding on their party executives. The Union Board would conduct its discussions and reach decisions on the basis of proposals made by the Executive. Decisions would be taken by a qualified majority. Unanimous agreement would be necessary on political matters for which no provision is made in the European Treaties.

The Union Board would also fix the Union budget and the contributions of the national parties.

The *European Executive* would have a limited number of members e.g. four for the present EEC or six for the enlarged Community of the Ten. There would no longer be any need for each national party to be represented on the executive. The German, Italian, French (and British) parties could be allowed one representative each on the Executive while the Benelux parties would have one representative between them (as would the Danish and Norwegian parties). The

Irish party (if it wishes to join the Union) would present a separate problem.

The members of the Executive would be elected by the Congress acting on a proposal of the Union Board. It would be permissible for them to be members of a national party executive (without holding special office) but not of the Union Board.

The task of the Executive would be to submit proposals to the European Union Board in complete independence but within the framework of decisions taken by the Congress. These proposals would be fixed by a simple majority in the Executive. Proposals could be made in all sectors of Community activity. The central national decision-making bodies of the affiliated parties could submit draft proposals to the Executive which would forward them to the Union Board with a favourable or unfavourable opinion.

Many improvements and amendments could probably be made to the structure I have outlined above. The need for this form of co-operation arises from the shift in the structure of power in the European Communities from the national to the trans-national European level.

APPENDIX

Resolution about Europe Adopted by the Dutch Socialist Party (Partij van de Arbeid) during the Congress Held in Amsterdam on 6 February 1971

The Congress,

1. Considering that in the process of economic integration and the emergence of power the Social Democratic movements in the European Communities are lagging far behind in integrating and co-operating with each other;
2. Considering that effective democratic control in an expanding Europe presupposes first and foremost wider powers for the European Parliament and a trans-national alliance of like-minded political movements;
3. Considering that the Social Democratic groupings in the European Communities should receive considerable reinforcement from the accession of the United Kingdom, Norway and Denmark;
4. Instructs the Party Executive to draw up a proposal in 1971 for a European Congress of the Social Democratic parties, to be convened if possible in 1972, and to submit this proposal as

soon as possible to the parties co-operating in the Liaison Office of the Socialist Parties of the European Communities, to the parties co-operating in the Socialist Group of the European Parliament, and to the Socialist Parties of the countries that have applied for membership of the Communities;

5. Invites the Party Executive to draw up, as the Dutch contribution to the decisions of the Congress, a draft plan for a European Social Democratic emergency programme and submit this for discussion, through sister parties, to all who wish to achieve a union of the progressive movements in Europe on this basis;

6. Believes that this European Congress must be able to secure the agreement of all the parties present to the taking of decisions binding on the parties and groupings represented there, and that it must lead to a federative partnership with the acceptance of majority decisions as a transitional phase towards the creation of a progressive European party;

7. Instructs its Executive to put forward proposals to a Party Congress, before the European Congress is held, concerning the emergency programme to be drawn up at the European Congress and the line to be followed by the Party's representatives.

Michael Steed

The European Parliament: the Significance of Direct Election *

THE POSSIBILITY THAT THE PARLIAMENT OF THE ENLARGED EUROPEAN Community may, wholly or in part, be elected directly within the next few years must excite both advocates of European unification and students of that curious political phenomenon, the European Community.[1] The event is still exceedingly problematical; no attempt is made here to assess just how much so. But the demand for direct election, and specific proposals to that end, have been actual for just over a decade and are worth analysing both as they relate to the possible future event and as they relate to other known factors – the existing state of organized political forces in Western Europe and the role of elections in the political life of member-states.

PROPOSALS FOR DIRECT ELECTION

Proposals for a directly elected parliament of the European peoples are as old as the first stirrings of the federalist movement.[2] In the debate after the 1939–45 war they moved a little closer to the centre of the stage but failed to get there. The Hague Congress in 1948 rejected a proposal for a directly elected European Assembly. At this period a directly elected European representative body was seen as a constituent assembly for a new political entity, even with revolutionary overtones. Had it materialized, it might have proved a means by which a European Union would have been created in a short space of time through direct popular participation. The very ambitiousness of the idea probably ensured that it was not to be taken seriously before a framework of European integration was established through inter-governmental action. At the outset European integration was constructed through inter-governmental

[1] The writer perhaps ought to state that he falls into both categories.
[2] Thus in R. N. Coudenhove-Kalergi, *Pan-Europa*, Vienna, 1923.

* Vol. 6, No. 4, Autumn 1971.

co-operation and the more radical federalist hopes of direct action became a fading inspiration.

Nevertheless, the Common Assembly of the ECSC, and in due course today's European Parliament had the possibility of direct election written into the Treaties. The *relance européenne* of the mid-1950s and the striking initial success of the EEC encouraged hopes that the sector-by-sector gradualist approach would bring political integration indirectly. Article 138 of the Treaty of Rome made the European Parliament the initiator of direct elections.[3]

The European Parliament moved with due speed to take up this opportunity. In October 1958 its committee on political affairs and institutional questions set up a sub-committee (later to be termed a working party) under the chairmanship of Fernand Dehousse to study the problems of instituting direct elections. The Dehousse working party prepared its report thoroughly. Between June and November 1959 meetings were held in each of the six national capitals with ministers and party leaders. Both these investigations and the proposals themselves bear every mark of the working group's intention that its scheme should be acceptable to the Community's member governments. Its work was completed in January 1960. With inconsequential amendments, its essential proposals proceeded, via approval by the committee on political affairs and institutional questions in March 1960, to the European Parliament in May 1960, which adopted them as a draft convention for submission to the Council of Ministers.[4] At this point the proposals came up against the deepening rift between the Gaullist government of France and the other five governments and no further progress was made.

The Dehousse proposals were essentially gradualist and saw direct elections as series of steps rather than as a stride. They pro-

---

[3] Article 138, § 3: The Assembly shall draw up proposals for election by direct universal suffrage in accordance with a uniform procedure in all Member States. § 4: The Council, acting by means of a unanimous vote, shall determine the provisions which it shall recommend to Member States for adoption in accordance with their respective constitutional rules.

[4] The report to the European Parliament and the convention adopted was published in October 1960 by the Publications Services of the Communities as *Vers l'élection directe de l'Assemblée parlementaire européenne*. An English translation of the report and the convention, together with the debate in the European Parliament, appears in *The Case for Elections to the European Parliament by Direct Universal Suffrage: Selected Documents* published by the Official Publications Office of the European Communities in September 1969 (pp. 22–245).

vided for a transitional period, following the end of the third stage of
the establishment of the Common Market, during which one-third
of the members of the European Parliament (which was to be trebled
in size to 426 members) were to continue to be indirectly elected.
Despite the Treaty requirement of 'a uniform procedure', the
electoral system was, for this transitional period, to be decided by
member states. Indeed there were few elements of uniform procedure in the proposals at all: a common minimum age for voting of
21 (which only affected the then Netherlands provision for 23), a
rather notional but symbolically important right of candidates to
stand outside their own state, and a refund of certain election
expenses which would be supranationally regulated by the bureau
of the European Parliament were the essential ones apart from the
date of election. Despite some argument for leaving each national
delegation to be elected on a nationally fixed date, it was agreed to
fix a common election day[5] and a common term of five years.
However, Dehousse was considerably more advanced in the direction of uniformity than the proposals published in 1958 by the
European Movement itself.[6] These had reservations about a common
election date, proposed none of the other three elements of uniformity mentioned above and indeed suggested that only half the
parliament should be directly elected. In its own words 'it avoided
recommending some proposals which were attractive in their
logical or progressive character but which risked being badly
received by national governments or parliaments'.[7] Thus carefully
were the proposals emanating from the proponents of integration
adjusted to the philosophy of working through national governments and of working by gradual stages.

Optimism about the imminence of direct election slowly receded.
Dehousse had talked of direct elections by 1962;[8] in 1962 Roy Price
wrote of 'aiming at a first election . . . in 1966 or 1967';[9] by 1967 the
prospect was quite different. The question was occasionally raised in
the European Parliament and in March 1969 a debate was staged on

[5] Strictly speaking the convention provided for a common date (a Sunday)
with national discretion on geographical or traditional grounds to have an
alternative polling day on the day before or the day after.
[6] Pamphlet: *Vers l'élection au suffrage universel direct de l'Assemblée Parlementaire
Européenne*, published by the Mouvement européen.
[7] *Op. cit.*, p. 7.
[8] F. Dehousse, '*Des élections européennes en 1962?*' in *Communes d'Europe*,
March, 1960.
[9] R. Pryce, *The Political Future of the European Community*, London, 1962, p. 90.

the failure of the Council of Ministers to consider the convention of May 1960 and the legal means open (under article 175) to remedy this failure.[10] In May 1969 the Council acted on the resolution passed by the Parliament by instructing the Committee of Permanent Representatives to consider the matter; but it gave no impression that this was any more than a way of avoiding the embarrassment of the use of article 175.

Meanwhile initiatives were being taken at a quite different level. In each of the six national parliaments bills or motions for direct election of that parliament's delegation to the European Parliament have been introduced. The greatest use of this procedure has been in Italy where, after several bills and motions introduced by deputies and senators, the Italian section of the European Federalist Movement collected in the first months of 1969 two hundred thousand signatures for a 'people's initiative bill'. These initiatives faced several problems. The Treaty requires that national delegations to the European Parliament be appointed by national parliaments from among their own members. The proposals therefore envisaged that those directly elected be then formally appointed by the national parliament; but the need to ensure that they be members of the national parliament created problems of the timing of the election. An election coincident with or shortly after each national election would make it easy to restrict candidature for the European election to those successful in the national election but would de-emphasize the European character of the election. An election held outside the period of national elections would highlight the European character of the election (especially if two or more states fixed the same date) but might mean that some members elected would cease to be eligible during their terms. In the event none of these initiatives has been pressed to a successful conclusion although the majority of the Community's political parties have accepted the principle of direct election.

With the successful completion of negotiations for enlargement in 1971, a new *relance* is foreseen by many. The time may shortly appear ripe for a fresh supra-national initiative to be taken and discussions in federalist circles are being held in anticipation of this. Whatever may appear or occur, it is worth noting that the potential situation is unlike that of earlier initiatives – the idealistic plans for

[10] Article 175 provides that institutions of the Community may refer a case where, in violation of the Treaty, the Council fails to act to the Court of Justice 'to have the said violation placed on record'.

launching the European idea after the war, the Dehousse plans for carefully fitting into the stages of the Common Market or the various national initiatives to find a way of breaking into the impasse of the European Parliament of the late 1960s. Fresh proposals must fit into the actual situation of a functioning Community in which responsibility for power exercised at Community level is channelled via national governments and legitimized through the responsibility of national governments to their peoples. This makes even more critical a question which has dogged all argument for direct elections already: just how they are intended to relate to changes in the Community's political system.

ARGUMENTS FOR DIRECT ELECTION.

The overwhelming bulk of the substantial body of argument for direct election which has amassed over the years is not susceptible to precise analysis in this respect. The debate, if that is the correct word in the circumstances, has been dominated by proponents (opponents have been happy to leave their case to the immobility of national governments) who have not had to meet reasoned argument. Advocacy of direct elections, indeed, is only partially directed towards its nominal goal. If popular belief in the norms of democracy and in the objective of European integration can be mobilized into popular demand for the specific proposal of direct election, that is in itself an advance for integration, whether or not direct election results. During the period when Gaullist intransigence was blocking any progress in the desired direction (or providing a convenient excuse for other governments) advocacy of direct election has provided a very useful symbol.

Nevertheless, one can extract plenty of concrete argument for direct election which is related to intended effects on the political system of the Community. It is convenient to divide these into four parts, in ascending order of the extent to which changes in that political system are implied.

The least adventurous arguments relate to the legitimacy of power now exercised by the Commission and the possibility (and legitimacy) of modest extensions of that power. Even without any additional powers going to the European Parliament (although the argument does presuppose increased prestige and influence), its direct election would enhance the authority of the main supranational organ, the Commission. This would help it to resist en-

croachments by national governments and might facilitate the
extension of its power.

The force of this argument may appear as limited as the present
powers of the Commission. It hardly envisages a stable situation and
most advocates of direct election would place it as distinctly subsidiary to the arguments envisaging direct accretion of power to the
European Parliament itself. Nevertheless it is worth distinguishing
from the latter, for it can lead to different conclusions about the
holding of direct elections. Arguments of this sort were widely used
in the first European parliamentary debate on direct election and the
anxiety voiced at that time that European elections might fail to
attract a high turnout was clearly concerned with the legitimizing
function of elections.[11]

But most proponents of direct election have linked their demand
with a complementary demand for powers for the European
Parliament, normally in the fields of budgetary control and of Community decisions of a legislative character. This has led at times to a
somewhat sterile argument between proponents as to which might
come first, if both aims could not be achieved simultaneously. On
the one hand a directly elected parliament could strengthen the
demand for the granting of powers to the European Parliament
because it would have produced politicians committed to obtaining
powers in order to justify their election; on the other, direct
election of a parliament without powers could prove a fiasco
through lack of interest both from elector and political leader.

The linking of the two demands, and the arguments associated
with them, evidently spring from the orthodox view of parliamentary government as practised in Western Europe. They also reflect
an institutional view of how European integration is to be promoted. If associated with increased powers, direct election is *ipso
facto* a good thing from the point of view of European integration.

In the third group come those arguments which link direct
election with alterations in the Community's political system. These
range from giving the European Parliament some secondary role in
the appointment of the Commission, to it taking on some of the

---

[11] Thus the French members of the study group which drew up the European
Movement's proposals argued that making the date of the election of the
French delegation to the European Parliament coincide with another election
(they suggested the municipal elections in France) was necessary in order to
avoid massive abstention and to that end opposed a common date for the
election.

functions of a constituent assembly in the deciding of major steps towards political union. They include arguments that direct election would be a means of creating political leadership inside the Community – which in this context would seem to be the hope that the direct election campaign would be a means whereby some national political leaders could establish supra-national standing, thus providing the European Parliament with a few members with the resource of supra-national prestige.

Such arguments cover a variety of means by which direct election may achieve given effects. The last example necessarily presupposes only a common period of election campaign, although certain conditions of the campaign might facilitate or frustrate it. Most, however, presuppose some grant of power by agreement of national governments – from the very specific agreement that would be required for the European Parliament to acquire a role in the appointment of the Commission, to the much more vague agreement that might be involved in an undertaking that a directly elected European Parliament could take part in creating a European Political Union. It is possible that this latter could come earlier than agreement on giving the Parliament legislative or budgetary powers, thus side-stepping the chicken-and-egg controversy over powers and direct election altogether. The election of the Parliament in such conditions would be fraught with uncertainty about how far the majority views that emerged from the election could have effect, but the possibility of a real effect would be present. The campaign might open up a debate on European unification and would provide an opportunity for federalists to seek to mobilize support.

This group of arguments shifts the focus from the legitimizing function of elections to the function of elections, and of the campaigns which precede them, in mobilizing and expressing opinion. It may be argued that most election campaigns in Western European states are ritual affairs which hardly perform this function. Yet examples to the contrary exist, a very striking one being Jean-Jacques Servan-Schreiber's successful campaign in the Nancy by-election in admittedly exceptional circumstances. But the first direct election of a European Parliament could also prove an exceptional circumstance.

The fourth set of arguments for direct election is less often voiced although it is sometimes implicit in a minor way in the formulation of other arguments: direct election as a means to the creation of trans-national political forces. The success of the integration of Europe will depend on how far European-wide parties which effectively bind together national political forces can arise. Direct election seen as a means to achieve this may complement the functions already discussed, but in the view of some, at any rate, this is the key function although the others may be more easily defended in public.

There is abundant evidence from other federations that political parties play a key role in the successful integration of different states. Both the union of Singapore with Malaysia and the first Nigerian Federation broke down with party systems that reflected state interests rather than combining them. The Civil War in the USA occurred at the point where the party which did not integrate Northern and Southern interests came to power in the White House. Conversely the integrating party not merely combines state interests but by providing political loyalties which cut across state loyalties, it strengthens the federal loyalty.

The existing party groups in the European Parliament cannot perform this function except for a tiny number of already European orientated politicians. To fulfil the role required, fully structured mass parties are needed, through which recruits to the higher positions in the party and in the European Parliament move upwards. Direct election will not of course produce such parties overnight but it could provide a necessary major stimulus. Furthermore, the precise arrangements for the election might play a significant part in stimulating or discouraging such parties. The timing of the election may prove important: should it wait until trans-national parties are beginning to form so that there is something to be stimulated or can one rely on the fact of a common European election to bring about common European parties? Certainly, insofar as it is this argument which has priority, the answers to many questions about the appropriate arrangements for direct election are different from what they would otherwise have been.

SOME EVIDENCE FROM NATIONAL ELECTIONS IN EUROPE

An election is a familiar part of the political life of each of the states making up the enlarged Community; it is worth, therefore, looking at the role that elections perform at national level to see how far the familiar functions are intended to be reproduced by a direct European election. Two functions performed by national elections seem particularly pertinent.

In every parliamentary election in the member-states the elector is being given the opportunity to influence the character, in party terms, of his government. A British general election exhibits this most clearly but the majority of the member-states where post-election negotiations for coalitions occur, or are the rule, also have recent experience of the results of an election changing directly and decisively the political character of their government. Even where *immobilisme* is most entrenched, in Italy, an election still affords opportunity to shift the centre of gravity of the coalition. Even in one-party Northern Ireland the 1969 election determined the political character of the ruling party. And even in quasi-presidential France both the 1967 and 1968 election campaigns were very directly related to the prospects for and authority of the government.

Yet even the most optimistic supporters of a European Parliament do not envisage that a decisive role in the appointment of the Commission, let alone something more like a government, would be acquired before the first direct election. How far might the absence of this familiar major function of national elections prove an impediment to a European election? It is impossible to tell but it clearly concerns some of those who argue for direct elections. It needs to be borne in mind by some who make direct comparisons between European and national elections. It may prove a strong argument to be deployed against direct election if and when debate about the matter is really joined.

An entirely different function of elections is one that is performed in both one-party and multi-party states. An election is the time when the citizen is called upon to demonstrate by his vote his loyalty both to the territorial area of his state and his form of government, following a campaign in which both loyalties are played on. In one-party states this function is more obvious. In multi-party states it is not the less important a function for the state because the elector is more free to indicate his dissent from that loyalty by voting for a party which contests the territorial integrity of the state, or for one which contests its form of government or, in some cases, by abstaining. Because the elector has had a certain freedom not to do so, the regular demonstration that the vast majority freely vote for parties which express loyalty both to the nation-state and to the constitutional order is all the more satisfying. In fact the whole presentation of the election campaign in the media will normally have been reinforcing those loyalties by emphasizing the issues which affect the national community as a whole and by exhibiting the constitutional order at its most democratic; in fact elements contesting those loyalties may well have found it difficult to make their case heard. Frequently parties which set out to some extent to contest these loyalties find that participation in an election tames them.

Conversely a fragile state embarks on a relatively free election at its peril. A striking case is the Federation of Rhodesia and Nyasaland whose federal government called an election to reinforce its authority in 1963 only to find that authority very gravely undermined by the successful boycott of the election. The 1918 election in Ireland demonstrated that the large majority of Irish people had rejected the territorial integrity and the constitutional order of the United Kingdom; the 1971 election in Pakistan demonstrated how far East Bengal's loyalty to the Pakistani state was diminishing.

A European election would probably replicate the normal loyalty-reinforcing function of national elections. The hope that it would help to create a European consciousness has several times been expressed in its favour. Insofar as the campaign was conducted at the European level and insofar as electors saw the election as a European one, it is arguable that nothing else would do so much to create a sense of involvement in the new European Community. But a great deal would depend on how the media, the parties and the governments presented the election. It would depend above all on the election taking place at the same time in all states.

Conversely, it is not inconceivable that direct election might put the European Community at greater risk in certain circumstances. If at some stage there was tension between one member-state and the rest of the Community, that state's government might prefer to seek compromises in private dealings with the Community's then executive organ and with other governments, although taking up public stances threatening the break-up of the Community. If a European election were to take place at this point, it is possible that the population of this state might demonstrate its estrangement from the continent-state at the polls, thus pushing its government into a more extreme position than that government (conscious for instance of economic consequences) would otherwise have wished. Such a scenario is certainly unlikely at the moment, but far from impossible in the future. An election is a testing-time which normally consolidates the integration of the state but which can occasionally work in the opposite direction.

Another feature of national elections, particularly marked in Britain, which could prove relevant is the way in which voters have increasingly used elections which are subsidiary to the main national election to register a protest vote against an unpopular government. British municipal elections and parliamentary by-elections have shown a rising anti-government vote in recent years. Between the peak of the labour government's unpopularity in May 1968 and a then record level of the conservative government's unpopularity in May 1971, there was a swing in votes of 26%; in June 1971 a by-election in Hayes & Harlington suggested an additional swing against the government of some 5%. In no other state has a floating protest vote of anything like 30% been measured but there are signs in French parliamentary by-elections and in West German *Länder* elections of analogous behaviour. Other states, notably Italy show much more steady party loyalty by voters in elections at different levels. But as the increase in the potential floating protest vote is a by-product of the weakening of ties of class, ideology and religion by which parties have traditionally maintained their voting-flocks, it is probable that this phenomenon will be an increasing feature of elections in Western Europe.

A European election which was clearly seen by the electorate to be a European election and to matter as such would presumably not be affected by this phenomenon. But insofar as the significance of a European election was not so communicated, electors would be liable to use it in the same way they are increasingly doing with other elections which are mid-term to national parliamentary general elections. The extent to which this might affect the outcome can be seen by calculating the likely results of the election of a British delegation to the European parliament at the spring 1968 or summer 1971 peaks of British government unpopularity. The British government, on both occasions, would have been put in a minority of approximately 65:35 in votes (similarly in seats if the election was by a proportional system) and of more than 85:15 in seats under the single-member seat plurality voting system.

If such behaviour, even to a much smaller degree, were observable in European elections it would have two results both very undesirable from the point of view of proponents of direct election. Political parties and commentators would note it and regard, at any rate partly or in some countries, the European election as a prestige contest for the parties within the context of national politics. This expectation would surely reinforce the behaviour (something of a similar self-fulfilling prophecy may well be at work in British municipal elections now) and establish a behaviour pattern from which it could be difficult to break out. If this happened, European elections would clearly fail to meet objectives set for them and by demonstrating that the European political level was seen by the electorate as so distinctly secondary to the national political level would certainly set back the progress of European integration.

The second result would be more likely if such behaviour occurred in one or two states only: it is quite probable that such behaviour is the more likely to occur where it already exists in national politics and where the relevant national government is already unpopular. In that case the relevant national government would be likely to oppose any increase in the role of a European Parliament wherein its own national representatives were of a different political hue from itself. If such behaviour were to persist in that state's part of a European election it would tend to cause tension between that state and the rest of the Community.

Curiously the one way to avoid this danger is a procedure which in other respects works right against the objectives set for direct election: to hold the election of each national delegation to the European parliament separately and simultaneously with national elections.

PROBLEMS OF HOLDING A DIRECT ELECTION.

From the foregoing it is evident that optimal arrangements for the initial direct election must vary accordingly to the objectives set for it in terms of the Community's political system and of one's judgement of the likely reaction of, among others, political parties and the electorate. The simple question of whether to have a common polling day and a common term of election can take on several different lights. Usually this forms a minimum uniform element in the election procedure whenever that is elaborated by proponents. Clearly only with a uniform polling day and therefore common campaign can one have any hope that direct election will raise European consciousness among the electorate, facilitate the emergence of a European political leadership or encourage trans-national political forces. But, primarily concerned with the effect of a high abstention rate on its legitimizing role, the French minority in the European Movement's study group opposed a common date,[12] from a pro-European point of view. Similarly in view of its attitude to mid-term elections, one could argue from a European point of view that the

---

[12] See footnote 11, p. 143.

British electorate might do less harm to European integration if European elections coincided separately with national elections.

A verdict on the electoral system depends on similar assessments. The Dehousse scheme has obvious merits of avoiding an issue on which it would be difficult to get agreement and if the priority is to legitimize supra-national power and obtain powers for the European Parliament as soon as possible, it is the obvious solution. But differing national electoral systems could prove a significant disincentive towards national parties reorganizing on a trans-national basis while some features of a uniform electoral system could aid the emergence of trans-national parties. A parallel dilemma appears in the initiatives towards national election of national delegations. These have enthusiastic federalist sponsorship and if one should succeed it would be hailed as a great victory. But direct election occurring through a series of national initiatives, each operating under different rules and each viewed as selecting national delegations to the supra-national parliament, might present serious disadvantages if this entrenched national political forces and electoral habits before a supra-national election could stimulate more supra-national attitudes to the event.

As for the electoral system itself, proposals have generally avoided the issue. But Birke, in a thorough and comprehensive study of some of the problems of holding direct elections, provides full and cogent reasons for the use of a proportional representation system from the point of view of European integration.[13] These are reinforced by the grave disadvantage of the main rival system, voting in single-member constituencies, in a new federal situation: by distorting the relative representation of parties according to states this could seriously hinder the growth of trans-national parties.[14] But it

[13] W. Birke, *European Elections by Direct Suffrage*, Leyden, 1961. Part 3.
[14] This characteristic of the single-member seat system is not widely recognized. The tendency to produce false identification of parties in certain regions can be very clearly seen if the results of the 1970 British general election are broken down by regions:

	Votes (%)		Seats	
	Con	Lab	Con	Lab
East Anglia	53	41	17	1
Northern Ireland	54	12	8	—
South-West	51	34	35	6
Home Counties	54	34	79	5
Northern	41	55	10	29
Scotland	39	45	23	44

may be very difficult for these reasons relating to supra-national considerations to be appreciated by national politicians with established views on electoral systems based on national experience or party interest.

However, at least the question of a common electoral system has received some attention. Another matter of electoral arrangements fraught with difficulties but potentially critical for the success of an initial direct election does not seem to have been considered in any proposals: that of the broadcasting arrangements. Yet it may very well lie in the hands of the television and radio media to determine whether the campaign acquires a European coherence; the press, relying on material written in national languages and on national circulations could follow but hardly lead. A scenario for a coherently European campaign could necessitate recognition of certain Europe-wide party spokesmen, probably expressing themselves in either English or French, with appropriate speeches, interviews, press conferences and confrontations broadcast over the whole continent. If national party interests, language and other technical difficulties resulted in the issues of the campaign being transmitted almost exclusively through national party leaders in national languages, with familiar national interviewers and commentators, one can imagine that a very different image of the campaign would be conveyed to electors. The interesting question is not so much what would happen (which is difficult to plan ahead) but how decisions about what would happen would be taken.

An example of how different broadcasting conventions reflect and transmit different conventions about what a party system is can be seen in existing national practices about allocation of time to parties. In Britain the arrangements entrench a two-large-and-one-small party system: smaller parties are effectively not recognized for all the minute concessions made to them recently. The multi-party system of the Fifth Republic was presented clearly as a two bloc

	Votes (%)		Seats	
	Con	Lab	Con	Lab
Wales	28	52	7	27
Yorkshire	40	52	16	34
United Kingdom	48	43	330	287

Because the United Kingdom is, apart from Northern Ireland, a well integrated state this gross distortion of party support in certain regions does not matter when it balances out at national level. But in a nascent federation in which an integrating party system had yet to grow up, it could prove disastrous.

system by the arrangements in the last two legislative elections for equal time between the government parties (as a pair) and the various opposition parties (taken together). But a party system in Norway which in 1969, after four years of non-socialist coalition rule, had emerged as more of a two bloc system was presented in a rather different light by the traditional eve-of-poll Norwegian television confrontation marathon. Each party (right down to the Communist Party which had received 1·4% of the votes in the previous election) had equal time for its spokesman (together with the Prime Minister and a second Labour Party representative); there was every incentive in the form of the discussion for each government party to differentiate itself from the others. If Europe-wide political broadcasts are to play a part in a campaign, some preparations must be made for decisions on how to recognize parties and leading spokesmen in the new situation.

The examples of the common date, the electoral system and the broadcasting arrangements suffice to show some of the ways in which arrangements for the initial direct election could crucially affect the behaviour of both parties and voters in a situation for which there are no precedents. In turn these affect the judgement of whether or not it seems likely that direct election could fulfil the objectives, particularly the more ambitious ones, of its proponents.

Like those who consider direct election of the European Parliament as the key to democratization of the Community institutions, this article has confined itself to an orthodox view of how the matters at issue – legitimation, the formation and competition between parties and so forth – operate in West European democracies. It can well be asked whether this is the right approach. Several ideas for a radically different approach towards combining a *relance* with democratization have begun to circulate, a typical example of which is the proposal for a directly elected collegial executive instanced by David Coombes.[15] A little thought will demonstrate that many of the problems which arise in the context of seeking to achieve the desired objectives through direct election of the European Parliament can be much more easily met in the context of such ideas. The one problem is that, if getting down to the details of direct election of the present Parliament in the present Community may err on the side of unrealism, what Coombes terms 'the alternative means' might seem at present to belong to Utopia.

[15] D. Coombes, *Politics and Bureaucracy in the European Community*, London, 1970, pp. 317–18.

Jacques-René Rabier

Europeans and the Unification of Europe *

AMONG THE TOOLS USED TO STUDY SOCIAL, AND MORE PARTICULARLY political phenomena, the part played by public opinion surveys continues to grow, in spite of the tentativeness of some and the blunders of others. The study of the process of European integration and, more generally, of every process of regional integration has not escaped this. Indeed, it can be asked whether the most decisive progress in the theory of European integration has not been brought about by the very close co-operation between political scientists and the opinion poll experts.[1] Carrying out the intention which was expressed in this journal in 1967, the Press and Information Services of the Commission of the European Communities have tried, in the last two years, to promote a study in depths of the attitude towards the Common Market and the unification of Europe in the six founder countries.[2]

Between 1968 and 1970, three phases of the study were undertaken, in which, under our direction, representatives of the European institutes of the groups 'International Research Associates' and 'Gallup International' collaborated with an American specialist, Professor Ronald Inglehart (Ann Arbor and Geneva).

During the first phase, in 1968, 216 boys and girls, divided into three age groups (11–12, 15–16 and 19–20) were interviewed in depth, under the supervision of psychologists, in order to discover the common characteristics in each age-group as well as the differences between those who were interviewed.

In 1969, a pilot questionnaire was tried out on a sample of 486 young 'Europeans' aged, half and half, between 15 and 16 and 19 and

---

[1] Cf. Stéphane Bernard: 'Esquisse d'un modèle du processus d'intégration européenne', *Integration*, Vierteljahreshefte zur Europaforschung, 4/1970, Bonn, pp. 308–20.

[2] See my article, 'The European Idea and National Public Opinion', *Government and Opposition*, Vol. 2, No. 3, April–July 1967, pp. 443–54.

* Vol. 6, No. 4, Autumn 1971.

20. This international sample was not aimed at any particular section of the population under study but was as heterogeneous as possible, in order to supply the maximum information about the relations between the answers to the different questions.

In 1970, finally, a poll of a representative sample of the population over 16 was undertaken in the six countries of the European community. A questionnaire made up of fifty questions was sent to 8752 persons, 2021 in Germany, 2046 in France, 1822 in Italy, 1298 in Belgium, 1230 in the Netherlands and 335 in Luxemburg.

It is not possible to resume here all the information gathered during the two first phases of this study. Certain of the hypotheses formulated in the course of these two phases have been validated in the course of the third. Others have for the time being been put to one side, either because they do not seem to be firm enough to be given priority in a research project somewhat restricted by lack of time and money, or because the exploration of some age-groups seemed less urgent in view of the wide objectives of the research. Thus, for example, the study of the attitudes of those under 16 has not been followed up, in spite of the very interesting verbal and graphic material received.[3]

The results obtained from the poll itself have been or will be the object of extremely interesting and profound analyses, but nothing has as yet been published as a whole.[4]

In giving these new insights to the public – and to the public in a country which has reason to be interested in the political attitudes of the 'citizens' of the Europe which is taking shape, we would like to conclude by appealing to researchers in the various disciplines concerned. On the one hand, these facts are far from having yielded all the information to be drawn from them, no matter how valuable the first analyses quoted at the beginning of this article may be. On the other, this kind of research must be periodically renewed in order to follow the change of attitude which comes with time.

---

[3] See Jacqueline Bissery: 'Comment l'idée de l'Europe vient aux plus jeunes' et 'Comment les jeunes Français voient l'Europe politique'. *Communauté européene*, No. 131, June 1969, pp. 30–2, and No. 134, September 1969, pp. 25–7.

[4] See Ronald Inglehart: 'Public Opinion and Regional Integration', *International Organization*, World Peace Foundation, Boston, Mass., Vol. XXIV, No. 4, Autumn 1970, pp. 764–95; 'Ongoing Changes in West European Political Cultures', *Integration*, Vierteljahreshefte zur Europaforschung, Bonn, 4/1970, 250–72; 'The Silent Revolution in Europe', shortly to appear in the *American Political Science Review* and 'Changing Value Priorities and European Integration', which will be published in the *Journal of Common Market Studies*, Oxford.

Lastly, it would be highly desirable to extend this research to other countries, in order to make possible wider international comparisons, especially between the countries which for twenty years have been engaged in the process of European integration and those who desire to join them.

Below will be found unpublished information on:

Exposure to information media and the degree of information.
Contacts abroad and the degree of confidence towards certain foreign peoples.
Attitudes regarding the unification of Europe.
The degree of social and political participation.

INFORMATION MEDIA AND DEGREE OF INFORMATION

Exposure to information media

About seven persons out of every ten watch the news broadcasts on television every day (48%) or several times a week (20%). Only 12% never watch the news. The Netherlands and Germany are the two countries where exposure to television is strongest; the four other countries are almost equal. Radio takes second place as a source of information: six Europeans out of ten listen to the news daily (45%) or several times per week (16%); 17% never listen to the news. The Netherlands and Germany again head the list, closely followed by France and Luxemburg. The press comes in third place: four Europeans out of ten read the political news in the newspapers every day (27%) or several times a week (14%); 25% never read the news. The Netherlands, Luxemburg and Germany are in first place.

The total exposure index to information media, calculated by simply adding together the percentages of persons most exposed (maximum: 300 points), places the Netherlands and Germany first (201 and 194, respectively), followed by Luxemburg. For France, Italy and Belgium, exposure is below average for the Community.

Degree of information

The study of the degree of information was made with the aid of several questions: one was on the knowledge of the names of countries belonging to the Common Market and another, in each country, on knowledge of the name of the Prime Minister and Minister of Foreign Affairs of that country.

In the Community as a whole, 36% of those polled correctly gave

TABLE 1

Exposure to Information Media

(of 100 persons polled, aged 16 and over)

	EC	G	B	F	I	L	N[5]
Watch television news programmes							
Every day	48	60	41	46	36	37	57
Several times a week	20	19	20	16	24	21	24
Listen to the news on the radio							
Every day	45	50	30	48	36	46	52
Several times a week	16	15	15	15	20	16	13
Read the political news in the newspapers							
Every day	27	34	19	25	19	42	38
Several times a week	14	16	11	13	15	12	17
Exposure index	170	194	136	163	150	174	201

the composition of the Common Market, 63% in Luxemburg and 49% in the Netherlands. These percentages may seem rather low; they are explained by the fact that many people add certain countries (for example, Switzerland) or forget one (for example, Luxemburg). In fact, the six countries are named on the average by more than half the people questioned: France and Germany by eight out of ten; Belgium, Italy, and the Netherlands by about seven out of ten; and Luxemburg by five out of ten.

The name of the Prime Minister of their country is given by 90% of the persons polled (only 77% in Belgium) and the name of the Minister of Foreign Affairs by 64% of the persons polled (48% in Belgium and 34% in France.) In France, as can be seen, the percentages are the same for persons who correctly give the six coun-

TABLE 2

Degree of Information

(out of 100 persons polled, aged 16 and over)

	EC	G	B	F	I*	L	N
Give the exact composition of the Common Market	36	39	34	31	35	63	49
Give the name of the Prime Minister	90	98	77	84	—	91	87
Give the name of the Minister of Foreign Affairs	64	84	48	34	—	73	96

(*) There was a governmental crisis in Italy when the poll was taken.

[5] European Community – Germany – Belgium – France – Italy – Luxemburg – Netherlands.

tries of the Common Market (31%) and those who give the name of
the Minister of Foreign Affairs.

CONTACTS ABROAD AND DEGREE OF CONFIDENCE TOWARDS FOREIGN PEOPLES

Contacts abroad

Do Europeans of countries of the European Community travel
outside their country? To the question: 'In which country have you
spent at least one day?', almost seven out of ten (68%) give at least
one country. In other words, only three out of ten (32%) have not
travelled outside their country. But this proportion increased to
54% where the Italians are concerned.

TABLE 3

Contacts Abroad

(out of 100 persons polled, aged 16 and over)

	EC	G	B	F	I	L	N
Have spent at least one day in:							
No country	32	20	18	32	54	1	14
One foreign country	18	15	17	23	18	13	14
Two foreign countries	14	16	16	13	12	12	16
Three countries	11	15	14	10	6	17	15
Four countries and over	25	34	35	22	10	54	40
No answer	0	—	—	—	—	3	1

TABLE 4

Degree of Confidence towards Foreign Peoples

(out of 100 persons polled, aged 16 and over)

	EC	G	B	F	I	L	N
Express great confidence or rather great confidence towards the following peoples:							
The Swiss	78	86	77	77	70	78	84
The Americans	69	77	69	59	67	71	75
The British	61	72	70	55	49	65	66
The French	52	58	74	—	43	63	51
The Germans	45	—	52	48	39	28	60
The Italians	31	26	41	34	—	26	32
The Russians	23	17	20	29	25	11	24
The Chinese	9	7	8	9	10	5	8

Degree of confidence towards foreign peoples

The degree of confidence towards the various peoples of the world is particularly high towards the Swiss, Americans and British, and expecially low towards the Chinese.

It can be seen that the rating of the various foreign countries is almost the same in the six countries of the European Community:

The Swiss lead in all cases, with particularly high scores in Germany and the Netherlands.

The Americans (USA) are everywhere in second place, except in Belgium where, along with the British, they are preceded by the French. Their score is particularly high in Germany and the Netherlands.

The British come in third place, with a relatively low score in Italy. The Russians and the Chinese everywhere occupy the last two places. The degree of confidence towards the Russians is especially low in Luxemburg.

As concerns the three countries of the Community on which the persons polled had to give an opinion, all three occupy a middle position on the list. The French come first except in the Netherlands, with high scores in Belgium and Luxemburg; the Germans follow them, with relatively low scores in Italy and especially in Luxemburg; the Italians come in third place.

One might be surprised that the persons polled in the countries of the Community more frequently expressed their confidence towards people who are not part of that Community (Swiss, Americans, British) than towards their own partners within the Community (France, Germany, Italy). This is because the image people have of each other is a complex phenomenon, made up of very many factors: historical, geographical, political, cultural, etc. More serious studies would make it possible to get a clearer idea of these images, of which confidence is only one aspect. Saying that two groups understand each other is like saying that each of them believes that the behaviour of the other is predictable; saying that they have confidence in each other is like saying, in addition, that each expects from the other favourable behaviour towards it. These favourable behaviours may be expected in very different sectors of activity: cultural, economic, and military co-operation, even integration in the same political system. The images – even favourable – that one people has about the others may represent very different things. Moreover, each of these images is the result of images formed in each social group constituting that people.

Therefore, the above results may be considered data the interpretation of which is especially delicate.

ATTITUDES TOWARDS THE UNIFICATION OF EUROPE

What characterizes the present poll is that it was not limited to gathering more or less vague opinions related to problems in which the people polled feel themselves more or less involved. It attempted to go further by gathering much data on the image that the Europeans have of unified Europe or of the Common Market, on the degree of their belief in or attachment to it, on their analysis of the results of the Common Market, and on their expectations concerning the results (favourable or unfavourable) that the unification of Europe could produce.

We will here examine in turn:

Overall attitudes regarding the political unification of Europe.
Attachment to national symbols.
The geographic extension desired for the Common Market.
The form of political organization desired for a unified Europe.
The image of the United States of Europe: what is expected of it and what is feared from it.
The analysis of the effects of the Common Market and the degree of attachment to the Common Market.
The degree of attachment to the unification of Europe.

Overall attitudes towards the political unification of Europe

Four questions make possible a first indication of overall attitudes towards the evolution of the Common Market, towards the political creation of the United States of Europe, towards the election of a European parliament by direct universal suffrage, towards the formation of a European government and towards the vote for a president of the United States of Europe, of a nationality other than that of the person polled. A fifth question makes it possible to measure a rate of overall attachment to the unification of Europe.

'Are you for or against the evolution of the Common Market towards the political creation of the United States of Europe?'

TABLE 5

Evolution of the Common Market towards the Political Formation of the United States of Europe

(of 100 persons polled, aged 16 and over)

Expressed themselves:	EC	G	B	F	I	L	N
For	70	69	62	63	77	77	75
Against	10	10	10	13	6	5	14
Don't know or did not answer	20	21	28	24	17	18	11

TABLE 5a

The Evolution of the Common Market towards the Political Formation of the United States of Europe

(out of 100 persons who expressed an opinion)

	EC	G	B	F	I	L	N
For	87.5	87	86	83	93	94	84
Against	12.5	13	14	17	7	6	16

'Are you for or against the election of a European Parliament by direct universal suffrage, that is, a parliament elected by all the citizens of the member countries?'

More than six people polled out of ten and eight out of ten of those expressing an opinion are 'for'. Italy and Luxemburg are again first.

TABLE 6

Election of a European Parliament by Direct Universal Suffrage

(of 100 persons polled, aged 16 and over)

Express themselves:	EC	G	B	F	I	L	N
For	64	63	56	59	71	70	60
Against	12	12	12	16	8	11	21
Don't know or did not answer	24	25	32	25	21	19	19

TABLE 6a

Election of a European Parliament by Direct Universal Suffrage
(of 100 persons who expressed an opinion)

	EC	G	B	F	I	L	N
For	84	85	82	79	90	86	74
Against	16	15	18	21	10	14	26

'*Would you be in favour of having, above the government (of your country), a European government responsible for common policies in the fields of foreign affairs, defence, and economics?*'

Here again, six persons polled out of ten and seven out of ten of those expressing an opinion are 'in favour'. The favourable replies are considerably more frequent in Italy, and considerably less in the Netherlands and Luxemburg.

TABLE 7

Formation of a European Government
(of 100 persons polled, aged 16 and over)

	EC	G	B	F	I	L	N
Expressed an opinion:							
For	58	56	52	53	67	47	49
Against	23	23	19	28	16	36	37
Don't know or did not answer	19	21	29	19	17	17	14

TABLE 7a

Formation of a European Government
(of 100 persons who expressed an opinion)

	EC	G	B	F	I	L	N
For	72	71	73	65	81	57	57
Against	28	29	27	35	19	43	43

'*In case of the election of a president of the United States of Europe by universal suffrage, would you or would you not vote for a candidate who was not (of your nationality) if his personality and his programme corresponded better to your ideas than those of the candidates (of your nationality)?*'

Almost seven persons polled out of ten and almost eight out of ten of those expressing an opinion were in favour. The Germans, Dutch and Luxemburgers more often gave a positive answer to this question, which may be considered an indication of opposition to nationalism or of acceptance of a European democracy.

TABLE 8

The Vote for a President of the United States of Europe of Another Nationality (of 100 persons polled, aged 16 and over)

	EC	G	B	F	I	L	N
Expressed themselves:							
For	66	70	54	63	64	68	71
Against	19	14	23	23	22	19	19
Don't know or did not answer	15	16	23	14	14	13	10

TABLE 8a

The Vote for a President of the United States of Europe of Another Nationality (of 100 persons who expressed an opinion)

	EC	G	B	F	I	L	N
For	78	83	70	73	74	78	79
Against	22	17	30	27	26	22	21

'*Would you say that you are very favourable, rather favourable, indifferent, rather opposed, or very opposed to European unification?*'

In a way, this question incorporates the attitude probed by means of the four preceding questions. Three-quarters of the persons polled and eight out of ten of those expressing an opinion are in favour of the unification of Europe. The differences from country to country are insignificant. The 'Europeans' seem somewhat more numerous in Italy, somewhat less numerous in Belgium. Whether one considers the persons polled or only the persons who expressed an opinion, the percentage of those opposed approaches ten percent only in France and the Netherlands.

Attachment to national symbols

One question makes it possible to measure approximately an attitude which may be considered opposed to a pro-European attitude: the attachment to certain national symbols such as currency, Olympic teams and the flag.

TABLE 9

General Attitude towards the Unification of Europe
(of 100 persons polled, aged 16 and over)

	EC	G	B	F	I	L	N
Expressed an attitude:							
Very favourable	34	39	31	24	40	52	30
Somewhat favourable	40	37	35	46	38	24	44
	(74)	(76)	(66)	(70)	(78)	(76)	(74)
Indifferent	11	13	16	11	7	14	11
Rather unfavourable	4	4	3	6	4	2	7
Very favourable	2	1	2	2	1	2	3
	(6)	(5)	(5)	(8)	(5)	(4)	(10)
Don't know or did not answer	9	6	13	11	10	6	5

TABLE 9a

General Attitude towards the Unification of Europe
(of 100 persons who expressed an opinion)

	EC	G	B	F	I	L	N
Favourable	81	81	76	79	87	81	78
Indifferent	12	14	18	12	8	15	12
Unfavourable	7	5	6	9	5	4	10

'*Would you be favourable, opposed, or indifferent to the currency (of your country) being replaced by a European currency, to the team (of your country) in the next Olympic Games being incorporated into a European team, and to the flag (of your country) being replaced by a European flag in solemn ceremonies?*'

One person polled out of two was in favour of replacing the national currency with a European currency. On the other hand, the percentage of persons opposed to the Olympic team of their country being incorporated into a European team is, in all countries except Luxemburg, higher than the percentage of those in favour. As for the national flag, it is still a symbol to which they are attached, although out of ten persons polled, throughout the countries of the Community, three are in favour and two are indifferent to its being replaced by a European flag in solemn ceremonies. It is in Germany that the European flag would be most easily accepted.

TABLE 10

Attachment to National Symbols

(of 100 persons polled, aged 16 and over)

Attitude towards:	EC	G	B	F	I	L	N
a *European currency*							
Favourable	51	52	49	51	51	63	47
Opposed	23	26	23	23	21	13	23
Indifferent	18	14	21	18	18	19	27
Don't know or do not answer	8	8	7	8	10	5	3
a *European Olympic Team*							
Favourable	27	25	26	34	24	53	20
Opposed	43	51	36	36	41	20	54
Indifferent	22	18	27	22	25	21	23
Don't know or did not answer	8	6	11	8	10	6	3
a *European flag*							
Favourable	27	35	26	22	24	26	19
Opposed	52	41	48	61	57	57	57
Indifferent	15	18	20	11	11	12	21
Don't know or do not answer	6	6	6	6	8	5	3

Geographic extension desired for the Common Market

Two questions were asked on this subject: one concerning membership of Great Britain in the Common Market, and the other concerning various other countries which one might or might not like to see join.

'Are you for or against the entry of Great Britain into the Common Market?'

About seven persons out of ten and about nine (out of ten) among those who expressed an opinion are in favour of the entry of Great Britain into the Common Market. It is in France and Italy that the most opposition is found.

TABLE 11

Attitude towards the Entry of Great Britain into the Common Market

(of 100 persons polled, aged 16 and over)

Expressed themselves:	EC	G	B	F	I	L	N
For	67	70	65	60	65	72	82
Against	11	9	7	15	12	6	7
Don't know or did not answer	22	21	28	25	23	22	11

TABLE 11a

Attitude towards the Entry of Great Britain into the Common Market
(of 100 persons who expressed an opinion)

	EC	G	B	F	I	L	N
For	86	89	90	80	84	92	92
Against	14	11	10	20	16	8	8

'*Among the following countries which are not members of the Common Market, are there any that you would like to see join? Which ones?*'

Among the persons polled in the countries of the Community, it is Switzerland and Denmark which, far exceeding the others, gained the most votes. Then, Spain (mentioned more frequently in France and Germany), East Germany (Germany and France), Poland (France and Germany). The USSR comes last, with a somewhat higher score in France than in the other countries of the Community.

TABLE 12

Countries One Would Like to See Enter the Common Market
(of 100 persons polled, aged 16 and over)

	EC	G	B	F	I	L	N
Mention the following countries:[6]							
Switzerland	63	67	57	62	59	64	70
Denmark	59	76	46	52	43	54	78
Spain	39	42	30	45	33	25	29
East Germany	25	29	16	26	22	13	16
Poland	23	24	15	28	19	15	18
USSR	18	16	12	23	18	12	16
None of these countries	5	3	10	8	6	6	3
Don't know or did not answer	15	12	22	14	19	20	12

Forms of political organization of unified Europe

Two basic formulas of organization of the relations between states in a politically unified Europe, or a Europe in the process of unification, may be distinguished: inter-governmental co-operation and the establishment of a 'supra-national' confederal or federal government. Theoretically the creation of a centralized European state may also be imagined.

The question posed makes it possible to evaluate the orientation of

[6] The persons polled could give several answers.

the persons questioned concerning these three types of organization. The majority of the Europeans of the six countries of the Community (56% of the persons polled and 64% of those who were for one of the three formulas or against all three) are in favour of the formation of a European government which would concern itself with the most important questions, leaving to each national government the responsibility for its own particular problems.

The formula of simple inter-governmental co-operation received the votes of fewer than two persons out of ten.

TABLE 13

Forms of Political Organization of Unified Europe

(of 100 persons polled, aged 16 and over)

	EC	G	B	F	I	L	N
Favour one of the three types of political unification:							
1. There is no government on the European level, but the governments of all the countries meet regularly to decide common policy.	16	16	14	18	13	19	18
2. There is a European government which concerns itself with the most important questions, but each country retains a government which concerns itself with its own particular problems.	56	52	51	62	57	63	58
3. There is a European government which concerns itself with all questions, and the member countries no longer have a national government.	11	15	9	7	10	5	13
4. None of these formulas	4	4	6	3	4	1	3
5. Don't know or did not answer	13	13	20	10	16	12	8

TABLE 13a

Forms of Political Organization of Unified Europe

(of 100 persons who expressed an opinion)

	EC	G	B	F	I	L	N
1. No European government, but intergovernmental co-operation.	18	18	17.5	20	15	22	20
2. A European government concerning itself with the most important questions.	64	60	64	69	68	72	63
3. No more national governments	13	17	10	8	12	6	14
4. None of these formulas	5	5	8.5	3	5	–	3

Image of the United States of Europe: expectations, hopes and fears

We have just seen, and this confirms all previous polls, that the great majority of 'Europeans' favour the unification of Europe, and even favour a supra-national form of organization of a unified Europe. But one criticism is often made of such polls: Do the persons polled know what is involved? Do they feel concerned, implicated? What images do they have of a unified Europe, and what do they expect of it exactly?

One may already answer that the percentage of persons polled who 'don't know and do not reply' is not very high, which is already a sign of a certain consciousness of being concerned and implicated. For example, for the four questions pertaining to the evolution of the Common Market towards the political formation of a United States of Europe, to the election of a European Parliament by direct universal suffrage, to the formation of a European government above the national governments, and to the vote for a 'foreign' candidate for the presidency of a United States of Europe, the average percentage of persons not expressing an opinion is 19·5% for all the Community (28% in Belgium, and 13·5% in the Netherlands). For the question concerning the general attitude towards the unification of Europe, the percentage of 'no' answers is 9% (13% in Belgium and 5% in the Netherlands).

But it may still be objected that, even for those who express an opinion (positive or negative) the unification of Europe is a vague, unreal notion and perhaps corresponds to an ideology unconnected with reality.

It was to answer these objections that the following question was asked, designed to present to those polled a certain number of opinions, in relation to which they were to express an opinion by giving their degree of approval or disapproval.

A first conclusion is that the great majority of persons polled (more than eight out of ten) affirmed their national pride: the percentage is 82% for the countries of the Community as a whole (92% in Luxemburg and 71% in Germany).

The conservatives, that is to say, those who are hesitant concerning any change in the present situation, those who fear certain negative effects of the integration of Europe (loss of national culture and originality, increase in the cost of living and in unemployment), or those who believe that the unification of Europe is impossible because of the diversity of languages, represent two to three persons out of ten. The Luxemburgers seem to be the most conservative, followed by the Belgians and the Dutch. The Italians are the most open to change.

Approximately one person out of two expressed resigned or ethnocentric opinions rather close to conservatism: for 55% 'the fact cannot be changed that the strong always dominate the weak'; for 46%, there are too many foreign workers in their countries.

As for the pro-European attitudes, clearly in the majority, they seem to revolve around five images or major motivations:

Europe, a third force between America and the USSR: 67% of those polled (69% to 64% in Germany, Belgium, Italy and France; 57% in the Netherlands; 46% in Luxemburg).

Europe, a means for European scientists to catch up with the Americans: 62% of those polled.

Europe, a means of improving the situation of the less-favoured classes: 61% of those polled.

Europe, a first step towards a world government which would eliminate wars: (66% to 54% in Germany, Belgium, Italy and France; 47% in the Netherlands; 40% in Luxemburg).

Europe, a means of improving the living standard for everybody: 59% of those polled (71% in Italy).

TABLE 14

The Image of the United States of Europe: Expectations, Hopes, Fears
(of 100 persons polled, aged 16 and over)

	EC	G	B	F	I	L	N
State that they accept, either fully or for the most part, the following propositions:							
I am proud to be (. . .)	82	71	88	88	86	92	82
The United States of Europe should become a third force, equal to that of the United States of America or the USSR.	67	69	67	64	66	48	57
Within the framework of the United States of Europe, European scientists could catch up with the Americans.	62	63	50	64	59	55	60
In the United States of Europe, the less-favoured classes of the population would have a better chance of improving their situation.	61	59	55	55	69	53	66
The United States of Europe would be a first step towards a world government which eliminates wars.	59	66	60	54	58	40	47
In the United States of Europe, the living standard would probably be higher.	59	51	57	55	71	59	60

The fact cannot be changed that the strong always dominate the weak.	55	61	63	61	42	70	53
In principle I have nothing against foreign workers, but there are really too many in our country.	46	54	62	60	16	53	59
In the present state of affairs things are going rather well for us; so, why change?	30	44	44	27	13	51	31
In the United States of Europe, the various peoples would risk losing their culture and their originality.	27	29	29	29	19	29	45
The unification of Europe is impossible since we speak different languages.	21	20	25	25	20	19	20
In the United States of Europe life would be even more expensive and there would be an even greater risk of unemployment.	18	20	22	19	13	25	21

Limiting the analysis to the questions directly related to Europe, we note again that there are a few differences between the countries. The Germans, Belgians and French clearly favour the motivation theme: 'Europe, a third force'. The Italians and the Luxemburgers are particularly sensitive to the idea of a 'general improvement of the standard of living', and the Dutch to the idea of an 'improvement of the situation of the least-favoured classes.'

As concerns the risks inherent in a unification of Europe, the one relatively most feared is loss of cultural originality, especially in the Netherlands. Risks of an economic nature are feared by only two persons out of ten, and even fewer in Italy (13%).

Appreciation of the effects of the Common Market and degree of attachment to the Common Market.

Two questions made it possible to measure the attitudes towards the Common Market: one concerned an opinion of the effects of the Common Market on the living standard of the persons polled, and the degree of attachment to the Common Market.

Opinion of the effects of the Common Market.

'*Do you consider that the Common Market has had up to now a very favourable, rather favourable, rather unfavourable or very unfavourable effect on your living standard?*'

The conclusion is surprising at first glance; although the great majority of those polled were favourable to the unification of

Europe, and, although this favourable view was accompanied, as we have seen, by a rather precise picture of the forms that unification could adopt and the goals it could make it possible to attain, only four people out of ten stated that they had noted favourable effects of the Common Market on the living standard. It is true that, out of the six other persons, four did not answer and two only stated they had noted unfavourable effects.

These results could mean that the effects of the Common Market on 'the man in the street' are really insignificant, or that, although they are not negligible, they are hardly noticed. The first interpretation is not very plausible, when one takes into account what is known about the increase in trade between the countries of the Common Market; but what is important from the viewpoint that interests us here is less the objective situation than the image of it that is obtained. Actually, if the relatively high percentage of 'no answers' is eliminated, it may be noted that the favourable effects largely predominate: in the proportion of seven to three for all persons who replied (somewhat more in Belgium, Germany and Luxemburg; somewhat less in the Netherlands and France). The 'no answers' undoubtedly come from persons not sufficiently informed, or badly integrated in a society whose restraints and injustices are not differentiated. Moreover, one notices that it is in the three countries where the index of exposure to the means of collective information is the highest (Netherlands, Germany and Luxemburg) that the 'no answers' are fewest.

TABLE 15

Opinion of the Effects of the Common Market on the Living Standard
(of 100 persons polled, aged 16 and over)

Believe that the Common Market has had, up to the present, the following effect on the living standard:	EC	G	B	F	I	L	N
A very favourable effect	5	6	6	2	4	6	5
A rather favourable effect	37	43	36	30	36	42	45
Total 'favourable'	42	49	42	32	40	48	50
A rather unfavourable effect	14	11	8	18	12	13	22
A very unfavourable effect	4	4	2	4	4	2	5
Total 'unfavourable'	18	15	10	22	16	15	27
Don't know or did not answer	40	36	48	46	44	37	23

TABLE 15a

Opinion of the Effects of the Common Market on the Living Standard
(of 100 persons who expressed an opinion)

	EC	G	B	F	I	L	N
Very favourable effect	8	10	12	4	7	9	6
Rather favourable effect	62	67	69	56	64	67	58
Total 'favourable'	70	77	81	60	71	76	64
Rather unfavourable effect	23	17	15	33	22	21	30
Very unfavourable effect	7	6	4	7	7	3	6
Total 'unfavourable'	30	23	19	40	29	24	36

Degree of attachment to the Common Market

*'If you were told tomorrow that the Common Market has been given up,
would you feel great regret, a little regret, indifference, or relief?'*

Although the favourable effects of the Common Market have
been noticed only by four out of every ten persons polled in the
countries of the Common Market, the people are attached to it. Six
persons out of ten would feel regret if the Common Market were to
disappear. This would tend to prove that, among those who did not
answer the question on the effects of the Common Market, and even
among those who state that they have felt unfavourable effects,
there are some who are favourably inclined towards it. It is in the
Netherlands and Germany that giving up the Common Market
would cause the most regret.

TABLE 16

Degree of Attachment to the Common Market
(of 100 persons polled, aged from 16 years and over)

	EC	G	B	F	I	L	N
If they were told tomorrow that the Common Market has been given up, they would feel:							
Great regret	28	38	27	21	22	20	40
A little regret	34	30	26	37	38	37	28
Indifference	24	16	32	30	28	28	20
Relief	5	6	3	5	3	4	5
Don't know or did not answer	9	10	12	7	9	11	7

Degree of attachment to the unification of Europe

This attachment to an idea or a project can only be measured
indirectly. Two questions were asked for this purpose: one on the

personal sacrifices that the persons polled would be willing to bear
so that unification could be effected, and the other on the influence on
the choice of electors or future electors, of the orientations of the
political parties towards the unification of Europe.

Acceptance of personal sacrifices

'*Would you be disposed to make certain personal sacrifices, for example
financial, so that European unification could come about?*'

Somewhat more than one-third of those polled declared that they
are disposed to make such sacrifices: it is in the Netherlands and
Germany that the percentages are highest, in Belgium that the
percentage is the lowest.

TABLE 17

Acceptance of Personal Sacrifices to Achieve the Unification of Europe
(of 100 persons polled, aged 16 and over)

Degree of willingness to make certain per-sonal sacrifices)	EC	G	B	F	I	L	N
Entirely willing	8	13	5	5	7	6	9
Rather willing	27	29	18	22	29	31	34
Not very willing	22	24	19	22	20	21	19
Unwilling	34	27	47	41	20	34	32
Don't know or did not answer	9	7	11	10	10	13	6

*The influence of the orientations of the political parties towards the unifi-
cation of Europe in the choice of electors or future electors.*

It may be supposed that attachment to a party or a political
tendency is generally stronger than attachment or hostility to a
project such as the unification of Europe. However, it was interesting to cause a kind of conflict of attitudes in the minds of those
polled between their political preferences and their orientation
towards Europe. Hence the question, coming immediately after that
in reply to which those polled indicated the party for which there
would be the greatest chances of their voting if elections took place
tomorrow for the selection of deputies:

'*If this party took a position contrary to your ideas concerning European
unification, do you believe that you would certainly, probably not, or
certainly not, vote for another party?*'

More than four persons polled out of ten in the countries of the Community as a whole stated that they would vote certainly (19%) or probably (25%) for another party in case of a conflict of attitudes concerning the unification of Europe. It is in Germany, Italy and the Netherlands that orientation towards Europe would most frequently predominate over preference for a party.

TABLE 18

Influence of the Orientations of the Political Parties towards the Unification of Europe in the Choice of Electors or Future Electors

(of 100 persons polled, aged 16 and over)

	EC	G	B	F	I	L	N
Would vote for a party other than the preferred party:							
Certainly	19	14	16	17	27	23	22
Probably	25	37	16	18	21	20	24
Probably not	22	28	18	20	16	15	20
Certainly not	16	10	24	26	12	29	18
Don't know or did not answer	18	11	26	19	24	13	16

SOCIAL AND POLITICAL PARTICIPATION

Satisfaction and optimism

'Are you satisfied with your present living conditions?'

In the Community as a whole, two-thirds of those polled are satisfied with their present living conditions. In Italy, and above all in France, a large percentage of unsatisfied persons is noted, in this latter country it is even somewhat in the majority.

'Do you think that your conditions will improve, especially during the next five years?'

On the whole, the optimists and the pessimists almost balance out, but the former are clearly more numerous in terms of percentage than the latter in Italy and in Belgium, and far fewer in Germany and the Netherlands. The case of Italy is characteristic of a country where a strong minority of unsatisfied people exists, but, among those who expressed an opinion, a strong majority were optimists. On the other hand, in France the percentage of optimists is lower than that of the dissatisfied.

The types of participation studied are:

Personal participation in political activities (and interest or lack of

TABLE 19

Satisfaction with regard to Present Living Conditions
(of 100 persons polled, aged from 16 years and over)

	EC	G	B	F	I	L	N
Satisfied with their present living conditions	64	77	80	46	59	85	80
Not satisfied with their present living conditions	30	16	17	48	37	11	18
Don't know or do not answer	6	7	3	6	4	4	2

interest in politics), according to the attitude of the person polled.
The sentiment of closeness to a political party, whatever it may be.
Attachment to that party.
Membership in a trade union, whatever it may be.
Sympathy for a trade union, whatever it may be.
Attachment to that trade union.
Membership in a religion.
Religious practice.

Participation in politics and attitude towards parties.

'*Do you personally participate in political activities, or do you follow
politics with interest without actively participating, or does politics not
interest you more than other things or not at all?*'

TABLE 20

Degrees of Participation in Politics
(of 100 persons polled, aged 16 and over)

	EC	G	B	F	I	L	N
Personally participate in political activities	4	3	3	4	5	2	3
Are interested in political activities without participating actively	36	36	17	42	33	41	47
Are no more interested in politics than in other things	31	43	23	26	22	34	25
Are not at all interested in politics	27	16	54	27	34	20	23
Don't know or did not answer	2	2	3	1	6	3	2

Very few of the persons polled stated that they personally participate in political activities: 4% for the Community as a whole,
without any great differences from country to country. The great
majority may be divided into three almost equal fractions: 36%

state they follow politics with interest without actively participating (47% in the Netherlands and only 17% in Belgium). 31% state that politics does not interest them more than other things, 27% say they are not at all interested in politics (54% in Belgium). It is in the Netherlands and France, and secondly in Luxemburg, Germany and Italy, that the citizens more frequently feel concerned with politics. Belgium comes at the very end, far behind. It has already been seen that the Netherlands also has the highest index of exposure to information media, whereas Belgium has the lowest.

'As for you, is there a political party among the present parties to which you feel closest?'
'Do you feel a deep or only slight attachment to this party?'

About six persons polled out of ten (56%) feel closer to one particular party: 64% in Germany, 60% in Italy, 57% in the Netherlands, 49% in Luxemburg, and only 39% in Belgium. Once again Belgium is distinguished by a relatively high apolitical sense. Among those who feel closer to one political party, one-third are deeply attached to that party, and this time the Belgians are first (with Luxemburg): about half of those who are close to a party are deeply attached to it. Lastly, out of all those polled, the proportion of those who are deeply attached to one particular party is on the order of one person out of five: a bit more in Italy, Luxemburg, and the Netherlands, a bit less in the three other countries. This proportion corresponds to half the number of those who feel concerned with politics.

TABLE 21

Closeness to a Political Party and Attachment to that Party
(of 100 persons polled, aged 16 and over)

	EC	G	B	F	I	L	N
Feel closer to one particular political party	56	64	39	44	60	49	57
Of these, the following number							
Are deeply attached to that party	17	15	18	13	22	22	22

Participation in a trade organization

'Are you a member of a trade organization?
'If not, without being a member do you nevertheless feel favourably inclined towards some trade organizations?'
'Do you feel very attached to that organization, or only a bit, or not at all?'

Two persons polled out of every ten in this representative samp-
ling of the whole population of the European Community are
members of a trade organization. Among those who are members of
or favourably inclined towards a trade organization, in one out of
three states he is very attached to that organization.

TABLE 22

Attitude towards a Trade Organization: Membership, Goodwill, Attachment
(of 100 persons polled, aged 16 and over)

	EC	G	B	F	I	L	N
Are members of a trade organization	20	18	29	23	17	24	23
Are favourably inclined towards a trade organization	14	8	13	20	14	9	23
Total	34	26	42	43	31	33	46
of whom:							
Are deeply attached to that trade organization	10	7	14	15	9	29	11

These percentages must be interpreted cautiously; on the one
hand they concern representative national samplings of the total
population aged 16 years and over, and not wage-earning workers
only. Furthermore, some self-employed persons replied that they
belonged to or were favourably inclined towards a trade organization
(farm federation, management association, etc.).

Religious participation

Nine persons polled out of every ten declared that they professed a
religion: only 68% in the Netherlands. The Catholic religion is
very much in the majority in Luxemburg, Italy, France, and Belgium.

TABLE 23

Membership in a Religion and Religious Practice
(of 100 persons polled, aged 16 and over)

	EC	G	B	F	I	L	N
Declare that they profess a religion	91	96	85	89	91	99	68
The breakdown is as follows:							
Catholic religion	69	43	83	85	90	98	31
Protestant religion	20	52	1	3	1	1	35
Other religions	2	1	1	1			2
and							
Attend services at least once a week	37	29	51	23	56	52	42
Do not profess any religion	9	4	15	11	9	1	32

In Germany and the Netherlands, the Protestants somewhat out-number the Catholics.

For the whole of the population, almost four persons polled out of every ten stated that they attended religious services at least once a week: more than 50% in Italy, Luxemburg, and Belgium; only 23% in France.

To end this chapter on social and political participation, the per-centages will be compared of persons who show not only member-ship in a political, trade or religious organization, but a more profound commitment to it.

Religious practice is definitely more marked than political or trade-organization commitment, and this is true in countries as different as, for example, Italy and the Netherlands.

TABLE 24

Comparison between the Different Types of Participation in Society-Oriented Activities

(of 100 persons polled, aged 16 and over)

	EC	G	B	F	I	L	N
State they personally participate in political activity	4	3	3	4	5	2	3
Are deeply attached to a trade organization	10	7	14	15	9	29	11
Are deeply attached to a political party	17	15	18	13	22	22	22
Frequently practise their religion	37	29	51	23	56	52	42
Participation Index	68	54	86	55	92	105	78

Stanley Henig

The Mediterranean Policy of the European Community *

THE MEDITERRANEAN POLICY OF THE EUROPEAN COMMUNITY[1] FORMS an important part of its general external policy. Since this paper can, therefore, be considered as a case study, it is worth trying to define at the outset the concept of 'external policy'. The Treaties did not delegate to the common European institutions any of the powers of foreign policy-making traditionally exercised by the nation state, but the granting of wholesale economic competences and the consequential obligation of evolving a common commercial policy ensured that the Community would come into direct contact with non-member states. Through its diplomatic relations with other countries,[2] the Community has become an actor on the international stage, whilst the scope of its external relations has frequently exceeded that of purely commercial policy.[3] It is both meaningful and useful to consider the Community as exercising an external policy – a kind of half-way house to full foreign policy. While any study of Community policy – formation and substance – may help to illuminate the integration process, external policy is particularly important for those who assume that the scope of integration will continue to increase. Should the Community ever be granted powers of foreign policy-making, then the methods and procedures used to formulate external policy will be particularly relevant. The importance of the Mediterranean is that this is not an area for which the Community acquired a policy at birth as it did with the overseas

[1] Legally there is not one Community, but three resulting from separate treaties and sharing common institutions. In this paper 'Community' will be synonymous with EEC and reference to the Treaty of Rome means the EEC treaty.

[2] The Community has formal diplomatic relations with about one hundred third countries, but in most cases it has only exercised the right of passive legation i.e. it receives ambassadors, but rarely appoints them.

[3] On the Community's general external relations, see S. Henig, 'The External Relations of the European Community', PEP/RIIA., London, 1971.

* Vol. 6, No. 4, Autumn 1971.

associates in Africa. During the last thirteen years, though, the Community has slowly built up a global view of its attitude towards the area, so that it is now possible to talk of there being a 'Mediterranean policy'.

Europe's southern sea – '*mare nostrum*' – has always played a major political and economic role as a link with, rather than a barrier from, other continents. It has a direct strategic importance for two members of the EEC, but for every country in Western Europe it straddles vital routes of communication with other parts of the world. The EEC came into existence at the very moment when the traditional political dominance of Western Europe in the Mediterranean was being successfully challenged. In the post-Suez era the Community has been deeply involved in the twin problems of adjusting relations between Western Europe and the developing countries of the Mediterranean to the post colonial epoch and of trying to maintain some influence for Europe in its own 'back yard' in the face of growing military involvement by the two super-powers.

It is normal to assert that the Community is a political organization, although its formal competences are practically exclusively economic, and the evolution of Mediterranean policy lends support to the claim. Since the Community's political institutions are not autonomous from those of the member states, they are available as instruments of, and vehicles for, national foreign policies. The inter-play of national political motivations has helped to shape the Mediterranean policy which has, therefore, never been entirely conditioned by economic factors. Indeed the evolution of Mediterranean policy is an interesting case study in the integration of national policies in an area where decision-making has not been exclusively delegated to the common institutions.

From the Community's inception national motivations in the Mediterranean region have been very different. During the early period France's major concern was to endeavour to contain the spread of Arab nationalism. After the traumas of Suez and Algeria had faded, French policy has been directed at asserting European and her own national leadership in the area. The change-over in 1967 was immediately and noticeably evident in Community policy. In contrast German motivations have been primarily economic, constantly seeking enlarged outlets for her exports of goods and capital. However, even Germany has not been able completely to avoid the political problems of the area: the break in diplomatic relations with certain Arab countries was another national action carrying important repercussions for Community policy. For many years Italy lacked the confidence to pursue any kind of Mediterranean policy and her major motivation in that area was economic protectionism: many of the goods produced by other Mediterranean countries compete directly with her own. Recently she has, though, increasingly asserted her interest in the political and economic stability of the region around her: significantly she is one of the few countries to enjoy good relations with both Israel and the Arab states. Inevitably the range of interests of the Benelux countries is less wide, but they have enjoyed spectacular increases in their exports to the region. In addition, the Netherlands has been the consistent and unyielding champion of generous treatment for Israel.

For the developing countries in the Mediterranean, the major importance of Western Europe is as a source of capital and development aid and a destination for exports. In general Mediterranean production is complementary to that of Western Europe where most of it has been sold. Whilst the common external tariff involved little real threat to exports of raw materials, the common agricultural policy posed problems for sales of certain foods. In any case the existence of the common external tariff and the common agricultural policy gave Mediterranean countries an obvious inducement to try to establish a privileged relationship with the Community. Clearly special relationships for all might do no more than transfer certain financial resources away from the Community and towards the Mediterranean countries, but even that would be a contribution to economic development. As the Community's prosperity has increased there has been a wave of applications for special relations finally including every country except Albania, Libya and Syria.

The types of relationships which the Community can establish with third countries are laid down in the Treaty of Rome. European countries may seek membership under article 237, but by implication this is limited to those with democratic political systems and at a similar stage of economic development. Any country may apply to become associated under article 238 and thus share in some or all of the Community's activities. Whilst there is still no doctrine of association, it has always been assumed that the relationship implies a commitment to free trade between the Community and its associate. In addition part four of the Rome Treaty makes provision for a special kind of association with overseas dependencies and, significantly, gives the Community a competence in development aid outside its own boundaries. Part four also constitutes a declaration of intent for continued association as such countries become independent.[4] Finally articles 111 and 113 – the former during the transitional period, the latter thereafter – enable the Community to enter into preferential or non-preferential trade agreements with third countries. Such agreements do not necessitate the same kind of organic links as membership and association.

THE FIRST PHASE OF EEC MEDITERRANEAN POLICY.

The development of the Community's Mediterranean policy falls readily into two periods. During the first, up to the mid-1960s, the community entered into bilateral agreements with Greece, Turkey, Israel, Lebanon and also Iran.[5] Policy was characterized by a fairly scrupulous regard for the rules of the General Agreement on Tariffs and Trade (GATT). These laid down that any tariff reductions must be extended to all on an *'erga omnes'* basis, unless special dispensation was granted by a two thirds vote of the members. The establishment of new tariff preferences was otherwise only permissible if two or more countries were setting up a free trade area or customs union according to a precise time-table laid down in advance and covering substantially all of the trade between them. The second broad feature of the period was that the agreements sprang from no coherent philosophy on the kind of external policy which the Community ought to be operating. They reflected only a general desire to demonstrate a liberal, internationalist outlook, so long as that was consistent with economic self-interest. Nonetheless a number of general considerations can be discerned behind the series of 'ad hoc' decisions which constituted Mediterranean policy.

In the first place it was generally assumed that a customs union or free trade area had to be based on either article 237 or article 238 – that is to say the new partner would either join or become an associate of the Community. Since such a relationship would be essentially political, no decision to establish a customs union or free trade

---

[4] The treaty also included declarations of intent to establish associations with some former colonies which were already independent – Libya, Morocco, Tunisia. At the time of signature, Algeria was part of France.

[5] Although Iran is not formally a Mediterranean country, relations with the Near East involve similar political and economic problems. Some consideration will be given to this agreement since it played a part in the evolution of Mediterranean policy.

area could be made on purely economic criteria. Secondly there was general agreement that external agreements should not interfere with the autonomy of Community institutions or in any way jeopardize their functioning. The third consideration must be expressed in a more negative form – there was no agreement at all on any kind of doctrine of association, either on its essential ingredients or on the qualifications for eligibility. One view would have limited the relationship to those countries eligible for full membership so that article 238 would have applied exclusively to Europe and would have implied a transitional arrangement. In complete contrast was another view that any country eligible to join should not be given a 'soft option': on that basis no European country could permanently be associated. Finally, it must be remembered that in 1960 the European Community's achievements could only be measured in terms of progress towards internal free trade and a common external tariff. The latter was considered to be a symbol of the drive towards unity, and the eagerness of non-members to circumvent this obstacle to participation in the expansion of the Common Market was matched by Community fear that to allow this might negate the whole purpose of its existence.

Juxtaposing all these considerations, Community external policy was bound in a strait jacket. Since no Mediterranean country could aspire, on economic grounds, to full membership, the practical choice lay between association and a non-preferential trade agreement. The only legal method of granting tariff preferences was in the context of a customs union or free trade area which could only be based on association, implying organic links of a political kind. Non-preferential tariff reductions would be useful for a country which was the major supplier for a particular item – such as Greece for raisins or Turkey for figs or Iran for Persian carpets – but if the country seeking a bilateral agreement were not the major supplier for its important exports, Community action was very difficult. In the first place the Community had obviously to take account of its own domestic producer interests. Whilst member states might be willing to make a concession to help a particular third country in the context of a special agreement with it which might involve also some counter-concessions, they would be much less willing to make the sacrifice if the particular country involved were gaining much less than some others who were not party to the agreement and offering nothing in exchange. Secondly, the Community might at a later date find itself negotiating with those other countries: its bargaining position would have been weakened by making such important concessions in advance. One example will suffice to illustrate these points. Israel's most important export was citrus, but she certainly was not the major supplier. Any *erga omnes* concession in the 1964 agreement would have given much greater benefit to Spain and Morocco with whom the Community had not yet reached the stage of active negotiations. In view of the existence of an important Italian citrus industry such a measure was clearly excluded from the scope of a bilateral agreement with Israel. Indeed a major problem in the establishment of Mediterranean policy was the fact that so many countries in the area, including Italy, produced the same or similar products. The logic of this situation might have suggested a product by product approach on a multilateral basis. However in the early 1960s the Community did not feel itself ready to embark upon this, especially in advance of the common agricultural policy, whilst it did want – for a variety of political reasons – to give some response to the various applications. In the light of this general analysis the history of the first five negotiations and agreements with Mediterranean and Near Eastern countries is worth some study.

The first to apply for a special relationship was Greece, her approach occasioned by fear of economic isolation after the emergence of the European Free Trade Association (EFTA) as a rival to the EEC. In turn the exigencies of the split in Western Europe determined the six to do all in their power to demonstrate the superiority of their organization by the acquisition on generous terms of a first associate. The Community was simply not ready to formulate any kind of general policy, but felt it quite unacceptable to ask Greece to wait. In consequence all caution was, uncharacteristically, thrown to the winds, the Community reached its first external agreement and, in so doing, prejudiced the future course of Mediterranean policy. Although the Community denied that the terms of the Treaty of Athens were a precedent, its overall form could only be that. Henceforth, the Community would always be impelled to respond to bilateral applications. Instead of indicating the course of a future multilateral Community policy towards the Mediterranean, the Greek agreement effectively prevented its emergence.

The Treaty of Athens of 1961 established an association based on a customs union which would come into existence over a twenty-two year period during which Greece would benefit from intra-

Community treatment for her exports,[6] although her own rate of tariff disarmament would be much slower. In addition the six member states agreed to make funds available via the Investment Bank to help with Greece economic development – an early demonstration that lack of formal Community competence need not necessarily preclude policy innovations. More questionably the Community agreed that in exchange for full Greek acceptance of the common external tariff she should be given veto rights for a period of twelve years over future changes for five items of particular interest.[7] This concession created all kinds of difficulties for the Community in subsequent negotiations with other countries and it has never been repeated. The ultimate object of the association was the preparation of the Greek economy for full membership for which she was eligible at the time by virtue of her formally democratic institutions. Association was thus temporary although of long duration. During the twenty-two years there would be measures of harmonization to bring Greek economic policy and practice in line with the Community. The problem was that the Council of Association – which embodied the organic link – lacked any enforcement powers. Effective measures of harmonization would, of course, imply Greece losing all economic autonomy without being able directly to influence the real centres of decision making in the Community. In fact harmonization worked badly up to the time of the Greek *coup d'état* in the aftermath of which the Commission eventually took action to discontinue the flow of financial assistance and effectively reduce the association to a state of suspended animation.

Initially there were expectations that negotiations with Turkey might be pursued simultaneously with those with Greece, but this was prevented by the anti-Menderes coup. In the interim the novelty of acquiring associates had worn off and there were fears that the Community's autonomy might be damaged if too many bilateral associations were established. The Turkish economy was even more backward than the Greek, so that the concept of harmonization would have been inappropriate. Rather than establish an association involving a meaningless panoply of arrangements and undertakings, the Community would have preferred a limited agreement giving Turkey commercial and financial assistance. This implied granting

[6] All industrial goods and her most important agricultural exports. Other agricultural items would depend on the progress of harmonization, see below.

[7] The Community retained the right to make only limited changes without Greek approval.

tariff concessions for four important exports for two of which – nuts and figs – Turkey was the major supplier. However, this was not the case for the other two – raisins and tobacco – which were also products for which the Community had surrendered some negotiating rights by the Athens agreement. The only way round the institutional problems of GATT and the Greek agreement was to acquire a second associate.[8] In any case the Turks were absolutely insistent that they should not formally be treated any differently from Greece. Finally it was decided that the transitional period during which a customs union would be established should be preceded by a five year preparatory period during which Turkey would receive financial assistance and preferential tariff measures for the four products. The Council of Association later added other products to this list. Nonetheless, although GATT in a sense enforced the Turkish association, the failure to give any detailed indication of the time-table for the establishment of free trade constituted a technical breach of the strict letter of GATT – a harbinger of what was to come during the second phase of Mediterranean policy.

Whilst there were no ostensible objections to an organic political relationship with Greece and Turkey, the case of Israel – a persistent early suitor – summed up virtually all the irreconcilable problems. Geographically non-European, Israel was ineligible for full membership, so that any association would have been permanent. The exigencies of the Arab-Israel conflict ruled out such a close political link, certainly as this would have been the first such arrangement, and with it either a customs union or free trade area. However, Israel simply could not be given meaningful help by *erga omnes* tariff reductions, for on her major exports she was not the major supplier. Given that preferential arrangements were excluded, the Community could only offer a collection of miscellaneous tariff measures – suspensions[9] of tariffs for products of which Israel was an important supplier and for specially created sub-items[10] where most benefit

[8] As an associate Turkey would no longer be considered a third country, so that Greece would have no veto rights on any tariff benefits she received. On this and other negotiations see S. Henig, *op. cit.*

[9] Not the same as reductions which would have been permanent. A tariff suspension – in this case they were mostly by 20% – was formally temporary, pending the next round of general GATT talks in which it could be negotiated as a concession against counter-concessions by other suppliers.

[10] Generally the Community's tariff schedule has sought to limit the number of different items. In this case sub-headings, such as different kinds of bathing costumes, were created, so that concessions could be made for Israel without giving too much for nothing to other suppliers.

might go to her, accelerating the movement of certain high national tariffs to the ultimate common external tariff and removal of quantitative restrictions. These measures give marginal benefit to about 10% of Israel's exports to the community and when the three year agreement expired in 1967 she made no move for renewal. Pending the second agreement, the Community kept the concessions in force unilaterally. Attached to the agreement was a declaration that Israel would be consulted in the event of an agreement with any other major producer of oranges and from this was to spring the 'orange policy' which was one basis for the second phase of Mediterranean policy. Finally a joint committee was set up. Lacking any kind of secretariat or organic existence outside its members, it constituted a less obvious political link than a Council of Association.

Iran actually approached the Community after Israel, but agreement was reached first in late 1963. For her major non-oil exports to the Community Iran was the most important external supplier[11] and an agreement was rapidly reached granting non-preferential tariff quotas for carpets, raisins, dried apricots and caviar. In contrast the Lebanese negotiations – once it had been established that no tariff concessions were possible – moved off in another direction. In addition to establishing most favoured nation treatment in trade between the parties, the 1965 agreement allowed for technical co-operation – another extension beyond the formal competence of the Community.

By 1964 the Community had only reached bilateral agreements with four non-member countries – all in the Mediterranean and Near East regions and producing goods to some extent in competition with Italy. The last stage of the Greek negotiations caused an internal Community crisis when the Commission exceeded its mandate in granting an extra concession on tobacco sales to the Italian market. Since the commercial contents of the Turkish and Israeli agreements also involved products of interest to Italy, she considered that she was making undue sacrifices as part of an unbalanced external policy. The breakdown of the negotiations for enlargement gave Italy – a champion of British entry – the opportunity to express her concern at the impact on the balance of the Rome Treaty of a plethora of external agreements in one area only. Whilst Italy's motivations were mainly economic,[12] her actions were to give a

[11] i.e. apart from Community members and associates.

[12] However she was also interested in the question of an Austrian association to which her attitude was hostile so long as no measures were taken to curb Tyrolese terrorists.

doctrinal impetus to Community Mediterranean policy. Although the so-called Italian memorandum of 1964 has never been adopted as formal Community policy, its main arguments have played a major role during the second phase in the Mediterranean. The principles emerging from the memorandum can be readily summarized. Since membership was reserved for European countries alone, this ought to be their normal relationship with the Community. The only valid form of permanent association would be along the lines laid down in part four of the Rome Treaty applying to former colonies. For countries not falling into either category and for European states not wanting full membership, the only possible arrangement would be a trade agreement in accordance with articles 111 and 113. Italy did not rule out the possibility of such agreements being preferential, but she insisted that some priority had still to be given to the Community's own producers to safeguard the benefits of actual membership. The implications of these arguments were that preferential agreements with Mediterranean countries might fall short of customs unions or free trade areas and they need not be based on article 238. These concepts and the practical implications of the need to safeguard Italian produce – particularly oranges – were to be crucial determinants of Mediterranean policy after the mid-1960s.

THE SECOND PHASE.

The first period of Mediterranean activity yielded five agreements which arose out of no clear doctrine and produced no coherent policy. After marking time for several years, during which the Kennedy round was successfully completed, the Community has since 1968 in rapid succession reached agreements with Morocco, Tunisia, Yugoslavia, Turkey (additional protocol for transitional period), Spain, Israel (second agreement) and Malta. There is now both a doctrine and a coherent, if limited, policy.

The determinants of policy during the first phase were the rules of GATT, the persistence of Mediterranean countries in seeking special relations, the Community's general desire to accede to these requests and its unwillingness to establish organic political links with countries such as Israel and Spain. Increasingly strong Italian insistence on safeguarding her own economic interests left the Community with no room for manoeuvre unless one of these factors changed. Given the Community's growing economic and political

strength in world affairs and the basic belief that it should pursue a
dynamic policy in this neighbouring region, the obvious solution
was to bend the rules of GATT. It would be possible to enter into a
long discussion about the value to the world economy of these rules
and regulations, but it would be neither conclusive nor wholly relevant. It is, though, worth remembering that GATT was structured
at a time of almost complete world economic domination by the
USA and it reflects the pre-occupations, interests and prejudices of
that country. At the time most European countries were themselves
in the position of seeking economic aid from the USA. All international institutions reflect the constellation of political and economic forces at the moment of inception. The testing time for the
survival and durability of the institution comes when that constellation changes. Today the economic relationship between Western
Europe|and North America is very different, but the rules of GATT
have undergone no substantial change. In the circumstances once
the Community had demonstrated its general economic liberalism
through participation in the Kennedy round, it felt justified in
blowing a hole through the middle of GATT's most cherished regulation as the only means by which it could establish a viable framework for relations with the Mediterranean.

Two countries, Spain and Israel, and one product, oranges, bear
the prime responsibility for this new development. Each of the
countries had its champions amongst the member states, the Netherlands and Germany strongly advocating a much enlarged agreement
with Israel, whilst France, with some support from Germany,
sought'to establish the basis for a developing relationship with
Spain. However, there was also a strong feeling that organic links of
a political kind should be rejected – in the Spanish case because of
her undemocratic institutions, and in the Israeli case for fear of
damaging relations with the Arab countries. In both cases tariff
arrangements would only give real benefits if they were preferential
and extended over a large number of products. The final solution was
to establish free trade areas based on article 113, but by bringing
them into effect slowly and non-automatically to preserve the
primacy of relationships based on articles 237 and 238. The Community has claimed that the ultimate commitment to free trade,
however vague, should be sufficient to compensate for the technical
infraction of GATT occasioned by the absence of a detailed time-
table. The argument is hard to sustain, for neither of these agreements,
nor for that matter the association with Malta, possess automatic

mechanisms for bringing about free trade on substantially all the commerce between the parties. The member states and the Commission are all well aware that this amounts to somewhat more than a technical infraction, but this policy also represents the only one on which agreement can be reached. Even the Netherlands – on record as being strongly opposed to the multiplication of exceptions and derogations from GATT – prefers this type of solution to the twin alternatives of an association with Spain or no agreement at all for Israel.

The one product, oranges is easily the most important in the citrus group, but its market in the Community is virtually static. Whilst Italy is self-sufficient, the other five import 96% of their needs from non-Community sources. Only 15% of the five's imports come from outside the Mediterranean area and mostly at times of the year when those countries are not producing. For Spain, Morocco and Israel oranges have been a major item in exports to the Community and all have sought special terms. Concessions for any one Mediterranean producer can only be at the expense of the others, although it can be argued that tariffs are not the major determinant of trade in this kind of product.[13] A reduction in the general tariff barrier might conceivably redistribute some marginal financial resources from the Community to the producer countries, although this is by no means certain[14] and is effectively ruled out by Italian insistence on adequate protection for her domestic market and exports to the other five. The Community has finally laid down a series of regulations which protect Italian production by imposing certain price requirements on all imports, but then admit Mediterranean produce on a variety of preferential terms. The importance of this product for the exports of many countries has placed the 'orange policy' at the very core of Mediterranean policy and its techniques have to some extent been copied in dealing with other products involving similar problems.

When the association agreements with Morocco and Tunisia came into effect they granted these countries a reduction of 80% in

[13] Harvests, quality and taste are at least equally important. During the 1960s and in the absence of preferential treatment Israel increased her share of the Community market, whilst that of Algeria fell markedly. For full details see S. Henig, *op. cit.*

[14] Since it is doubtful if limited price reductions would cause any increase in demand, and the producer countries would hardly be likely to come together and charge higher prices as this would involve agreement between Algeria and Israel!

the tariff on oranges. Simultaneously, and in advance of any bilateral agreements, the Community granted a unilateral reduction of 40% for Turkish, Israeli and Spanish produce. Whilst the concession for Turkey could be placed in the context of the association, which GATT had formally accepted, the Community had to apply for a special waiver for the preferential reductions granted to Israel and Spain. The outcome in GATT confirmed the fears that the Community had always entertained about recourse to this procedure which required a two-thirds favourable majority vote: opinion was so hostile that the request was finally withdrawn. The Commission then proposed to the Council of Ministers that the 40% reduction should be extended *erga omnes* for that part of the year which covered the major Mediterranean harvests. In a series of near farcical proceedings Italy objected in principle although she would still have received the normal price guarantees, but then seems to have offered to be out-voted, to which France in her turn objected on her own principles. Finally the Council put into effect a little known but apparently 'established' procedure for withdrawing the concessions. This involved consultation with the European Parliament and by the time it had been accomplished the major producing season for 1969–70 was over in both Israel and Spain. By the time the next one arrived each country had its own agreement which restored the orange concession and which was dressed up as a free trade area. There was no longer any need to seek a GATT waiver, and the onus was on that organization to refuse by straight majority vote to accept the new agreements. The position now is that Community and Greek oranges enter free of duty, those of Morocco and Tunisia receive an 80% reduction and those of Turkey, Israel and Spain one of 40%. Presumably Algeria would be eligible for the 80% reduction and Cyprus for the 40%.

The Community now possesses the framework for relations with Mediterranean countries in the light of which the agreements with Turkey (transitional phase), Morocco, Tunisia, Spain, Israel (second agreement) and Malta can be examined. A basic point is that the legal framework for any agreement is not necessarily reflected in its commercial contents: although relations with Israel and Spain are based on article 113 and the others on article 238, the commercial arrangements differ in extent rather than kind. In particular the ethos of the Maltese agreement, formally based on article 238, is much closer to that of the Spanish and Israeli agreements than it is to the others. Although a major part of the exports of all these countries, save Malta, consists of agricultural produce, there are no firm arrangements for free entry to the Community in this sector. Instead each country receives limited concessions on products of particular interest. In the industrial sector the Community grants free entry for Turkey, Morocco and Tunisia, whilst Malta, Spain and Israel are granted preferential reductions of 70, 60 and 50% respectively.[15] However, the concessions for Spain and Israel come into effect gradually over a four year period. All these countries give counter-concessions, but only Turkey is formally committed to granting free entry at the end of a specific twenty-two year period. This is also the only agreement to envisage a customs union rather than a free trade area as the ultimate basis for partnership. In contrast Morocco grants only non-preferential tariff measures on products of interest to the Community, although her acceptance of the principle of special treatment is demonstrated by some preferential concessions on quotas. The extent of counter-concessions seems determined more by the relative economic strength of the partner country than by the magnitude of the Community's own reductions. Amongst the other countries, Spain and Israel give the most and Tunisia the least, although the percentage reduction is always less than that given by the Community. It is, though, worth remembering that all these countries have a considerably higher tariff barrier than does the Community, so that a smaller percentage reduction may actually be greater in absolute terms. In consequence the actual advantages gained by Community exporters in comparison with other suppliers to these markets may be greater than those given to the Mediterranean countries on the Community market.[16] Since it is now accepted in both GATT and UNCTAD[17] that developed countries should not seek reciprocal measures from the developing

[15] The present agreement with Spain also makes an optional provision for this reduction to be increased from 60 to 70%. All the agreements contain some exceptions to the general arrangements for industrial produce – absence of any concession, reduced rate or tariff quotas. This is in contrast to Greece where there are no exceptions on the industrial side to the rule of free entry.

[16] Thus the agreement with Israel granted an overall tariff reduction of 42% (i.e. allowing for exceptions) reducing the barrier facing her exports from a notional average 7·5% to 4%. In contrast the Israeli reduction of just over 16% reduced the average barrier facing Community goods from a notional 42% to 36%. In absolute terms, therefore, the price of the average Community goods in Israel would drop by more than the price of the Israeli goods inside the Community.

[17] United Nations Conference on Trade and Development.

in exchange for help given to their exports, the Community's defence of its breach of the strict rules of international trade – that this is the only way in which it can make a contribution to the economic development of the Mediterranean – must be weakened. Indeed it is possible to bring a charge of economic colonialism against the Community and it may be significant that Morocco – the partner spiritually closest to the third world ethos – gives the least in the way of counter-concessions. If ever serious negotiations do open with Algeria, this whole question is likely to prove a major problem. Finally, all the agreements look forward to a further phase in relations. In the Turkish case this will only commence in the 1990s as a prelude to possible full membership. The other arrangements are of much shorter duration: all the agreements require renegotiation during the 1974–76 period on an enlarged basis which in the cases of Spain, Israel and Malta is specifically to involve the progressive elimination of the remaining obstacles to trade.

No specific mention has yet been made of the community's bilateral agreement with Yugoslavia. The first with a communist country, it falls rather outside the scope of other Mediterranean agreements. This agreement established most favoured nation treatment between the partners as well as accelerating certain Community tariff concessions agreed in the Kennedy round. The most important commercial clauses modified the import levies on beef and cattle, thus helping an important Yugoslav export. In general the major significance of this agreement is political, for it could be the precursor for a normalization of relations with other Eastern European states, of whom Albania is the other Mediterranean country.

Most of the other Mediterranean countries – Algeria, Libya, Lebanon, Egypt, Cyprus and Gibraltar – seem likely to establish their own special relations with the Community during the next few years. As a condition for finally agreeing to open negotiations with Israel in 1969, France insisted that the Community express a willingness to establish similar agreements with other countries in that area. Her own diplomacy conjured up applications from Lebanon for the second time and Egypt. Negotiations are now proceeding for preferential trade agreements. It also seems probable that Algeria will shortly be forced to drop her 'colonialist' jibes and take more seriously the Community's willingness to negotiate a new relationship. As part of France when the Treaty of Rome was signed, Algeria has for the most part received intra-Community treatment ever since.

This is likely to come to an end for one important export in at least some parts of the Community market when the new wine regulation comes into effect. On the other hand, Libya – secure in her oil wealth – seems less likely to take up the original declaration of intent, unless she feels entitled as a matter of course to the same treatment as Egypt. Conceivably the last motivation might ultimately affect Syria as well, although she has so far shown no interest in the Community. Finally relations with Cyprus and Gibraltar seem likely to be settled – in different ways – in the context of the general enlargement negotiations.

FUTURE ORIENTATIONS

There has recently been growing dissatisfaction inside the Community with the present Mediterranean policy. Whilst there is general acceptance of the twin propositions that the Mediterranean is a crucial area for the Community and that it can be given special treatment not extended elsewhere, the limitations of that treatment have aroused concern inside both the Commission and the European Parliament. Four types of criticism have been advanced. In the first place, it is claimed that however politically motivated the policy may have been in theory, its actual orientation has been largely determined by the exigencies of the Community's own agricultural problems. Mediterranean policy has even been described as 'a non-policy based on a pre-occupation with oranges'. Secondly, the plethora of bilateral agreements and their provisions for consultative mechanisms must slow down the working of the Community's own institutions. At the same time it seems doubtful whether the new partnerships add anything significant to the political weight of the Community in world, or even Mediterranean, affairs. Thirdly, the commercial substance of the agreements hardly makes a major contribution to the real economic problems facing the Mediterranean. In the agricultural sector, tariff reductions do not necessarily lead to increased exports by the countries supposed to benefit. In some cases the largest benefit may go to Community consumers rather than to Mediterranean producers. Finally, it is argued that the Community has not turned its attention directly on the major political problems confronting the Mediterranean – the Arab-Israel conflict and the military domination by external naval power.

There are various strands to the debate which is beginning to take place on these propositions, but there is general agreement that a

major difficulty lies in the Community's lack of certain competences even on the economic side. A comparison has been made
between the Community's powers under part four of the Treaty of
Rome when dealing with African countries and its more general
powers in external policy. The major difference is that the Community is able to be much more intimately concerned with the
problems of economic development within African countries. On
the other hand, lack of formal Community competence has not
prevented financial assistance for Greece and Turkey and the technical co-operation agreement with Lebanon. It seems likely that the
argument about competences in the Mediteranean will be a strand in
a more general debate about extension of the Community's powers,
but meanwhile some further progress on the traditional 'ad hoc'
basis is not to be precluded.

The reformers have advanced a number of propositions on which
a third phase of the Mediterranean policy may be based, especially
when it comes to the renewal and enlargement of present agreements
in the period 1974–76. First, although it is recognized that policy may
still have to be expressed in the form of various bilateral agreements,
there should be still more conformity in their contents. Instead of a
patchwork quilt of commercial arrangements, the Community
should proceed much more on a product by product basis. Secondly
measures should be taken directly to assist Mediterranean production: development aid, technical assistance, provision of services
and organization of marketing have all been proposed. Thirdly,
Mediterranean countries can be helped to diversify their production
and exports, in the industrial as well as the agricultural spheres. This
would help to alleviate the problems posed by the various countries
competing against one another for limited markets. Finally, all these
economic measures ought to be placed in a political framework.
Through them the Community ought to aim to involve itself in
finding solutions to problems facing the Mediterranean and in
particular the Near East conflict.

Interestingly enough the only practical progress so far has been
on the last point. Quite independently of the question of increased
competences – to which she would in any case be opposed – France
has taken the lead in using the institutions of the Council of Ministers
to examine and discuss the problems involved in the Arab-Israel
conflict. Whilst the results have done little more than indicate the
range of national differences on this problem – and the French
attitude is sufficiently partial at present to occasion considerable

doubts about her motivations – it seems likely that the Community will increasingly interest itself in such political issues. Given the internal and institutional problems which will confront the Community when enlargement takes place, it seems unlikely that any formal proposals for increased competences for the institutions will be accepted in the near future. In the long term the scope of integration seems more likely to be extended by the member states expressing the political will to take actions technically beyond the scope of the Community, but nonetheless through the established joint procedures. This has been done at various times already during the evolution of Mediterranean policy, but clearly the scope of the Near East conflict goes way beyond the technicalities of giving financial assistance to Greece and Turkey. It can be argued that the fundamental motivation for the establishment of the European Community was a desire to change the basic relationship between Europe and the rest of the world. An opportunity and a challenge to produce the first manifestation of this presents itself in the Mediterranean.

Helen S. Wallace

The Impact of the European Communities on National Policy-Making* †

THE NOW FAIRLY EXTENSIVE LITERATURE ON THE EUROPEAN Communities, much of which sets out to analyse 'the European decision-making process', has tended to concentrate on how this process looks from the perspective of the Community itself and of its institutions. National governments and actors in the six political systems have been discussed primarily in so far as they are participants in the Community system. However, if we are to reach an understanding of the impact of the Communities on national processes, then some attention must be given to how the Communities are viewed from the national capitals, to the extent to which Community business impinges on the governmental systems in the member states and to the importance given to European matters among the competing issues which vie for prominence in national politics. Any analysis of the politics of European integration which looks from the Communities outwards makes the assumption that European issues are the only ones that count; but if those same issues are examined from a national perspective, we need to ask whether they represent simply one bundle of issues among many, or whether they have come to add a new dimension to the full range of governmental business and political debate. In other words, has the advent

  * This article is based on the concluding paper presented to a seminar held at Manchester University during the academic year 1970–1 on 'Decision-Making in the European Communities'. The author is indebted to the other papers presented (by European and British civil servants and by scholars in the field of European integration) and to the other participants for raising many of the ideas discussed in this article. Substantive evidence for the arguments presented is derived from the existing literature, from papers given in the Manchester seminar and from conversations with participants in the process in Brussels and in Bonn.

  † Vol. 6, No. 4, Autumn 1971.

of the European Communities changed the political configuration of the six national systems, and, if so, marginally or fundamentally?[1]

Clearly a broad approach is required into which can be incorporated a range of relevant questions, an approach which covers the domestic policy-making process.[2] The advantage of this is that it embraces both the procedures used for formulating policy and the involvement, whether actual or potential, of political actors in the process as they affect the decisions reached. Proponents of European integration might argue that to ask those questions about national policy-making familiar from more conventional studies of domestic politics would risk a failure to appreciate the revolutionary nature of the supranational experiment. But if the 'founding fathers' were correct in their assumption that the logic of the European Communities is to transform the politics of Western Europe, then what we should expect to find are unconventional answers to conventional questions.

The more striking aspects of the impact of the Communities on national policy-making will be illustrated by reference to three major areas:

(1) the European Communities as an issue area[3] in national politics;
(2) national actors concerned with the European issue-area;
(3) the implications of the growing arena of Community activity for national policy-making.

---

[1] Studies of the European Communities since their establishment, both European and American, have been overwhelmingly Community oriented. Some studies have, however, been made of the relationship between the Community and national levels, notably in *Institutions Communautaires et Institutions Nationales dans le Développement des Communautés*, Institut d'Études Européennes, Université Libre de Bruxelles, 1967, and *La Décision dans les Communautés Européennes* (based on a conference held in Lyons in 1966 and published, under the direction of Pierre Gerbert and Daniel Pépy, by the Université Libre de Bruxelles in 1969).

Two German projects on the relationship between national governments (particularly the German government) and the EEC are now reported to be under way, one under the auspices of the Deutsche Gesellschaft für Auswärtige Politik, the other directed by Professor Karl Kaiser at Saarbrücken.

[2] The phrase is used here as defined by Charles E. Lindblom, in *The Policy-Making Process*, Prentice Hall, 1968. For discussions of the distinction between the foreign policy and domestic policy processes see James N. Rosenau, 'Foreign Policy as an Issue Area', in Rosenau (editor), *Domestic Sources of Foreign Policy*, Free Press, New York, 1967, and William Wallace, *Foreign Policy and the Political Process*, Macmillan, London, November 1971.

[3] The concept of 'issue area' is taken originally from Robert A. Dahl, *Who Governs?*, Yale University Press, New Haven, Conn., 1961.

THE EUROPEAN COMMUNITIES AS AN ISSUE-AREA IN NATIONAL POLITICS

The governments of the Six, like all governments, are faced with a mass of demands and recurrent problems competing for attention and for solutions. Where does Europe figure in this competition? Is it accorded similar treatment to other issues? How has the treatment accorded to European issues at the national level affected the attitudes of the six governments to the progress of integration and specifically to the development of the institutional structure of the Communities?

The weight of the evidence so far available suggests that the Communities have not penetrated dramatically into the national political scene, but have rather been confined predominantly within the executive (particularly within some departments) and within the sphere of certain national elites.

Some argue that this relates to the nature of the Community process: that, for example, 'it would not be an exaggeration to characterize the entire Community as essentially bureaucratic and technocratic'.[4] Why should this be so? In part it is a consequence of the predominant role played by Ministries of Foreign Affairs in coordinating national positions on community policies and in setting the parameters of overall national policies. Despite the economic and social policy orientation of the Treaties, their adoption resulted from specific foreign policy actions by the six governments and their implementation has continued to be regarded at the national level as primarily a pursuit of a foreign policy objective. To some extent the consequence has been an erosion of the traditional distinction between foreign policy and domestic policy, a factor of which British diplomats have been particularly aware in considering the potential British governmental response to membership of the Communities. 'The most important lesson for the United Kingdom', a member of the Foreign and Commonwealth Office recently observed, 'is the prospect of the amalgamation of the two areas of foreign policy and domestic policy which, in the past, it has been possible to keep more or less separate'.

In the administrations of the Six, foreign affairs officials meet regularly with their colleagues from domestic ministries to discuss

[4] Leon N. Lindberg and Stuart A. Scheingold, *Europe's Would-be Polity*, Prentice Hall, Englewood Cliffs, New Jersey, 1970, p. 79.

and to coordinate community matters.[5] In the West German administration there has been a shift from the Chancellery to the Foreign Office as the coordinating department – although strictly speaking the Foreign Office shares responsibility with the Ministry of Economic Affairs. The bulk of coordination is handled by the weekly meetings of experts, chaired by a Foreign Office official, which agrees point by point the instructions to the Permanent Delegation; if agreement is not reached at this level, the point of contention is sent to the fortnightly meeting of State Secretaries (from the Chancellery, Foreign Office, Ministries of Economic Affairs, Agriculture and Finance, with representatives of other functional ministries as occasion requires) or very occasionally to a meeting of ministers. The prominence of the Foreign Office has resulted partly from the growing respectability for West Germany of an active foreign policy.

In Belgium coordination is organized at the administrative level by the inter-ministerial Economic Committee and at the political level by the Ministerial Committee for Economic and Social Coordination, with the Ministry of Foreign Affairs often playing the role of arbiter. In principle instructions to the Permanent Delegation are centralized through the Ministry of Foreign Affairs, but in practice the formal machinery does not function smoothly, leaving much of the regular coordination to the Permanent Representative himself, this being possible because of the government's situation in Brussels.

In France coordination on major issues operates partly through the 'Inter-ministerial Committee for questions of European economic co-operation,' which dates from 1948 and has its own secretariat, and partly through the 'Technical Inter-ministerial Committee for questions relating to the application of the EEC and ECSC treaties', which has come increasingly under the competence of the Prime Minister. But the role of the Quai d'Orsay remains central in defining policy options, particularly through its 'General Direction for economic and financial matters', and in controlling the Permanent

[5] Detailed accounts of the national coordinating machineries are to be found in *La Décision dans les Communautés Européennes* in the series of articles on 'la préparation nationale de la décision communautaire' (pp. 165–255) by Theodor Holtz (Germany), Marie-Paule Mahieu (Belgium), Pierre Gerbet (France), Marco M. Olivetti (Italy), Guy de Muyser (Luxembourg) and Robert de Bruin (Netherlands). My information on Germany is supplemented by talks with various officials during a recent visit to Bonn.

Delegation. In Italy the role of the Ministry of Foreign Affairs is
even more central, as it is specifically charged with the coordination
of all matters concerned with the Rome and Paris Treaties. At the
administrative level there exists a Committee of Directors General
from the major ministries convened by the Foreign Affairs Ministry and at the political level there is the 'Committee of Ministers for
international action on economic policy', usually chaired by the
Minister of Foreign Affairs. In addition the Foreign Affairs Ministry organizes groups of experts for specific problems, an activity
which is particularly significant as the distance between Rome and
Brussels impedes direct contact between national experts and the
Communities.

In Luxemburg too the Ministry of Foreign Affairs has the
central responsibility for coordination and has tended to provide
the full staff of the Permanent Delegation. The Luxemburg case is
rather special in view of their reliance on the Belgian administration
for much that concerns the Communities. In the Netherlands the
decentralized system of administration has meant that coordination
has not been clearly secured, particularly as there is uncertainty as to
the demarcation of competences between the Ministries of Foreign
Affairs and Economic Affairs. Weekly coordination is through an
official committee convened by the Ministry of Foreign Affairs;
questions not resolved at this level go to the Commission of Co-
ordination which precedes the Community Council meetings. The
uncertain demarcation of responsibilites between ministries has also
meant that the Dutch cabinet has become increasingly involved in
the process of coordination, primarily through its European Committee.

So the evidence suggest that the similarities in national patterns
are striking, although some governments have found more stringent
mechanisms for coordination than others. The similarities are not,
however, necessarily a reflection of similar political situations: for
example, the Dutch and Italian patterns reflect in different ways the
responses of the national administrations to their coalition governments. The aspect which is the most striking is the effort made by
Ministries of Foreign Affairs to reserve for themselves the position
of gatekeeper between the national and community systems, a position reinforced by the development of substantial functional expertise
on economic policies. Moreover, the tradition of the foreign policy
process has considerably influenced the handling of Community
issues in the degree to which debate has been concentrated within the

executive, partly because the foreign policy area tends not to be concerned with legislation and hence to avoid regular involvement with parliament or with pressure groups. Thus in a sense the erosion of the rigid distinction between domestic and foreign policy appears in this context to have made Community policy-making more like foreign policy-making than like domestic policy-making. This has been facilitated by the legislative process of the Communities, by which regulations take direct force at the national level. In part this concentration within the executive may account for the attention given by pressure groups to activity at a Community level.

The response of domestic ministries has not been to broaden the area of debate on particular issues, but rather to try to preserve their own autonomy by seizing upon issues within their competence as 'technical'.[6] Thus issues are 'de-politicized' and handed to 'neutral experts' for advice. Ministries of Foreign Affairs have seen their function as to sort out issues into 'political' and 'technical'. Such a division rests on an arbitrary decision of definition; often politically sensitive and far-reaching points may be concealed by a complicated 'technical' proposal. For example, the decision of the Council of Ministers of January 1970 to stabilize freight market conditions on the Rhine and Moselle rivers (by authorizing the payment of subsidies to barge owners who temporarily withdraw capacity from these waterways) has wider implications for German-Swiss relations at a high level.[7]

The pattern is one which minimizes participation. This is reinforced by the time table of decision-making. The welter of material to be reviewed is extensive and the need constantly to pass on instructions to the Permanent Delegations in Brussels leaves little time for thorough consultation at the national level. Failure to reach a decision on a coordinated national basis means either that the view of a particular government is absent from the matter in hand in Brussels or that the Permanent Representative is left to assume the attitude of his government. At this point the efficiency of the coordinating machinery is crucial. Another factor to be taken into

---

[6] This phenomenon is widespread. See Mahieu in *La Décision dans les Communautés Européennes*, p. 191 on Belgium, de Bruin in *ibid.*, p. 239 on the Netherlands, Holtz in *ibid.*, p. 177 on Germany.

[7] I am indebted for this example and the point which it illustrates to a discussion with a member of the German Foreign Office. For the decision itself see *European Community*, London, February 1970, p. 4. The same official estimated that 95% of Community issues were settled at the level of 'technical experts'.

account is the need for confidentiality in preparing bargaining positions for Council meetings.

Perhaps the most surprising aspect of the process is that it continues to work. Commentators have remarked that a crucial factor has been the personnel involved, that over the years more' or less the same group of key officials has been concerned with Community matters both in the Permanent Delegations and in the ministries in the national capitals.[8] Their familiarity with the issues involved, with the breadth of views to be taken into account and with each other, has made it possible for the wheels to be kept in motion. The members of these key groups are as concerned with selling a European line to their own government or ministry as with representing that government or ministry, whether through the Committee of Permanent Representatives or through the national coordinating machinery. The experience of those British civil servants concerned with the applications for membership over some ten years has been strikingly similar. But this elite-oriented approach has reinforced the pattern of trying not to extend the policy debate beyond those who 'really understand' the problems.

To set this adequately in the context of the national political scene requires more evidence than is available on the reaction of other political groupings not included in the charmed circle, on aspects such as intra-party discussions of affected policy areas or the accommodation of the consultative machinery of functional ministries to the problem. The exception in terms of studies so far published is agricultural policy.[9] Agriculture is moreover the significant exception to the pattern of an executive-dominated and non-participatory process described above. Yet it is the most highly integrated sector of community policy and has been portrayed as the model likely to be adopted as other sectors are integrated. However, a number of factors lead me to doubt that this will be the case. The relationship between government and agriculture is of a dif-

[8] E. Noel on 'Le Comité des Représentants Permanents' in *Institutions Communautaires et Institutions Nationales*, p. 12, and P. Gerbet in *La Décision dans Les Communautés Européennes*, p. 199.

[9] Giancarlo Ami, 'Le rôle respectif des institutions communautaires et nationales dans la mise en oeuvre de la politique agricole commune', in *Institutions Communautaires et Institutions Nationales*, pp. 115f., Hélène Delorme, 'L'adoption du prix unique des céréales', and J. R. Verges, 'L'élaboration du système de financement de la politique agricole commune', both in *La Décision dans les Communautés Européennes*. Note too the extent to which evidence from the agricultural sector is relied upon in more general works.

ferent order from that which obtains in other sectors of the domestic economy. In all European states agriculture receives considerable subsidies, and agricultural policy bears the mark of social as much as of economic considerations. The political power of agriculture is more effectively organized and more immediately brought to bear upon governments than that of most other sectors. The sensitivity of the agricultural market to daily fluctuations means that certain kinds of decisions have to be reached quickly and regularly through the Management Committees, and that the effects of those decisions are immediately evident to and readily identifiable by the farmers.

The evidence of public opinion surveys suggests a widespread agreement with the broad objectives of the Community.[10] Statements made by officials in ministries assume the principle of a commitment to European integration as an agreed political end. However, it does not follow from this support and commitment at a broad and generalized level that a parallel willingness exists on the part of national or sectional interests to subordinate their own interests on specific issues to a higher community interest. Furthermore the mode of resolving conflict adopted by the national authorities affects directly both the policy outcome at the Community level and the evolution of the institutions of the Communities.

This can be illustrated by the gradual shift of emphasis from the Commission to the Council and the Committee of Permanent Representatives (CPR). Much of the analysis devoted to this has concentrated on a number of contradictions in the role of the Commission.[11] These contradictions, it is argued, are founded in the dual administrative and political functions expected of the Commission and in the ambiguity of the relationship between the Commission and the Council. The shift of emphasis has also been seen as stemming in part from the failure to move from unanimous to majoritarian voting. Evidence cited has included the increasing attention given

[10] See for example Lindberg and Scheingold, *op. cit.*, pp. 45f; but note table 3·5 on p. 75 which shows the consistent discrepancy between the percentages showing support for a united Europe and those listing European problems as among the most important.

[11] D. Coombes, *Politics and Bureaucracy in the European Community*, London, PEP, Allen and Unwin, 1970; E. Noel and H. Étienne, 'Quelques aspects des rapports et de la collaboration entre le Conseil et la Commission', in *La Décision dans les Communautés Européennes*, pp. 33–55. Detailed information on more recent developments is drawn from papers presented in Manchester by H. Étienne on 9 February 1971, and by H. Nord on 10 November 1970.

by pressure groups to the CPR (although access is not easy), the establishment of *Comités de Concertation* (groups of high officials, convened by the CPR, often at the request of the Council, to investigate particular problems) and the tendency for Commission proposals to be channelled by the Council into the national administrative hierarchies. These factors are seen as undermining the policy-formulation role of the Commission.

However, it has also to be borne in mind that this shift stems not only from the development of the Commission but also from the volition of the national governments. The Council of Ministers is still primarily a meeting of the representatives of the six governments. In this it presents a close parallel with other inter-governmental organizations. The practice has been such as not to encourage the strengthening of the Commission, because, unless the Council and the CPR keep community policy-making within their control, the national machinery will cease to be able to keep pace. It might even be argued that for the role of the Commission as the formulator of policy to predominate would require almost the by-passing of coordinated national postures, with consultations with experts in various fields not depending so heavily on their selection by national governments.

The models of Community decision-making based on the early years of the EEC[12] described the detailed formulation of policy proposals as concentrated in the Commission. The procedure consisted of a compilation of dossiers through working groups of experts, studies by professional organizations, questionnaires to ministries and 'information meetings with national experts *in their personal capacities*'. These dossiers then formed the basis of consultation with professional organizations, the European Parliament and governmental experts called in by the Commission. Only then were the final versions of the proposals handed to the Council and CPR for a decision on acceptance or amendment.

More recently the trend has been for proposals to be presented to the Council in a more general form and for these then to be transmitted by ministers to the national administrators for thorough examination at various levels.[13] Papers are prepared individually by

---

[12] One such model was described by D. Sidjanski, in 'The European Pressure Groups', *Government and Opposition*, Vol. 2, No. 3, April–July 1967, pp. 400f.

[13] This trend was corroborated by H. Etienne and H. Nord in the papers cited above. More detail on the control of national governments over the participation of national experts can be found in the articles by P. Gerbet (p. 204) and M. Olivetti (p. 212) in *La Décision dans les Communautés Européennes*.

the six governments and collated in the CPR. The detailed work of the Commission continues, but can be disputed more vigorously by the national representatives on the basis of their own substantive study. This trend is reinforced by the developing efforts of the national coordinating machinery to keep a check on the experts involved in consultation with the Commission. Furthermore it has been a characteristic of national governments not to accommodate themselves to a process which would diminish their ability to press authoritatively a national attitude on any proposal, even though political tactics may on occasion lead a national attitude to be expressed in terms of a 'community solution'. The outcome of this maintenance of executive control at the national level has been to insulate the European issue-area from national politics and to lead to the pursuit of minimalist strategies.[14]

NATIONAL ACTORS AND THE EUROPEAN ISSUE-AREA

In the early days of the Communities commentators frequently remarked upon participation in Community decision-making as provoking 'a restructuring of activities and aspirations' for political actors, by which were understood 'high policy-makers and civil servants'.[15] The trend towards a Community spirit was anticipated as likely to intensify and to embrace a growing number of individuals and groups. The major potential obstacles to this evolution were seen as the pursuit of Gaullist policies, direct pressures to reduce the role of the Commission, or the enlargement and possible dilution of the Communities.

In practice, the minimalist strategies of the national governments and the routinization of the process of policy-making have tended to act as a barrier to this type of socialization in a more subtle manner. On the one hand the existence of the Communities has enhanced the role of some national administrators who have gained a new dimension of activity and responsibility. But, on the other hand, the national machineries have not involved large numbers of national political actors in the Community process.

At a specifically Community level the national actors most

[14] See the arguments made by Miriam Camps, in *European Unification in the Sixties*, Oxford University Press, 1967, Ch. VI, pp. 196f., and by Lindberg and Scheingold, *op. cit.*, pp. 287f..

[15] Lindberg, *The Political Dynamics of European Economic Integration*, Stanford University Press, California, 1963, p. 286.

involved are the members of the Council and of the Permanent Delegations. For the ministers the burden of attendance at Council meetings is large and increasing. It is especially heavy for Ministers of Foreign Affairs in view of their commitments to other international organizations and their programmes of bilateral visits.[16] This burden must to a degree diminish the attention that these ministers can give to their other administrative and political duties and must lead to some uncomfortable compromises in terms of preliminary discussion and briefing. One German official complained of the difficulty of briefing ministers adequately for Council meetings. For the Permanent Delegations the burden of work is equally strenuous. Their task is complicated by their dual role, which consists of the representation of national positions in Brussels and the explanation of decisions agreed in Brussels to the national administrations. The two functions require that members of the delegations keep abreast with the minutiae of both national and community developments. Indeed, the demanding nature of the role is said to make some national civil servants reluctant to serve in the Brussels delegations.[17] On the other hand a period as Permanent Representative certainly does not impede a civil servant's career, and may perhaps even further it.[18]

At the highest national level the actors involved are the ministers of the relevant departments (primarily Foreign Affairs, Economic Affairs, Finance, Agriculture and other departments such as Labour or Transport as required), their top officials and members of the relevant directorates within ministries. In practice, as was described above, Community matters seem on the whole to be settled at the technical level and only to receive the attention of the higher echelons of ministries if they are either contentious or of great political significance. It is sometime argued that this results

[16] In 1967 there were 37 Council meetings covering 68 days, distributed as 48 days for Ministers of Agriculture, 28 for Ministers of Foreign Affairs, 16 for Ministers of Economic Affairs, with a smaller number for other ministers. These figures include the presence of more than one minister per country at some meetings.

[17] This point was made in interviews with Dutch and German civil servants.

[18] Several former Permanent Representatives have moved on to high positions either in the Communities or in their national administrations. E. Noel, in his article in *Institutions Communautaires et Institutions Nationales*, p. 12, cites amongst others the examples of M. de Carbonnel (France) and M. Cattani (Italy), who each became secretary-general in their respective Ministries of Foreign Affairs.

from the consensual nature of the problems under discussion.[19] It is, however, equally plausible to argue that this technicalization has tended to submerge disagreement, and that this is facilitated by the compartmentalization of European issues within ministries. Inter-ministerial conflicts of opinion do exist,[20] although conflicts over matters concerning the Communities reflect in part a more general competition among central departments to assert their authority in the national administration. This competition has tended to provoke more comment from journalists than from political scientists, perhaps because of the difficulty of finding hard data. John New-house, in his discussion of the 1965–66 crisis and particularly the Bonn meeting between de Gaulle and Erhard in June 1965, writes: 'The endless in-fighting between responsible ministries had for the mo-ment been stilled in order to present a unified front'. The 'unified front' soon collapsed and added to the series of problems which lay behind the Luxemburg crisis. The 'in-fighting' can in part be attributed to the fragile balance of the German administration at that time, but it also relates to a more constant facet of policy-making in an area where decisions are not easily confined within individual ministries.

The role of the Ministries of Finance would be of particular interest to students of British politics familiar with the intricacies of Treasury control, and would certainly merit further study. Prior to the recent advances in plans for economic and monetary union, Ministries of Finance were peripherally and intermittently involved with Community matters. Other ministries have nonetheless had to take their views into account through their participation in the co-ordinating bodies, and from time to time Ministries of Finance have tried to exert a more positive role.[21] In West Germany there has been a sensitive relationship between the Ministries of Economic Affairs and of Finance. This has been accentuated by Professor Schiller, who has to some extent used the development of Com-munity policy to reinforce his own views on German economic policy, as for example over revaluation and the floating of the

[19] This argument appears regularly in discussions of the Communities. See, for example, Lindberg and Scheingold, *op. cit.*, p. 41, on the 'permissive con-sensus'.

[20] See the articles by Holtz (p. 177), Gerbet (p. 203), de Bruin (p. 254), in *La Décision dans les Communautés Européennes*; also John Newhouse, *Collision in Brussels*, Norton, New York, 1967, p. 96.

[21] See Mahieu (p. 185) and Gerbet (p. 198) in *La Décision dans les Communautés Européennes*.

German mark. This tension, which culminated recently in the merger of the two ministries, can only have been exacerbated by the added dimension of the European Communities. It will be revealing to see the impact of further progress towards monetary union on attitudes within the Finance Ministries.

The prominence of Ministries of Foreign Affairs, particularly in their transmission of instructions to the Permanent Delegations, has included efforts to control the channels of communication between domestic ministries and Brussels. In practice this control has more easily been exerted over written communication, and has failed to control direct communication by telephone between functional ministries and their seconded members in the Delegations. Traditionally, bilateral contacts between functional ministries in different national capitals have been handled by Ministries of Foreign Affairs, but in practice direct contacts have increased.[22] On occasion direct contacts have deliberately been made between German and French officials to find ways round impasses in Brussels.

The diplomatic content of the work done by functional ministries has increased. This is due to the involvement of officials in negotiation over Community matters and to the increasing foreign affairs dimension of many areas of domestic policy, including for example international transport problems or the growing international mobility of labour, neither of which areas is confined to Community level discussion. Functional ministries are involved, too, as the agencies for the implementation of community policy. For example, those substantial sections in the Ministries of Agriculture which deal with food markets and prices are now primarily concerned with the implementation of the Common Agricultural Policy.

The executive orientation of the handling of Community matters has militated against the representation of a wider section of national attitudes. In terms of the structures of the Communities this was intended to be counter-balanced by the European Parliament. Discussions of this institution have been overshadowed by the continuing debate over the powers of the Parliament and over direct elections. Given the lack of progress on both questions, some attention is due to the involvement of the six national parliaments in the process and to the activities of members of the European Parliament within their national parliaments. Michael Niblock has usefully

---

[22] See Mahieu, *ibid.*, p. 185.

illuminated these points in his study, *The EEC: National Parliaments and Community Decision-Making.*[23]

It has been a feature of the European Parliament, which distinguishes it from the assemblies of parliamentarians attached to other European international organizations, not to encourage its members to promote the discussion of European issues in their national parliaments. There have been two major reasons for this: the first has been the concern of Europeans to establish the identity of the European Parliament as the representative organ of the Communities; the second has been a desire not to isolate European affairs as a discrete area. Despite its weak powers the Parliament's activities are time-consuming in terms both of full sessions, which cover some thirty-five sitting days per year, and of committee sessions. Thus its conscientious members find it increasingly difficult to play an active part in their national parliaments, often endangering their domestic political careers. The list system by which members are elected to the Dutch Second Chamber has made it easier for Dutch members of the European Parliament than for their colleagues, in that they need to spend less time on extra-parliamentary activities. It should also be noted that frequently the members selected by the national parliaments to serve in Strasbourg have represented the pro-European wings of their parties, a factor which has to be taken into account in assessing their contribution at both levels.

The direct impact of the Communities on the national parliaments has been relatively limited. The accountability of governments is restricted by their ability to explain Council decisions as required by particular circumstances and by their inability to renounce those decisions. The evidence suggests that national parliamentarians are more concerned with general postures than with detailed examination of policy. The agricultural sector has been more thoroughly probed than other sectors for the reasons outlined above. The absence of detailed examination of most aspects of Community policy results from the lack of adequate information available to MPs, from their inability to influence their governments at the most crucial stages of policy formulation and from the highly technical nature of many of the issues. Those parliaments which have a well developed committee system, notably West Germany and the Netherlands, are somewhat better placed. But the low level of

[23] Chatham House/PEP, London, 1971. The author elaborates in this study on many of the points summarized below.

parliamentary control over European issues as much reflects a general problem of parliamentary control as it denotes a limited interest in the Communities.

The role of national interest groups has been discussed in the literature, principally in relation to the development of community-level groups. Sidjanski, in particular, has emphasized this,[24] partly to substantiate the arguments that elites and groups are highly adaptable to changing political situations, and partly to suggest their crucial role in building up support for further integration. A European strategy, he argues, is generally pursued where the groups can agree on a common position and it is only in the absence of agreement that national strategies are pursued. However, frequently agreement à Six can only be reached at a minimal level, leaving the national groups to press their particular views on their own governments. The German Trade Union Organization, for example, admits to concentrating its pressure on the Bonn government, because it feels that neither consultation with the Commission nor participation in the Economic and Social Committee is adequate.[25] On the other hand, the involvement of national groups with each other through groupings in Brussels does affect their attitudes and perspectives. The most striking example of this was the conversion of the German industrialists to the idea that economic planning was not a threat, as a result of its discussion in the Union des Industries de la Communauté Européenne. This in part accounts for the change of position by the German government, which facilitated the development of the medium-term economic programme.[26] Yet the predominant trend is for national groups to press their governments for a defence of their interests, and if necessary for a national antidote to an unfavourable Community policy.

This survey of national actors suggested that involvement is limited and is oriented to the development of coherent national positions, although the competitive relationship between ministries points to the difficulties of maintaining such cohesion. Fuller

[24] Sidjanski, op. cit., and in his paper delivered at Manchester on 27 October 1970.

[25] The information on the Deutscher Gewerkschaftsbund is drawn from a recent visit to their headquarters. For a description of the general attitudes of national interest groups see Werner Feld, 'National Economic Interest Groups and Policy Formation in the EEC', in Political Science Quarterly, September 1966.

[26] For a detailed account of the German government's changing views see Geoffrey Denton, Planning in the EEC, Chatham House/PEP, London, 1967.

information on the implementation of Community directives in national legislation might illuminate these difficulties further.[27] But to date the process of policy-formulation at the national level has tended to protect the political establishment, which has thus so far avoided the consequences of allowing European issues to be caught up in the normal process of domestic politics.

THE IMPLICATIONS OF THE GROWING ARENA OF COMMUNITY ACTIVITY FOR NATIONAL POLICY-MAKING

Two major sets of implications are of interest: the effect of existing community policies on the policy options available to governments, and the possible effect of the expansion of Community activity to include sectors which may erode more drastically the distinction between national and community policies.

Community policies have been restricted so far either to sectors like agriculture and tariff policy, which are relatively well insulated from other sectors, or to fairly limited aspects of other sectors. Spill-over from sector to sector has not occurred and even progress on policies like the free movement of labour and capital has had a lesser impact than many anticipated. The existence of such Community policies does close certain options for national governments, as, for example, the customs union has excluded tariff adjustments from the range of available policy instruments. Domestic economic planning has not yet been deeply affected. The French experience suggests that the work of the *Commisariat du Plan* has changed little.[28] There are several reasons for this, partly that French planning is less far-reaching than its public relations activities suggest, partly that the agricultural sector was never properly integrated, and partly that international agreements, which for their purposes include community agreements, have not been regarded as a component of the planning procedure, but rather as defining the parameters of action.

Evidence collated on the impact of Community policies on industrial management[29] suggests that the elimination of some of the obstacles to trans-national management has not had a great liberating

[27] Directives have not been much studied, but see the series in *Cahiers du Droit Européen*, covering in 1969 the Netherlands and in 1970 France.

[28] Gerbet in *La Décision dans les Communautés Européennes*, p. 199, and J. E. S. Hayward in a paper delivered at Manchester on 2 March 1971.

[29] Werner Feld, 'Political Aspects of Transnational Collaboration in the Common Market', in *International Organisation*, Spring 1970, pp. 209f.

effect. Few businessmen yet think in European terms; industrialists have not seen the European Communities as imposing a logic which makes it no longer reasonable to think in national terms. This is compounded by the persistence of many financial, legal and technical obstacles which make it easier to continue to use traditional patterns.

Perhaps the area of greatest impact has been the foreign policy area.[30] The development of a common commercial policy and the association with developing countries in Africa and the Mediterranean basin have considerably altered the range of instruments available to foreign policy-makers and the scope of their activities. However, overall the effect so far of Community activity on national policy-making has been at most restrictive: it has narrowed the parameters of action, but its positive effect on the way policy alternatives are posed has been small.

Areas of potential community agreement imply a more profound effect on domestic policy-making. The implementation of the value added tax and its imposition at a common rate may influence national fiscal policies extensively; the adoption of a statute for a European Company might alter the configuration of European industry.[31] More importantly, steps towards economic and monetary union, as envisaged in the Werner Plan, even if haltingly taken, are likely to affect national economic management substantially.[32] But it should be remembered that the experience to date has been that it is easier to reach agreement on something which it is simple to align in a technical sense, even though it may not go to the root of the problem in hand. Thus the principle of aligning exchange rates within the Community, even of establishing a common currency, may be agreed, but the far-reaching issues of economic management allied with it are more complex and more contentious: particular problems include the relationship between balance of payments equilibrium and the level of employment, and the existence

[30] This point was developed by S. Henig in a paper given at Manchester on 24 November 1970.

[31] See Peter Stephenson, 'Problems and Political Implications for the UK of introducing the EEC Value Added Tax', in *Journal of Common Market Studies*, June 1970, pp. 305f.; Community Topic no. 29, *Tax Harmonisation in the European Community*, European Communities Information Office, London, 1968; Dennis Thompson, *The Proposal for a European Company*, Chatham House/PEP, London, 1969.

[32] The points which follow derive from the Werner Report (published as a supplement to Bulletin 11 of the European Communities, 1970), and from a paper given at Manchester by Peter Oppenheimer on 9 March 1971.

of regional imbalances. The nature of these problems calls into question the very ability of the Community institutions to fulfil a central function of economic management.

A similar range of problems arises in the technological sector.[33] The recognition of the strength of American business in Europe does not automatically lead to an acceptance of the solutions required, solutions which rest upon European purchasing policies, European companies and European programmes. All of these presuppose hard decisions as to which country will benefit in which sector, and which companies will receive which contracts. Such hard decisions are not made easier by the importance of the industries involved in terms of national prestige, national employment and high earning capacity.

The first areas chosen for Community policies were among those thought in the 1950s to be central, but which have, in practice, left national policy-making relatively immune. Potential and scheduled community policies are of a different order. The form in which they emerge and the methods of implementation will be interesting for their effect on policy-making at the national level. The argument so far suggests that the six governments generally pursue a minimalist strategy, but it is an open question as to whether this trend will continue.

CONCLUSIONS

From this we may draw a number of tentative conclusions. First, the lack of academic attention to the impact of the Communities on national politics has resulted in a failure to relate the stagnation of the Communities in the late 1960s and the changing emphasis in the Brussels institutions to the process of national policy-making on European issues. The executive orientation of this process, especially the predominance of Ministries of Foreign Affairs, has influenced both the minimalist strategies pursued in Brussels and the minimizing of participation at the national level. As far as can be judged, each of the six governments has been affected in a broadly similar way, although more detailed investigation would probably unearth interesting differences related to the variations in national political style.

[33] I am indebted to the paper given by Roger Williams at Manchester on 8 December 1970 for the arguments presented here.

Secondly, although the attitudes of administrators and public opinion surveys substantiate a broad acceptance of European integration, the stuff of policy-making has been relatively compartmentalized in the national processes. European issues have, in practice, tended to be regarded as one bundle of issues rather than as a new dimension pervading the political spectrum.

Thirdly, despite the intensity of activity generated by the European Communities, their impact on the national level seems to be different in degree rather than in kind from that of other international organizations. For political integration of the character envisaged by the founders of the Communities to be achieved, changes at the national level are as important as the development of the Community institutions themselves. So far such changes have not been extensive.

These reflections all add up to a view which does not see economic integration gradually and painlessly moving towards political integration. This derives from an assessment of the behaviour of national governments as impeding such an evolution. Indeed for this to occur far more positive and deliberate actions on the part of governments would be necessary. Their negative attitudes have not prevented political leaders from embracing apparently progressive positions on the development of the Communities – the Werner Plan is an outstanding example. The contradiction lies in the gap between the adoption of broad proposals and their translation into practice in a heavily mutilated version.

Terkel T. Nielsen

European Groups and the Policy*†

ONE HIGHLY SIGNIFICANT ASPECT OF THE PROCESS OF INTEGRATION in the European Community is the transfer of social sectors from the national political systems to the Community system. One such sector is agriculture. This article will focus on a limited, but significant part of the activities performed by the Community institutions: the collective decision-making process with reference to the common agricultural policy.

The information used comes mainly from the following sources: structured interviews with 18 respondents in the Commission, the Council, and some European interest groups; several informal conversations; official Community publications; internal documents of COPA; and periodicals. The research strategy was inspired by the approach of systems analysis, and the decision-making process is considered as an information-processing activity implying the selection of one action from a number of available alternatives.[1]

Agriculture has a key position in the European Economic Community.[2] The principles of the Common Agricultural Policy

---

* The author wishes to express his gratitude to Rector H. Brugmans, The College of Europe, Bruges, for financial support which made it possible to carry out field research during the months of January and February 1969.

† Vol. 6, No. 4, Autumn 1971.

[1] See Dick Ramström, *The Efficiency of Control Strategies. Communication and Decision-Making in Organizations*, Stockholm, 1967, Chaps. 2 and 6 on the decision-making process.

[2] Cf. Leon N. Lindberg and Stuart A. Scheingold, *Europe's Would-Be Polity. Patterns of Change in the European Community*, Englewood Cliffs, N.J., 1970, on the agricultural sector in a Community context, pp. 141–81.

are: no restrictions on internal trade, joint finance of market organizations, and a common external trade policy. Through the market
organizations prices are stabilized at a uniform level above the
world market, external trade is regulated, and other measures taken.
The market organizations are controlled through a complicated
price mechanism. In the internal market prices can fluctuate between
the target price and the intervention price. A basic intervention price
is fixed for Duisburg. If the market price falls below the intervention
price, designated bodies intervene; if the price rises above the target
price the supply will be increased through imports from third
countries.

The task of the price mechanism in relation to imports from third
countries is to eliminate the difference between the price level in the
internal market and the world market through a system of variable
levies. When the imported products arrive at the Community
border (cereals in c.i.f. prices, dairy produce in free at frontier
prices) a levy is imposed, the levy equalling in principle the difference between the world market price and the target price. In practice
the levies imposed equal only the difference between the world
market price (c.i.f. price) and the threshold price, the difference
between the threshold price and the target price being equivalent to
the costs of transportation between the port of entry (in principle
Rotterdam) and the large consumer centres (in principle Duisburg,
the district with the largest deficiency of cereals in the Community);
thus the selling price is brought up to the level of the target price.
For other regions corresponding prices are calculated. In order to
support agricultural exports a system of export restitutions (corresponding to the levies) has been introduced; this system also includes
transportation costs. Furthermore, external trade is regulated
through a system of import and export certificates.

Actual market intervention is carried out by a number of national
intervention bodies operating at the national level, such as the Produktschappen in the Netherlands, the Einfuhr- und Vorratsstellen
in Germany, and ONIC and FORMA in France; these are controlled
by the Community authorities. Three types of intervention can be
identified: automatic intervention where the intervention bodies are
obliged to buy at the existing intervention prices (e.g. cereals, dairy
produce, sugar); non-automatic intervention where no action is
taken until the Community authorities have taken a decision; and
semi-automatic intervention where the price is fixed, but intervention only occurs under certain conditions.

Responsibility for the formulation and implementation of agricultural policy is divided between the Community level and the national level. With the achievement of a common Community policy covering almost the entire agricultural sector, collective decision-making takes place within the framework of the Community institutions, through a complex process involving a number of actors from the Community and from the member states.[3]

At the Community level the actors involved include the Commissioners themselves and their cabinets and the various Directorates General. Directorate General VI is responsible for agriculture. It consists of six directorates: 'A' responsible for external affairs, 'B', 'C' and 'D' for market organizations, 'E' for economic and structural questions and 'F' for the European Fund for Agricultural Guidance and Guarantees (FEOGA). Under these are twenty-four divisions and two sections concerned with legal harmonization. Other interested sections of the Commission include the Legal Service, the Statistical Office and the General Secretariat. The Council of Ministers, with its own secretariat, is involved both directly and through its subsidiary bodies: the Committee of Permanent Representatives (CPR) and the Special Committee on Agriculture with their respective working groups. The common agricultural policy has brought into existence a large number of special committees: the Management Committees, Committees of Regulation, Committees of National Experts and other consultative committees. The normal procedures of the Community also involve the Economic and Social Committee and the European Parliament.

The activity of these Community bodies takes place within a wider environment which affects the pattern of Community policy-making. Firstly there are the participants in the six national political systems: the governments, in particular the Ministries of Foreign Affairs, Economic Affairs and Agriculture, national intervention bodies, national interest groups, and various political and administrative elites. Secondly, there are the governments of third countries and the various factors which affect world market prices. Thirdly there are the Community-level interest groups.

[3] Cf. Lindberg and Scheingold, *op. cit.* on the political system and the problems of decision-making, pp. 64–100; Leon N. Lindberg, 'Decision-making and Integration in the European Community', *International Organization*, Vol. XIX, No. 1, 1965; Leon N. Lindberg, 'The European Community as a Political System: Notes towards the Construction of a Model', *Journal of Common Market Studies*, Vol. 5, No. 4, 1967, which has inspired the present concept of EEC authorities.

The national governmental bodies without question constitute the most important part of this environment. Apart from the national groups, however, the European groups are of considerable importance. A remarkable reshaping of the activities of interest groups has taken place since 1960, when some 80 European groups concerned to some degree with the agricultural sector could be identified as against some 130–140 today. Most are members of 'umbrella organizations'; the groups can be classified under the headings in Table 1.

TABLE 1[4]

EEC Interest Groups of relevance to the Agricultural Sector

Sector	Number	Central organization
Producers	15	COPA
Industry	55	UNICE/CIAA
Trade	38	COCCEE
Co-operation	9	COGECA
Trade unions	3	CISL/CISC
Consumers	3	Comité de contacte
Other sectors	10	
Total	133	

The organizational structure of the European groups as well as their significance and power varies considerably. Some groups are well organized institutions with an administrative apparatus, such as COPA and UNICE (the federation of employers organizations) that perform a significant interest aggregation and provide an accommodation of different positions and demands; others are just weak bodies the activities of which rarely extend beyond acting as a post box between the Commission and the national member organizations. The agricultural organizations are among the most important groups.

[4] Répertoire des organizations agricoles non gouvernementales groupées dans le cadre de la Communauté économique européenne; admission to the Répertoire is criterion of relevance.

UNICE = Union des Industries de la Communauté Européenne.
CIAA = Commission des Industries Agricoles et Alimentaires de l'UNICE.
COCCEE= Comité des Organisations Commerciales des Pays de la CEE
COGECA= Comité général de la Coopération Agricole des Pays de la CEE

Three types of channel link the national organizations[5] to the EC authorities. One channel passes through the national governmental bodies, the traditional and well known route; a second channel goes directly to the Community authorities where the groups try to exert pressure individually; by a third channel demands are funnelled through European groups which try to give priority to certain demands. During the early 1960s national groups seemed to prefer those channels which led through national government organizations; but today at least some agricultural groups tend to put more emphasis on the route through the European groups. This trend may be related to the evolution of the CAP and parallels the development from the period of construction to the present phase of management of the CAP.

COMMITTEE OF PROFESSIONAL AGRICULTURAL ORGANISATIONS OF EEC: COPA

As the agricultural umbrella organization, COPA is the most important group. Its national member organizations are the central agricultural organizations and its organizational structure consists of five major components. The Assembly is the controlling body and consists of representatives from the member organizations; it is concerned largely with major policy options. The Presidium contains one elected leader from each member state. It represents COPA and by its power to approve the decisions of the specialized sections it occupies a central position. The group of general experts which assists the Presidium is composed of representatives from the member organizations (mostly from the secretariats) and apart from preparing the meetings of the Presidium it considers a number of general problems in line with *la philosophie du COPA*. The Secretariat had in 1969 a staff of seven people with professional qualifications and clerical assistants; it is the centre of communication within COPA and also between the member organizations and the Community authorities. Some thirty specialized sections, working groups of various kinds, are either directly part of the COPA organization or are separate European groups (about 10). Their significance and independence of COPA varies considerably.

---

[5] See Werner Feld, 'National Economic Interest Groups and Policy Formation in the EEC', *Political Science Quarterly*, Vol. LXXXI, No. 3, 1966, on the activities of the national groups.

Most are organized according to agricultural products; some deal with questions in the legal, structural and social field. It is an official goal of COPA to centralize all interest group activities in the agricultural sector.

COPA has developed its own procedure for reaching decisions. In response to measures initiated in the Commission the Secretariat sends a questionnaire to the member organizations (to the relevant specialized section) by which their positions are indicated. The members of the section try to reach a common position on the basis of the answers and reports from the Secretariat. The decision of the section is then transmitted to the general experts, who examine it and often make a set of 'observations' on the position. The next phase takes place within the Presidium which has to approve the decision before it is transmitted to the Community authorities as a note or a formal *prise de position*. Particularly important problems are discussed by the Assembly. Throughout the whole process the Secretariat plays an important role through its part in defining the questions to be considered within the various component bodies.

COPA can be considered a 'gatekeeper' in the Community system. Demands from the member organizations emerge from the COPA process with a rather different content. In 1964 COPA was unable to reach a common position on the fixing of the cereal price because of the divergent positions held by the German, French and Dutch organizations. This sort of situation which paralysed COPA no longer exists. Divergent positions in specific sectors are still to be found; for example in November 1968 the Dutch organizations added a rider to the COPA position on the intervention price for milk powder, demanding a lower price of 46·50 units of account (1 ua = $1) as against the COPA demand for a price of 48 ua per 100 kilograms. However, such dissension has become increasingly rare. The annual price review presents particular difficulties, but although divergent positions persist, compromises are usually reached. When in 1968 the Commission proposed to lower the intervention price for butter, COPA as a whole strongly opposed this. There is evidence that the mode of conflict resolution within COPA may be changing from an accommodation on the basis of 'the minimum common denominator' or 'splitting the difference' to an 'upgrading of the common interest'. In 1967 the national organizations put forward different claims for the annual price review, yet they succeeded in reaching a common position demanding a general price rise of 5 per cent.

Moreover, in 1968, an agreement was reached to demand a *differentiated* rise of prices for each product concerned.

The initiative in agricultural policy generally lies with the Commission, and COPA responds to this stimulus. Thus the activities of COPA can be regarded as a process of feedback and response. COPA's behaviour is not always confined to a reaction; sometimes policy initiatives originate in COPA or its member organizations. For instance COPA has exerted considerable pressure upon the Commission to induce it to set up a new market organization for sheep products, and the Commission is actually planning a proposal for the Council on this. The absence of voting procedures probably has a stress-reducing function; if compromises turn out to be impossible all points of view are presented to the Community authorities. Political cleavages are based predominantly on national antagonisms, but sectoral problems also provoke clashes of interests. On cereals and dairy produce disagreement is, by and large, attributable to national differences, while disagreement on structural problems stems from both national and sectoral antagonisms. In general, stable markets and a fixed policy seem to facilitate the possibilities of accommodation in COPA.

Coordination of views among member organizations of the same nationality is least developed in the Italian groups and most in the Dutch groups. One reason for the lack of coordination among Italian organizations may be ascribed to the fragmentation of Italian agricultural interest groups; conversely the three central Dutch organizations have established a joint international secretariat to coordinate their activities, and the Landbouwschap which comprises both farmers' organizations and trade unions facilitates the coordination of positions. In the majority of cases the representatives are competent to bind their organizations, but this has been more difficult in bodies where member states, rather than organizations, are represented. In respect of the overall configuration of power there is evidence that the Presidium and the major specialized sections are particularly influential, but so too is the Secretariat with its easy access to relevant information and numerous contacts with the EC authorities. Finally it must be underlined that the interest articulation of the member organizations through COPA is the basis of COPA's existence. Any threat to use other channels challenges the survival of COPA. In June 1968 COPA and the trades unions were strong enough to establish a collective agreement on hours of work for 300,000 agricultural workers in the EEC.

PATTERNS OF DECISION-MAKING

The pattern of decision-making varies according to the type of decision and the bodies involved.[6] The definition of the type of decision affects the way in which it is handled. It may be classified as a guideline or a detailed decision, as a strategic or a tactical, as policy-defining or routine, or as 'political' or 'technical'. Article 189 of the Treaty of Rome divides Community decisions into Regulations, Directives and Decisions. In the operation of the CAP, Regulations are particularly important. They can be divided into Basic Regulations made by the Council and Implementing Regulations which are made either by the Council or by the Commission. Three patterns of decision-making can be distinguished.

The first pattern is the Council procedure. On a proposal of the Commission the Council produces a decision, after the proposal has been processed in either the Special Committee on Agriculture or the CPR, and sometimes after consultation with the European Parliament and the Economic and Social Committee. Basic regulations contain the essential rules of the market organizations; Implementing Regulations are decisions such as the annual price review, the basic principles of intervention, and the principles of calculating the other prices and levies. These decisions are 'general rules' and their main object is to control the Commission. The most important are the target and basic intervention prices of cereals and dairy products and other prices which define the structure of the policy; these are prices of high political significance, such as the threshold prices and the derivative intervention prices. These decisions are strategic policy decisions of high political saliency, which do not set out the details of the policy.

The second pattern is the Commission-Management Committee procedure. A Commission decision is submitted to a Management Committee which then gives an opinion on it. These decisions concern the terms of implementation of the market organizations, such as changes of the variable levies and export restitutions, the fixing of criteria or conditions of intervention and import and export certificates. They are fairly detailed, routine decisions of a technical and administrative nature.

The third pattern is the Commission procedure. These decisions

---

[6] See Giancarlo Olmi, 'Common Organization of Agricultural Markets at the Stage of the Single Market', *Common Market Law Review*, Vol. 5, 1967–68, on agricultural decision-making.

are non-discretionary, very detailed and technical routine decisions made at short and regular intervals, or very urgent decisions. These include decisions such as changes in export restitutions made between meetings of a Management Committee, but comprise most importantly decisions on the c.i.f. prices of cereals and free at frontier prices of dairy products.[7]

The Council Procedure   The Community authorities have constantly to adapt to changing circumstances. When a new problem arises the Commission produces a proposal for the Council. The initiative is taken in DG VI and instructions are transmitted to the relevant Division which investigates the background; the problem area is defined and information is collected to form a basis for decision. Contact may be made with other directorates and DGs and with division B-4 (which deals with the legal aspects and with problems of coordination). National governmental agencies and the Permanent Delegations may be contacted; the 'top management' of DG VI and the cabinet of M. Mansholt is kept informed; the cabinet and the commissioner often make contact with national administrative and political elites in order to ensure the adoption of the proposal in the Council. When a basis for decision has been constructed it is transformed into an *avant-projet*, the first partial decision. Sometimes an ad hoc group of top officials is set up to work out the details of the proposal, particularly for an important plan such as Mansholt's memorandum 'Agriculture 1980' on the modernization of agriculture.

Although it is not the norm the *avant-projet* may be submitted to a group of national experts for discussion, and the relevant Division with Division A-4 (responsible for contact with interest groups) may seek an opinion from the Consultative Committee. The next step is the transformation of the *avant-projet* into a *projet*, the second partial decision, which has then to be approved by the Director and deputy Director General before it is transmitted to the 'Round Table', a meeting of the Commissioner, and the Director General, his deputies, and the Directors. At the 'Round Table' the

[7] See David Coombes, *Politics and Bureaucracy in the European Community. A Portrait of the Commission of the EEC*, London, 1970, on the Commission as a European civil service, Chaps. 6 and 7; on the administrative, initiative, mediative, and normative functions of the Commission, pp. 234–42; and especially Chaps. 11 which treats the Commission as a bureaucracy with predominantly administrative and mediative functions.

Commissioner 'meets' his Directorate General. This constitutes an important decision and control centre in DG VI. The *projet* may be adopted, or returned to the Division, or approved after minor modifications. This circuit between the 'Round Table' and the Division may be repeated several times.

At this phase official consultation with other DGs and with the Legal Service takes place. While the Commissioners' working group on agricultural problems does not seem to play any significant role, the meeting of the chiefs of cabinet is very important. This committee prepares the meeting of the Commission; if the chiefs of cabinet agree on the proposal it will appear as a 'point A' on the agenda of the Commission, which means that the decision is usually endorsed by the Commission without discussion. Cases subject to disagreement are discussed by the Commission and changes may be approved at the meeting or through the 'written procedure'. Finally the proposal is transmitted to the Council.

In the Council the CPR stipulates the procedure to be followed. The SCA processes proposals on market organizations while questions of legal harmonization and fiscal, social, and structural problems are dealt with by the CPR. The Parliament is consulted on Basic Regulations and Implementing Regulations dealing with policy-defining prices such as target and basic intervention prices, while other prices such as threshold prices are not subject to consultation with the Parliament.[8] After discussion in the agricultural committee of the Parliament and in the political groupings, the proposal, a report, and the opinion are discussed in a plenary session: an opinion and a report are sent to the Council, where they appear on the agenda as a 'point B'. The Parliament is involved in the decision-making process at a rather late stage, and the procedure is merely consultative. Deadlines are short and only a few proposals are submitted to it for opinion; sometimes its opinions and resolutions arrive so late at the Council that there is no opportunity for them to influence the decision. As K. Neunreither states, 'le Parlement joue un rôle extrêmement reduit'.[9] The Economic and Social Committee is consulted on Basic Regulations and directives on legal harmonization. Its specialized section on agriculture drafts an

[8] On the consultation of the European Parliament, see Olmi, *op. cit.* pp. 402–4.

[9] Karlheinz Neunreither, 'Le rôle du Parlement européen' in *La décision dans les Communautés européennes*, ed. by Pierre Gerbet and Daniel Pepy, Brussels 1969, p. 126.

opinion which is often discussed in the heterogeneous 'groups', of employers, trades unions and other interests including the liberal professions, and then at the plenary session before being sent to the Council.

At the Council phase of the decision-making process three basic sets of communications can be identified: the internal communication among the various components of the Council; communications between the Council and the member states; communications between the Council and the Commission (the tandem Commission-Council).

Where the SCA is responsible the proposal is usually sent to one of its working groups. After discussion there the problem is referred to the full SCA which also receives reports produced by the Council Secretariat. If an acceptable compromise can be reached the proposal is sent to the Council as a 'point A' on the agenda, that is to say, the Council adopts the decision without discussion. Major political problems and disagreements are discussed in the Council as 'points B'. If the ministers cannot agree, the issue returns to the SCA, often with new instructions. This cycle, working group – SCA – Council, continues until a compromise has been accepted, and sometimes the CPR is drawn into the process. A similar pattern is found where the CPR is directly responsible.

Through the national delegations – drawn partly from the Permanent Delegations and partly from national ministries – a permanent stream of information about the state of affairs in the Council flows to the national governmental bodies, particularly to the Ministries of Foreign affairs and Agriculture. The permanent representatives and their deputies participate in coordinating meetings in their capitals and send letters and reports. The communication is two-way; instructions and other kinds of steering information constrain the Permanent Delegations and national civil servants taking part in the decision-making process. On the basis of the information fed back through the national delegations the national authorities are able to adapt to new situations in the Council. The degree of control over national civil servants and the Permanent Delegations varies from country to country and from case to case;[10] for instance the instructions of the German government are usually

<hr />

[10] See Jean J. A. Salmon, 'Le rôle des représentations permanentes' in *La décision dans les Communautés européennes* on instructions to the Permanent Delegations.

rather strict and detailed while the Italian instructions are rather general.

The Commission is represented at all levels of the negotiations of the Council and the groups under the Council by the General Secretariat of the Commission in the CPR, and by DG VI in the SCA and the working groups. These representatives are instructed, too; but the General Secretariat has a larger margin of manoeuvre than the national delegations. Information about the state of affairs is fed back to the higher levels of DG VI and the Commission which can then modify their positions.

As regards communication with the SCA and the working groups a copy of minor technical notes must be sent to the General Secretariat of the Commission. Working documents of little political saliency must be sent from DG VI through the General Secretariat for approval by the cabinets; other DGs are kept informed and then the documents are transmitted to the national delegations by the Council Secretariat or copies of the documents are sent to the Commission Secretariat before being circulated to the delegations. Official 'communications' of political relevance and all documents to be presented to the Council itself have to be approved either at the meetings of the Commission or by the 'written procedure'. Through the Commission's representatives information about responses to the communication is fed back, and the process continues.

The General Secretariat of the Commission distributes reports of meetings of the CPR to the Commissioners, chiefs of cabinet, and sometimes Directors General. DG VI and M. Mansholt are also informed through other channels; top officials of DG VI and experts from the Divisions attend the relevant meetings of the CPR, and the cabinet has contacts with the Permanent Delegations. At the subsequent meeting of the Commission new decisions are taken in response to the new situation in the CPR. In the Council itself the Commissioners or the chiefs of cabinet are present; at the meetings of the Commission decisions on new measures are made. All documents sent to the Council must be approved by the Commission or by the 'written procedure'. In the Commission DG VI, the General Secretariat, and the Commission itself are the central components of the tandem Commission-Council.

Proposals for compromise in the Council phase usually originate in the Commission, or from the member state acting as president of the Council, or from the Secretariat of the Council. The position of the Commission weakens when compromises come from any source other than the Commission. Although decisions of the Council can be adopted by majority vote hardly any decision on an agricultural problem has been taken through a ballot in the Council. Most of the market organizations and the financial organization have come into being through Marathon-sessions characterized by long exhausting negotiations, a fixed deadline or an ultimatum, and the elaboration of a 'package-deal' by the Commission. While parliamentary control is practically non-existent and the so-called triangle Council-Commission-Parliament must be considered a fiction, the important configuration is composed of the member states, the Council and the Commission.

The Commission – Management Committee Procedure. The Commission is linked to its environment by a network of communications. Daily or weekly the Division responsible for cereals, for instance, receives more than 25 different categories of input information. A considerable proportion of the data is received by telex from national governmental agencies. Information is also received through the committees of national representatives, through the Consultative Committees, directly from European interest groups, and from sources of information in third countries on world prices. The head of Division or the principal administrator supervises the construction of the decision base; contact is established with other directorates, DGs, and Ministries of Agriculture. Then an *avant-projet* is drafted, usually jointly with division B-4. The next phase is the discussion of the *avant-projet* in a Committee of national experts.[11] These experts cannot bind their government, but usually do not arrive without instructions. On the basis of the discussion in this committee, the Division is able to modify the *avant-projet* in order not to have it rejected in the Management Committee and tries to influence the national delegations to accept the position of the Commission. From time to time a *demande d'avis* is sent to the members of the relevant Consultative Committee. The Consultative Committees consist of representatives of European interest groups from various sectors, and COPA-COGECA have half the seats. Usually the interest groups cannot reach agreement and the Committee has to deliver an *avis dispersé*, because the groups represented in the committees – producers, traders, trade unions, consumers, foodstuff industry –

---

[11] Cf. Lawrence Scheinman, 'Some Preliminary Notes on Bureaucratic Relationships in the European Economic Community', *International Organization*, Vol. XX, 1966, on the 'bureaucratic interpenetration'.

defend different interests, particularly on agricultural prices, and thus take different positions in the Committees, the opinions of which must contain all points of view. The Consultative Committees deal predominantly with technical matters, meet rarely and at short notice, and deliver few opinions.

After discussion in the Committee of national experts, and possibly after receiving the opinion of the Consultative Committee, the *avant-projet* is transformed into a *projet*, which has to be approved by the Director and the deputy Director General, whom one respondent called 'the real power centre' of DG VI. Other DGs and the Legal Service are consulted, and finally the *projet* is submitted to the Management Committee for its opinion.

There is roughly speaking one Management Committee for each market organization. They are composed of national representatives and are presided over by a high official, from DG VI, who does not have the right to vote. The distribution of votes corresponds to that set out in Article 148.2.1 of the Rome Treaty and twelve votes are required for a committee 'opinion'. The Commission's decision is immediately applicable, but if the Committee delivers an 'unfavourable opinion' by casting twelve votes against the proposed decision, the decision of the Commission is sent to the Council, which must then take the decision. If the Committee delivers a 'favourable opinion' or cannot provide the qualified majority of twelve votes either for or against the Commission, the Council is not involved. The Management Committees 'may be considered as a sort of alarm system. When the Commission differs from an opinion ... this is a sign that a difficult situation or a serious problem exists'.[12] During the negotiations in the Committee the Commission can modify the *projet* or even withdraw it. The activities of the Management Committees are summarized in Table 2.[13]

Of the six cases communicated to the Council only one has been changed by the Council. The probability of an unfavourable opinion is thus 0·0026 and the probability of the Council changing a decision submitted to the Management Committees is 0·0004. This might indicate that the member states through the Management Committees, the Committees of national experts, and other channels control the behaviour of the Commission so effectively that

[12] Emile Noël, *How the European Economic Community's Institutions Work*, Community Topics, No. 27, p. 6.

[13] Data from QE no. 156/66, JO. p. 1634/67 of 27 April 1967; QE no. 289/69, JO no. C156/8 of 8 December 1969; QE no. 71/68, JO no. C66/56; QE no. 148/69, JO no. C124/2 of 23 September 1969.

TABLE 2

Opinions of the Management Committees until 30 June 1969.

Category	Number	Percentage	Changed by the Council
Favourable opinion	2046	89·46	–
No opinion	235	10·28	–
Unfavourable opinion	6	0·26	1
Total	2287	100·00	1

corrections are hardly needed; or it might indicate that the influence of the Management Committees is insignificant; or it might indicate that the Commission through the various feedback channels is able to regulate its own decisions so that the Management Committees do not reject them. Christoph Bertram thinks that as a result of the Management Committee procedure 'the Commission's authority has grown and its position in the Community has been strengthened'.[14]

The result of the procedure is communicated to the Permanent Delegations, and from then on DG VI does not take part in the decision-making. The next step of the normal programme is the 'written procedure'. The General Secretariat communicates the decision to the cabinets of the commissioners and if no objections have reached the Secretariat before a fixed deadline the decision is considered to have been adopted by the Commission. The decision-making process ends here. While the Management Committees deal with the direct administration of an agricultural sector, a number of Committees of Regulation provide a mechanism for co-operation between the Commission and the member states on the setting and operation of certain norms, as for example the Permanent Committee of Animal Feedstuffs and the Permanent Committee of Foodstuffs. The Committee of Regulation procedure has a pattern similar to the Management Committees, but an 'unfavourable opinion' and 'no opinion' both lead to the involvement of the Council.

[14] Christoph Bertram, 'Decision-Making in the EEC: The Management Committee Procedure', *Common Market Law Review*, Vol. 5, No. 1, 1967–68, p. 262. A quantitative indicator of autonomy (defined as an input/output ratio) provides evidence that the autonomy of the Commission has increased from 1962 to 1967; the input/output ratio of telex messages of DG VI was in 1962 0·92 (230/250) and in 1967 0·52 (1400/2700), and this indicates 'low' and 'high' autonomy, respectively; data from *Mitteilungen zur Gemeinsamen Agrarpolitik*, 14/1967, Press and Information Service of the European Communities, p. 6.

The Commission Procedure. There seem to be two different patterns. One is roughly similar to the procedure outlined above, but without the inclusion of the Management Committees and with less active participation by the Committees of national experts. The other is the 'Agri-telex' procedure.

The 'written procedure' is an important mechanism. Four types can be distinguished.[15] The *'procédure écrite normale'* has a deadline of five days; the *'procédure écrite accélérée'* has a considerably shorter deadline. The *'procédure écrite accélérée de type spécial'* was introduced with the modification in 1968 of the *'habilitations Mansholt'*, which authorized M. Mansholt in the name and under the responsibility of the Commission to make certain decisions on levies and restitutions; for these the deadline is at most one day and the objecting commissioner must moreover establish a majority for the decision to be changed. Presumably more than 6,000 'written procedures' are performed a year.

The 'Agri-telex' procedure is rather different.[16] The c.i.f. prices and free at frontier prices have to be fixed within very short deadlines, and take the form of decisions rather than regulations. When the relevant Division has calculated the price and it has been approved by the Director (in the case of significant changes by the deputy Director General too), DG VI in turn informs the governmental agencies by telex and the General Secretariat. The Secretariat operates a written procedure with a deadline of a few hours, after which it informs DG VI of the outcome, and DG VI in turn informs the governmental agencies by telex that the provisional prices are now definitive. The Secretariat then immediatly notifies the Permanent Delegations of the decision.

EUROPEAN INTEREST GROUPS AND THE DECISION-MAKING PROCESS

COPA provides a good example of the activities of European groups.[17] The Commission is COPA's main target. The Secretariat of

[15] See Hartmut Kirstein, *Les institutions communautaires*, College of Europe, Bruges, 1968 (unprinted paper).

[16] See Joachim-Friedrich Heine, 'Wie entstehen die Rechtsnormen der Europäischen Wirtschaftsgemeinschaft?', *Molkerei- und Käserei-Zeitung*, 16/1967, Hildesheim, on the 'Agri-telex' procedure.

[17] On interest group activities see Dusan Sidjanski, 'Pressure Groups and the European Economic Community', *Government and Opposition*, Vol. 2, no. 3, 1967; and Jean Meynaud and Dusan Sidjanski, 'L'action des groupes de pression'

COPA has contact with all levels and practically all Divisions of DG VI and with the Commissioner and his cabinet. On the whole direct personal contact is preferred, and the problem is to find the right man, one who takes part in decision-making, who has access to the relevant information and who has the appropriate authority. The most important contacts seem to be with people situated 'at the decisive middle level of communication and decision'[18] of DG VI, such as heads of Division. But in spite of good contacts with top officials 'the real lobby', as one respondent said, exerts pressure at a relatively low level of DG VI.

COPA is represented by its specialized sections in the Consultative Committees in the various meetings organized by DG VI, and sometimes too in meetings with national experts. Examples of subjects considered in Consultative Committees are Community quality norms on barley for breweries and on cereal and rice prices, the determination of commercial centres for derivative intervention prices, and on the butter surplus. COPA is also consulted on general political problems; for example its general experts are responsible for COPA's opinion on the problems of the 'Medium Term Economic Policy'. While the specialized sections are primarily responsible for technical matters, the meetings of the Presidium which takes place every six to eight weeks with M. Mansholt and the top officials of DG VI cover key political issues. In the early years of the CAP these 'summit meetings' dealt with the general problems of the construction of a common policy, for instance the establishment of common market organizations in 1962 and 1963,and with a general exchange of positions. But today they tend to consider specific political options on for example the butter surplus or the memorandum on 'Agriculture 1980'. This plan was developed by a small ad hoc working group of top officials from DG VI (including the Commissioner) and COPA kept in touch with the problems at various stages, both through informal and confidential information at an early stage and through official consultations at later stages. Furthermore, recently the Presidium has been consulted on *avant-projets* for policy decisions.

A stable pattern of relationships between COPA and the

---

in *La décision dans les Communautés européennes*, ed. by Pierre Gerbet and Daniel Pepy, Brussels, 1969

[18] Karl W. Deutsch, *The Nerves of Government. Models of Political Communication and Control*, New York, 1966, p. 154.

Community authorities has developed. The first phase is to ascertain the new measures planned by the Commission on, for example, a market organization for chicory, or on major changes in the restitutions for fats. COPA tries to be informed as early as possible. The next stage is the transmission of technical notes to the Commission indicating COPA's position. Then the Secretariat tries to discover the impact of the note on the Commission. Finally a formal *prise de position* is forwarded. Parallel to these activities the Secretariat and other COPA representatives exert pressure on officials at various levels in DG VI. Meetings may take place with experts from the Divisions; the problem may be considered in a Consultative Committee; or if it is an important problem the issue may be discussed at a meeting with M. Mansholt. While COPA is in contact with most major centres of decision in the Commission there are very few contacts with the Management Committees.

COPA and CIAA (representing the foodstuffs industry) are regarded by the Commission as the most important European groups in the agricultural sector. COPA is especially important for cereals and CIAA for dairy produce. In DG VI it is felt that the information passed from interest groups to Commission on dairy products is considered to be important, and in some cases even decisive; information on cereals is much less important, but occasionally decisive. Information on legal harmonization is felt to have 'a certain importance'. Moreover it must be remembered that COPA is consulted far more intensively on 'technical' than on 'political' matters. Sometimes the transmission of positions and pressure exerted by COPA results in an *avant-projet* being changed. It is widely held in the Commission that its decisions would have been substantially different had it not been for consultations with such interest groups as COPA. In practice the Commission takes COPA's demands into account to the extent that they are compatible with the goals of the Commission, or as one respondent said, 'when the demands are realistic', adding that during recent years COPA's demands have become considerably more 'realistic' than in the early years of the CAP.

There is little contact with the European Parliament, although important views are communicated to it. Through over-lapping membership and assistance to the agricultural representatives of the Economic and Social Committee, COPA devotes some efforts to influencing its opinions; but COPA considers the ESC relatively less important than it was in the early days of the EEC. Apart from communicating views and sending telegrams at the moment of decision of the Council sessions, there is little contact with the Council. On the other hand the agricultural groups at the national level exert strong pressure on national policy makers participating in Council negotiations.

SOME CONCLUSIONS

The agricultural sector represents the most highly integrated area of Community activity. The common agricultural policy is implemented by a pattern of intensive intervention and a system of market organizations which have been in operation for a considerable period. Consequently stable practices and routines have been established. In this respect the agricultural sector is significantly different from other sectors which have not yet acquired such precise policies or become subject to regular Community management. Therefore, the patterns of decision-making outlined above cannot yet be regarded as typical for all sectors, either in terms of the behaviour of the Commission or in terms of interest-group activity. With the possible exceptions of the internal commercial market and social affairs, the access of interest-groups to Community institutions has been less regular and less institutionalized than for agricultural groups.

It is difficult to assess the weight of influence exerted by the various participants in the agricultural decision-making process. A high degree of participation is not necessarily correlated with effective influence. For example, DG VI is very active at a number of levels, but its actual authority is heavily circumscribed both by the provisions of the Regulations and by the 'bureaucratic penetration' of the Commission by national representatives through the web of Committees.

It has been suggested that national agricultural groups tend to funnel an increasing number of demands through COPA at the expense of national channels. But as the national policy makers are still of vital importance in determining strategic policy decisions in the Council negotiations, and since COPA has much poorer access to the Council than to the Commission, national groups inevitably continue to represent their interests through national governmental bodies. The question as to whether a national or a community approach predominates is thus partly a question of emphasis and partly a question of the kind of problem involved – for instance according to whether it is a political or a technical matter. COPA and the national agricultural groups act simultaneously at community level and national level. Although compromises in COPA are generally adhered to, the national groups may follow their own policy towards their respective governmental bodies. COPA has succeeded in reaching accommodation on significant and contentious subjects such as agricultural prices. Although deviating positions still occur they occur less and less frequently.

COPA approaches systematically all or nearly all major decision centres of the Community authorities with the Commission as their chief focus. The national groups are most important at the Council stage.[19] COPA can be said to exercise some influence on the way in which the market organizations operate and where COPA's demands are compatible with the goals of the Commission they seem to be taken into account. Very detailed decisions can hardly be influenced; and on major political options it can be argued that power is concentrated in the national governments, although it is quite likely that COPA may have some influence at this level to the extent that it can maintain a united agricultural front. Consequently it can be argued that COPA has been more successful in influencing the way in which the CAP has been implemented than in influencing matters of detail or the definition of strategic policy options.

[19] Cf. Wilhelm Gieseke, 'Die berufsständischen Organisationen der Landwirtschaft in der agrarpolitischen Willensbildung der EWG', *Agrarpolitik in der EWG* ed. by Theodor Dams *et al.*, Munich, 1968, p. 218, 'nur die systematische Einschaltung auf allen Stufen der Beschlussfassung bringt Aussicht auf Erfolg'. Dr Gieseke occupies a high position in COPA.

Michael A. Wheaton

Literature on the Political Problems of European Integration

THE BOOKS AND ARTICLES LISTED BELOW ARE A SELECTION FROM the vast amount of material now available on this topic. A brief description of the content of the work is given in the case of the more important items in each of the sections.

SPECIALIST PUBLICATIONS

(a) *Agenor – a European Review* (Brussels) Monthly.
(b) *Agra Europe* (London) Weekly.
(c) *Common Market* (The Hague) Monthly.
(d) *Common Market Law Review* (London) Quarterly.
(e) *European Review* (London) Quarterly.
(f) *Journal of Common Market Studies* (Oxford: Basil Blackwell) Quarterly.
(g) *Revue du Marche Commun* (Paris) Monthly.

BACKGROUND WORKS

(a) R. Albrecht-Carrie, *The Unity of Europe – an Historical Survey* (London: Secker & Warburg, 1966).
(b) M. Beloff, *Europe and the Europeans* (London: Chatto & Windus, 1957).
(c) M. and S. Bromberger, *Jean Monnet and the United States of Europe* (New York: Coward-McCann, 1969).
(d) M. Crouzet, *The European Renaissance Since 1945* (London: Thames & Hudson, 1970).
(e) M. T. Florinsky, *Integrated Europe* (New York: Macmillan, 1955).
(f) Lord Gladwyn, *The European Idea* (London: Weidenfeld & Nicolson, 1966).

(g) *European Integration*, ed. C. Grove Haines (Baltimore: Johns Hopkins, 1957).

(h) E. B. Haas, *The Uniting of Europe* (Stanford: Oxford, 2nd edition, 1968).

(i) L. Lindberg, *The Political Dynamics of European Integration* (London: OUP, 1963).
A major theoretical analysis of the process of political integration.

(j) R. Mayne, 'The Role of Jean Monnet', *Government and Opposition* Special Issue (London) vol. 2, no. 3, April/July 1967.

(k) M. Palmer and J. Lambert, *European Unity – a Survey of European Organisations* (London: Allen & Unwin/PEP, 1968).
A thorough if rather dull examination of European political integration in the post-war period. Includes sections on the EEC, NATO and EFTA.

(l) D. de Rougemont, *The Meaning of Europe* (London: Sidgwick & Jackson, 1965).

(m) D. de Rougemont, 'The Campaign of the European Congresses', *Government and Opposition* Special Issue (London) vol. 2, no. 3, April/July 1967.

(n) A. Spinelli, 'European Union in the Resistance', *Government and Opposition* Special Issue (London) vol. 2, no. 3, April/July 1967.

(o) D. W. Urwin, *Western Europe Since 1945* (London: Longmans, 1967).

EUROPEAN INSTITUTIONS (EXCLUDING THE EEC)

(i) *The Council of Europe*

(a) *Manual of the Council of Europe*, edited by officials of the Council (London: Stevens, 1970).
The most comprehensive and up-to-date account of the role and operation of the Council of Europe.

(b) K. Lindsey, *European Assemblies 1949–1959* (London: Stevens, 1960).

(c) A. H. Robertson, *The Council of Europe – its Structure, Functions and Achievements* (London: Stevens, 1956).

(d) A. H. Robertson, *European Institutions: Cooperation – Integration – Unification* 2nd ed. (London: Stevens, 1966).

(e) F. F. Ritsch, 'Origins of the Council of Europe. Part One: The Post-War Unity Movements to The Hague Congress', *Il Politico* (Pavia, Italy) vol. 35, no. 1, 1970.

(f) F. F. Ritsch, 'Origins of the Council of Europe, Part Two: The Governments Take Action', *Il Politico* (Pavia, Italy) vol. 35, no. 2, 1970.

(ii) *The European Coal and Steel Community*

(a) W. Diebold, *The Schuman Plan – a Study in Economic Cooperation* (New York: Praeger, 1959).
(b) L. Lister, *The European Coal and Steel Community* (New York: 20th Century Fund, 1960).
(c) H. Mason, *The European Coal and Steel Community – an Experiment in Supranationalism* (The Hague: Nijhoff, 1955).
(d) J. McKesson, 'The Schuman Plan', *Political Science Quarterly* (New York) vol. 67, no. 1, March 1952.
(e) W. M. Parker, 'The Schuman Plan – a Preliminary Prediction', *International Organisation* (Boston: World Peace Foundation) vol. 6, no. 3, Summer 1952.
(f) P. A. Reynolds, 'The Coal and Steel Community', *Political Quarterly* (London) vol. 23, no. 3, July/September 1952.
(g) F. Sanderson, 'The Five Year Experience of the European Coal and Steel Community', *International Organisation* (Boston: World Peace Foundation) vol. 12, no. 2, Autumn 1958.

(iii) *The European Defence Community*

(a) E. Haas and P. Merkl, 'Parliamentarians Against Ministers', *International Organisation* (Boston: World Peace Foundation) vol. 14, no. 4, Autumn 1960.
(b) *France Defeats the EDC*, eds. D. Lerner and R. Aron (New York: Praeger, 1957).
The most comprehensive account of the political pressures at work in France during the lengthy EDC negotiations.
(c) G. Mollet, 'France and the Defence of Europe', *Foreign Affairs* (New York: Council on Foreign Relations) vol. 32, no. 3, April 1954.

(iv) *The European Free Trade Area*

(a) F. Franck and E. Weisband, *A Free Trade Area Association* (London: University of London Press, 1970).
(b) Geneva Graduate Institute of International Affairs Study Group,

The European Free Trade Area and the Crisis of European Integration
(London: Michael Joseph, 1968).
An analysis of the possible role of EFTA in the future political
integration of Europe. Contains a particularly useful section on
Scandinavian attitudes towards an integrated Europe.
(c) G. A. Schopflin, 'EFTA – the Other Europe', *International
Affairs* (London) vol. 40, no. 4, October 1964.

THE EUROPEAN ECONOMIC COMMUNITY

(i) *General Works*

(a) R. Broad and R. Jarret, *Community Europe – a Short Guide to the
Common Market* (London: Oswald Wolff, 1967).
(b) J. Calman, *The Rome Treaty – the Common Market Explained*
(London: Anthony Blond, 1967).
(c) P. A. Cornelis, *Europeans About Europe* (Amsterdam: Swets &
Zeitlinger 1970).
(d) M. Curtis, *Western European Integration* (New York: Harper &
Row, 1965).
(e) J. F. Deniau, *The Common Market* 4th ed. (London: Barrie &
Rockliffe, 1967).
One of the best introductory works on the EEC.
(f) A. Etzioni, *Political Unification* (London: Holt, Rinehart &
Winston, 1965) chap. 7, 'The European Economic Community'.
(g) A. Etzioni, 'European Unification – a Strategy of Change',
World Politics (Princeton: New Jersey) vol. 26, no. 1, 1963.
(h) E. B. Haas, 'International Integration', *International Organisation*
(Boston: World Peace Foundation) vol. 15, no. 3, Summer 1961.
(i) W. Hallstein, 'Some of Our *Faux Problèmes* in the EEC', *World
Today* (London) vol. 21, no. 1, January 1965.
(j) R. Hartley-Clarke, *The Politics of the Common Market* (New
Jersey: Prentice-Hall, 1967).
(k) D. H. Hene, *Decision on Europe – an Explanation of the Common
Market* (London: Jordan & Sons, 1970).
(l) S. Holt, *The Common Market – the Conflict of Theory and Practice*
(London: Hamish Hamilton, 1967).
A good introductory guide to the EEC. Contains sections de-
signed specifically for the use of British businessmen.
(m) *The European Common Market and Community*, ed. U. W. Kitzinger
(London: Routledge & Kegan Paul, 1967).
A useful collection of documents.

(n) L. B. Krause, *The Common Market – Progress and Controversy* (New Jersey: Prentice Hall, 1965).

(o) P. H. Laurent, 'Paul Henri Spaak and the Diplomatic Origins of the Common Market, 1955–6', *Political Science Quarterly* (New York) vol. 85, no. 3, September 1970.

(p) R. Mayne, *The Recovery of Europe* (London: Weidenfeld & Nicolson, 1970).

(q) A. Silj, *Europe's Political Puzzle* (Cambridge, Mass.: Harvard University Press, 1967).

(r) J. F. Zaring, *Decision on Europe* (Baltimore: Johns Hopkins, 1968).

(ii) *Institutions of the EEC (General)*

(a) R. Cox, 'The Study of European Institutions', *Journal of Common Market Studies* (Oxford: Basil Blackwell) vol. 3, no. 2, March 1965.

(b) J. Lambert, 'Decision-Making in the European Communities', *Government and Opposition* Special Issue (London) vol. 2, no. 3, April/July 1967.

(c) L. Lindberg, 'Integration as a Source of Stress in the European Community System', *International Organisation* (Boston: World Peace Foundation) vol. 20, no. 2, Spring 1966.

(d) L. Lindberg, 'The European Community as a Political System, – Notes Towards the Construction of a Model', *Journal of Common Market Studies* (Oxford: Basil Blackwell) vol. 5, no. 4, June 1967.

(e) R. Mayne, *The Institutions of the EEC* (London: PEP/Chatham House) European Series no. 8, 1968.
A short but useful guide to the roles of the Community institutions and the possible difficulties of British adaptation to these institutions.

(f) W. Pickles, 'Political Power in the EEC', *Journal of Common Market Studies* (Oxford: Basil Blackwell) vol. 2, no. 1, November 1963.
A provocative analysis of the Community institutions. The author is particularly critical of the role and power of the EEC Commission.

(iii) *The Commission*

(a) D. Coombes, *Politics and Bureaucracy in the European Community* (London: Allen & Unwin/PEP, 1970).
A major study of the EEC Commission. Contains an excellent analysis of the conflicting roles of the Commission sub-structure.

(b) D. Coombes, *Towards a European Civil Service* (London: PEP/ Chatham House) European Series no. 7, 1968.

(c) C. Cosgrove and K. Twitchett, 'Merging the Communities – a Miletsone in Western European Integration', *Orbis* (Pennsylvania) vol. 13, no. 3, Autumn 1969.

(d) M. Gaudet, 'The Challenge of the Changing Institutions', *Common Market Law Review* (London) vol. 3, no. 2, September 1965.

(e) W. Hallstein, 'The EEC Commission – a new Factor in International Relations', *International and Comparative Law Quarterly* (London) vol. 14, part 3, July 1965.

(f) E. Hirsch, 'Relations Between the Officials of the European Communities and the Member States', *Government and Opposition* Special Issue (London) vol. 2, no. 3, April/July 1967.

(g) P.-H. J. M. Houben, 'The Merger of the Executives of the European Communities', *Common Market Law Review* (London) vol. 3, no. 1, June 1965.

(h) E. Kapp, *The Merger of the Executives of the European Communities* (Bruges: de Tempel, 1964).

(i) J. Linthorst Homan, 'The Merger of the European Communities' *Common Market Law Review* (London) vol. 3, no. 4, March 1966.

(j) A. Spinelli, *The Eurocrats – Conflict and Crisis in the European Community* (Baltimore: Johns Hopkins, 1966).
A stimulating analysis of the EEC Commission. The author argues that the Commission should take the lead in promoting political integration.

(iv) *The European Parliament*

(a) W. Birke, *European Elections by Direct Suffrage* (Leyden: Sythoff, 1961).

(b) W. Feld, 'French and Italian Communist Parties and the Common Market – the Request for Representation', *Journal of Common Market Studies* (Oxford: Basil Blackwell) vol. 6, no. 3, March 1968.

(c) M. Forsyth, *The Parliament of the European Communities* (London: PEP, 1964).

(d) *European Political Parties*, ed. S. Henig and J. Pinder (London: Allen & Unwin/PEP, 1969), especially chapter 12 'European Assemblies' by M. Forsyth.

(e) R. Pryce, 'The Future of the European Parliament', *Parliamentary Affairs* (London) vol. 15, no. 4, Autumn 1962.

(f) G. van Oudenhove, *Political Parties in the European Parliament* (Leyden: Sythoff, 1965).
A detailed analysis of the increasing cooperation of political parties at the European level.

(g) G. Zellentin, 'Form and Function of Opposition in the European Communities', *Government and Opposition* Special Issue (London) vol. 2, no. 3, April/July 1967, reprinted in *Studies in Opposition*, ed. R. Barker (London: Macmillan, 1971).

(v) *Other Institutional Aspects*

(a) G. Bebr, *Judicial Control of the European Communities* (London: Stevens, 1962).

(b) J.-P. Dubois, 'The Economic Interest Group at Community Level – the Institutional Context and Political Integration', *Common Market Law Review* (London) vol. 8, no. 2, April 1971.

(c) A. W. Green, *Political Integration by Jurisprudence* (Leyden: Sythoff, 1969).

(d) J. F. McMahon, 'The Court of the European Communities', *Journal of Common Market Studies* (Oxford: Basil Blackwell), vol. 1, no. 1, November 1962.

(e) E. Noel, 'The Committee of Permanent Representatives', *Journal of Common Market Studies* (Oxford: Basil Blackwell) vol. 5, no. 3, March 1967.

(f) D. Sidjanski, 'Pressure Groups and the EEC', *Government and Opposition* Special Issue (London) vol. 2, no. 3, April/July 1967.

(g) E. Wall, *The Court of Justice of the European Communities* (London: Butterworth, 1966).

(h) A. Von Gesau, 'The External Representation of Plural Interests', *Journal of Common Market Studies* (Oxford: Basil Blackwell) vol. 5, no. 4, June 1967.

(i) G. Zellentin, 'The Economic and Social Committee', *Journal of Common Market Studies* (Oxford: Basil Blackwell) vol. 1, no. 1, November 1962.

(vi) *Political Development of the EEC*

a) S. Bodenheimer, *Political Union – a Microcosm of European Politics* (Leyden: Sythoff, 1967).

An analysis of the attempts to create a European Political Community; contains a useful section on the Fouchet negotiations.

(b) S. Bodenheimer, 'The Political Union Debate in Europe – A Case Study in International Diplomacy', *International Organisation* (Boston: World Peace Foundation) vol. 21, no. 1, Winter 1967.

(c) M. Butterwick, 'Before and After December 23rd, 1963', *Journal of Common Market Studies* (Oxford: Basil Blackwell) vol. 3, no. 1, October 1964.

(d) M. Camps, *European Unification in the Sixties* (London: Oxford/RIIA, 1967).
A useful account of the development of the Community since de Gaulle's 1963 veto. Contains a detailed analysis of the 1965 crisis.

(e) M. Camps, *What Kind of Europe – the Community Since de Gaulle's Veto* (London: RIIA, Chatham House Essay no. 8, 1965).

(f) M. Camps, 'Britain and the European Crisis', *International Affairs* (London) vol. 49, no. 1, Januray 1966.

(g) N. Heathcote, 'The Crisis of European Supranationality', *Journal of Common Market Studies* (Oxford: Basil Blackwell) vol. 5, no. 2, December 1966.

(h) J. Lambert, 'The Constitutional Crisis of 1965–66', *Journal of Common Market Studies* (Oxford: Basil Blackwell) vol. 4, no. 3, May 1966.

(i) J. Newhouse, *Collision in Brussels – the Common Market Crisis of June 1965* (London: Faber, 1967).
A lengthy and well-documented account of the complex issues involved in the crisis.

(j) J. Pinder, 'Political Union in Europe', *Common Market Law Review* (London) vol. 2, no. 4, March 1965.

(k) D. Thompson, 'The EEC After the 1965 Crisis', *International and Comparative Law Quarterly* (London) vol. 16, part 1, January 1967.

BRITAIN AND THE EUROPEAN COMMUNITIES

(a) N. Beloff, *The General Says No* (London: Penguin, 1963).
A lively account of the Macmillan government's attempt to enter the EEC.

(b) R. Butt, 'The Common Market and Conservative Party Politics 1961–62', *Government and Opposition* Special Issue (London) vol. 2, no. 3, April/July 1967.

(c) D. Calleo, *Britain's Future* (London: Hodder & Stoughton, 1969).

(d) M. Camps, *Britain and the European Community 1955–63* (London: OUP, 1964).
An excellent account of Britain's early involvement with Europe, particularly the Macmillan government's attempt at entry.

(e) R. H. S. Crossman, 'British Labour Looks at Europe', *Foreign Affairs* (New York: Council on Foreign Relations) vol. 41, no. 4, July 1963.

(f) Federal Trust, *Britain and Europe Now* (London: Federal Trust, 1970).

(g) C. W. Frey, 'Meaning Business – the British Application to Join the Common Market, November 1966–October 1967', *Journal of Common Market Studies* (Oxford: Basil Blackwell) vol. 6, no. 5, March 1968.

(h) H. T. Heiger, *British Policy towards the Unification Efforts on the Continent* (Amsterdam: Sythoff, 1959).
Particularly good analysis of British attitudes towards the Coal and Steel Community and the European Defence Community.

(i) J. C. Hunt, 'Britain and the Common Market', *Political Quarterly* (London) vol. 30, no. 3, July/September 1959.

(j) D. Jay, *After the Common Market* (London: Penguin, 1968).
Argues against British entry, mainly on political grounds.

(k) U. W. Kitzinger, *The Challenge of the Common Market* (Oxford: Basil Blackwell, 1961).
Generally argues in favour of British entry.

(l) *The Second Try – Labour and the EEC*, ed. U. W. Kitzinger (London: Pergamon, 1968).
Contains a useful collection of documents and speeches on the Wilson government's attitude to Europe.

(m) Labour Party, *European Unity* (London: The Labour Party, September 1950).
Argues against any involvement with Europe on the grounds that socialism is incompatible with supranational institutions.

(n) J. Lambert, *Britain in a Federal Europe* (London: Chatto & Windus, 1968).

(o) C. Layton, 'Labour and Europe', *Political Quarterly* (London) vol. 33, no. 1, January/March 1962.

(p) R. J. Leiber, *British Politics and European Unity – Parties, Elites and Pressure Groups* (California: California University Press, 1970).
A particularly good study of both the Macmillan and Wilson government's attempts to enter Europe. Contains some useful

material on the role of the TUC and the FBI in forming party opinion.

(q) J. P. MacKintosh, 'Britain in Europe', *International Affairs* (London) vol. 45, no. 2, April 1969.

(r) A. Moncreif, *Britain and the Common Market* (London: BBC Publications, 1967).

(s) A. Nutting, *Europe Will Not Wait* (London: Hollis & Carter, 1960).

(t) W. Pickles, *Not With Europe – the Political Case for Staying Out* (London: Fabian Society, 1962).

(u) W. Pickles, *Britain and Europe – How Much Has Changed?* (Oxford: Basil Blackwell, 1967).
A restatement of the earlier Fabian pamphlet, arguing that Britain should not enter the EEC because of political considerations.

(v) E. Pisani *et al.*, *Problems of British Entry into the EEC* (London: PEP/Chatham House, 1969).

(w) R. L. Pfaltzgraff, *Britain Faces Europe* (London: OUP, 1969).

(x) I. Richard, A. L. Williams, G. Williams and G. Mathias, *Europe or the Open Sea* (London: Charles Knight, 1971).

(y) U. Sahm, 'Britain and Europe 1950', *International Affairs* (London) vol. 43, no. 1, January 1967.
A useful analysis of the Attlee government's views on European integration.

(z) P. Spaak, 'Britain and EEC Entry', *Foreign Affairs* (New York: Council on Foreign Relations) vol. 43, no. 3, April 1963.

(ai) M. Torelli, *Great Britain and the Europe of the Six* (Montreal: Annals of the Centre d'Études et de Documentation Européennes, 1969).
A rather brief consideration of the Wilson government and its attitude to Europe.

(bi) P. Uri, *From Commonwealth to Common Market* (London: Penguin, 1968).

A Selection of Command Papers

(a) *Anglo-French Discussions Regarding French Proposals for the Western European Coal, Iron and Steel Industries*, Cmnd. Paper 7970, 1950.

(b) *Britain and the European Communities – an Economic Assessment*, Cmnd. Paper 4289, 1970.

(c) *European Political Union*, Cmnd. Paper 1720, 1962.

(d) *Legal and Constitutional Implications of United Kingdom Membership of the European Communities*, Cmnd. Paper 3301, 1967.

(e) *Negotiations for a Free Trade Area*, Cmnd. Paper 648, 1959.

(f) *The United Kingdom and the Common Market*, Cmnd. Paper 1565, 1961.

(g) *The United Kingdom and the European Communities – Text of a Statement made by the Foreign Secretary at a WEU meeting at The Hague*, Cmnd. Paper 3345, 1967.

COMMUNITY MEMBERS AND THE EEC

(a) K. Adenauer, 'Germany and Europe', *Foreign Affairs* (New York: Council on Foreign Relations) vol. 31, no. 3, April 1953.

(b) B. Criddle, *Socialists and European Integration* (London: Routledge & Kegan Paul Library of Political Studies, 1967).
A study of the French Socialist Parties.

(c) J. B. Duroselle, 'De Gaulle's Europe and Jean Monnet's Europe', *World Today* (London) vol. 22, no. 1, January 1966.

(d) M. Fackler, 'The Franco–German Treaty', *World Today* (London) vol. 21, no. 1, January 1965.

(e) S. N. Fisher, *France and the European Community* (Ohio: Ohio State University Press, 1964).

(f) P. Galloise, 'The *Raison d'Être* of French Foreign Policy', *International Affairs* (London) vol. 39, no. 4, October 1963.

(g) B. Gardyne, 'Outbidding de Gaulle for the Soul of Europe', *Journal of Common Market Studies* (Oxford: Basil Blackwell) vol. 2, no. 1, July 1963.

(h) C. Johnson, 'De Gaulle's Europe', *Journal of Common Market Studies* (Oxford: Basil Blackwell) vol. 1, no. 2, December 1962.
Mainly a discussion of the Fouchet proposals.

(i) N. Johnson, 'The Era of Adenauer and After', *Parliamentary Affairs* (London) vol. 17, no. 1, Winter 1963–4.

(j) W. Pickles, 'Making Sense of de Gaulle', *International Affairs* (London) vol. 42, no 3, July 1966.

(k) J. Pinder, *Europe Against de Gaulle* (London: Pall Mall, 1963).

(l) C. Schmid, 'Germany and Europe', *Foreign Affairs* (New York: Council on Foreign Relations) vol. 30, no. 4, July 1952.
A statement of the German Social Democratic Party's antagonism to Europe in this period.

(m) F. R. Willis, *France, Germany and the New Europe 1945–67*, 2nd ed. (London: OUP, 1968).

By far the best account of Franco–German relations in the post-war period.

(n) F. R. Willis, *Italy Chooses Europe* (Oxford: Basil Blackwell, 1971).

EUROPE AND THE UNITED STATES

(a) G. Catlin, *The Atlantic Commonwealth* (London: Penguin, 1964).

(b) College of Europe, *Political Problems of Atlantic Partnership* (Bruges: College of Europe, 1969).

(c) D. Humphrey, *The United States and the Common Market* (New York: Praeger, 1968).

(d) G. Lichtheim, *Europe and America – the Future of the Atlantic Community* (London: Thames & Hudson, 1963).

(e) W. Lippmann, *Western Unity and the Common Market* (London: Hamish Hamilton, 1962).

(f) E. Mondel, *Europe Versus America* (London: NLB, 1970).

(g) R. L. Pfaltzgraff, *The Atlantic Community* (New York: Van Nostrand, 1970).

(h) R. L. Richardson, *Germany and the Atlantic Alliance* (London: OUP, 1966).

THE EEC AND THE WORLD

(a) C. A. Cosgrove, 'The Common Market and its Colonial Heritage', *Journal of Contemporary History* (London) vol. 4, no. 1, January 1969.

(b) I. D. Delupis, *The East African Community and the Common Market* (London: Longmans, 1970).

(c) W. Feld, *The European Common Market and the World* (New Jersey: Prentice Hall, 1967).

(d) W. Feld, 'The Associate Agreements of the European Communities', *International Organisation* (Boston: World Peace Foundation) vol. 29, no. 2, Spring 1967.
A comparative study of the trade agreements between African states and the EEC.

(e) B. W. Jackson, 'Free Africa and the Common Market', *Foreign Affairs* (New York: Council on Foreign Relations) vol. 40, no. 3, April 1962.

(f) M. Kohstramm, *The European Community and its Role in the World* (Columbia: University of Missouri Press, 1964).

(g) P. Okigbo, *Africa and the Common Market* (London: Longmans 1967).
(h) R. K. Ramazinni, *The Middle East and the European Common Market* (Charlottesville: University of Virginia Press, 1964).
(i) W. Zartmann, *The Politics of Trade Negotiations Between Africa and the EEC* (Princeton: Princeton University Press, 1971).

THE FUTURE OF THE EEC

(a) C. J. Friedrich, *Europe – an Emergent Nation?* (New York: Harper & Row, 1969).
(b) F. A. von Gesau, *Beyond the European Community* (Leyden: Sythoff, 1966).
(c) W. Hallstein, *United Europe – Challenge and Opportunity* (Cambridge Mass.: Harvard University Press, 1962).
(d) L. Lindberg and S. Scheingold, *Europe's Would-be Polity – Patterns of Change in the European Community* (Wisconsin: University of Wisconsin Press, 1969).
(e) S. de la Mahotier, *Towards One Europe* (London: Penguin, 1970). A well-balanced discussion of the advantages of a united Europe.
(f) J. Pinder and R. Pryce, *Europe After de Gaulle* (London: Penguin, 1969). An examination of the possibilities of a Europe organized on federal lines.
(g) R. Pryce, *The Political Future of the EEC* (London: Marshbank, 1962).

APPENDIX

*EXTRACTS FROM THE REPORT OF THE WORKING PARTY EXAMINING THE PROBLEM OF THE ENLARGEMENT OF THE POWERS OF THE EUROPEAN PARLIAMENT**

SECTION I: THE NEED TO REINFORCE DEMOCRACY IN THE COMMUNITY

In the preceding chapters, some of the reasons why the powers of the European Parliament must be strengthened have been mentioned at various points.

As already stated, the processes of democratic legitimation are far from absent from the structures and mechanisms set up by the Treaties. But, in the main, these processes are only indirectly connected with the Community, since they are derived from the national parliaments and take place via the national governments. It is only to a minor extent, in limited fields and with limited powers, that the Assembly intervenes as a true parliament.

The new assignments, arising from the economic and monetary union to be realized in the near future, call for an extension of the European Parliament's powers. This is because the development of the Community's fields of operation and powers involves transfer to the Community bodies of powers which, on the national plane, belong wholly or partly to the parliaments. The growth of the Community's powers must not result in a reduction of parliamentary powers. It may be true that the distribution of powers found in national systems (which in any case varies from country to country) cannot be applied lock, stock and barrel in the Community system (nor is such application desirable), but the losses of power by national parliaments must be compensated.

It may indeed be asked if this necessity, plain enough from the democratic point of view, is equally plain from the point of view of efficiency. It would be idle to deny that the entry into Community life of a Parliament with greater powers might, in a way, complicate the institutional set-up and even cause further bottlenecks in the end.

These fears can be overcome. The suggestions below take the fullest account of the dangers just pointed out. But, above all, it should furthermore be emphasized that strengthening the role of the European Parliament will fill up not only a sort of democratic vacuum but also certain gaps in the efficient working of the Community.

In this respect it should be observed that the Parliament is the only

---

* Reproduced with the permission of the European Communities, 23 Chesham Street, London, S.W.4.

Community institution where the parliamentary oppositions of the Member States are represented. High on the list of essential structures, both from the practical and the legal point of view, is an opposition which is not only permitted but is considered to be a key element in the constitutional system. It is one of the firmest tenets of modern political theory.

Certain discussions on basic problems have no real significance unless they engage both majority and opposition. This is particularly the case with discussions concerning the structures and meaning of modern societies, for example the relationship between quantity and quality, the balance between industrial growth and the quality of life, environmental problems, consumer protection, the control of monopolistic undertakings, regional policy and federal or decentralized democracy.

It is often in the parliaments, where the worries of day-to-day policy and administration are less inhibiting than they are in the governments, that imagination, creator of social innovations, not to say inventions, can give of its best.

There is, therefore, no general and inevitable conflict between the demand of democracy and the need for efficiency. Both must be satisfied. And this is what we shall try to do in the following pages.

SECTION II: THE INCREASE OF LEGISLATIVE POWERS

§1. PRINCIPLES

Reasons will be given below (chapter V) why it is neither vital nor desirable to make the increase of the European Parliament's powers dependent on its election by direct universal suffrage.

Moreover, the Parliament's powers have undergone a first increase without its waiting for a change in its method of recruitment, since the Treaty of Luxembourg of 22 April 1970 gave it greater budgetary powers. These powers are, however, limited by the fact that the most important items of expenditure are governed rigidly by decisions on which the Parliament can, at best, do no more than give its advice.

In theory it might be thought that the extension of the Parliament's powers follows from the idea that it should play a leading role in all that can be described as community legislation.

Such a theory would not tally with the general philosophy of the Treaties.

The Treaties do not reproduce at Community level the distinction generally made by national constitutions between the legislature and the executive. According to the original set-up of the Community, the Council is its legislature. Without attacking the very roots of the Treaties, we should not be able to substitute the Parliament for the Council in this role. So any increase of the Parliament's powers would have to be achieved not through replacing one body by another but through a system enabling the Parliament to participate in law-making decisions. It can be seen that this participation by the Parliament can develop from a simple consultative role into a real power of co-decision based on the Parliament's ability to accept or reject Council decisions.

Furthermore, it should be borne in mind that there is no general clause in the Treaties which defines the power of each institution. The Council's and the Commission's powers are explicitly allocated for specified fields, and there is a list of the cases in which the European Parliament must be consulted. Consequently, the solutions put forward must, in accordance with the Treaties, define case by case the increased powers considered desirable.

In addition, this examination will have to conform to certain general criteria.

Despite the usefulness of the idea that the European Parliament's powers should be increased systematically by reference to cases where Parliament has a consultative role under present law, the Working Party did not believe that this idea could be adopted, at least as a principle. Clearly it would have been simpler to decide that, in such cases, the Parliament ought to be given a more active part capable of leading to a power of co-decision, whereas in those fields where the Parliament at present plays no role, not even a consultative one, this exclusion should continue.

An approach such as this would have seriously misinterpreted the actual situation. For one thing, there are cases where consultation of the European Parliament is provided for by the Treaties, although these are not cases involving fundamental problems, bearing in mind that the questions concerned are often largely answered beforehand by the terms of the Treaties. On the basis of these hypotheses, there is no need to give the Parliament more than a consultative role, while strengthening and improving the consultative procedures.

On the other hand, there are cases where no provision has been made even for consultation of the Parliament, but which concern matters whose importance will grow as the Community develops, especially because of the economic and monetary union (see, for example, article 103 §2 of the EEC Treaty). Accordingly, consideration should be given to whether the Parliament's intervention should not be recommended in these cases, either by way of consultation or by way of co-decision.

A further consideration should be borne in mind. The Community lays down plans and programmes guiding its future activities, in the more or less long term. The documents concerned do not, strictly speaking, involve legislative decisions creating binding obligations, but they are nevertheless of considerable political importance. Here, too, the European Parliament ought to be heard, at least in a consultative capacity.

Finally, the Parliament's preliminary intervention obviously cannot extend to all special or urgent decisions which have to be taken from day to day or in a hurry, under a common short-term economic policy or a monetary policy. Moreover, national constitutional laws do not, in general, provide for parliamentary participation in working out such decisions. Parliament plays its part by *post facto* control.

These are the criteria taken for delimiting the fields in which extension of the powers of the European Parliament is envisaged as set out below.

§2. FIELDS AND STAGES OF EXTENSION OF THE POWERS OF THE EUROPEAN PARLIAMENT

From the very beginning, the Community, in order to define the ways and means of its development, has often resorted to the system of programmes whose parts were to be implemented in various stages. The resolution of 22 March 1971 concerning the economic and monetary union recently made use of this method. The Working Party considered it would be advisable to have recourse to it in order to implement the proposals put forward here.

In this context the Working Party recommends that the European law-making powers should be increased in two stages. Apart from the problem of political timing which would be raised by the need for the consent of the Member States to a broad and very quick expansion of the Parliament's powers, a transitional period should be foreseen in the course of which the Community institutions would adapt steadily and by trial and error, each in its own field and in its relations to the others, to the new system which is recommended.

In the first stage, Parliament would be given a power of co-decision (according to the procedures set out under 4 below) in the following matters, which, for simplicity's sake, are hereinafter called *list A*:

- revision of the Treaties;
- implementation of article 235 of the EEC Treaty and analogous provisions in the ECSC and Euratom Treaties;
- admission of new members;
- ratification of international agreements concluded by the Community.

Besides this, in the first stage the European Parliament would be given a power of consultation consisting in the right to ask the Council to reconsider a subject, and hence a suspensive veto, in the following fields, (called *list B*):

EEC TREATY
- article 43 (common agricultural policy);
- article 54 §3, g (guarantees required of firms);
- article 56 (special treatment for foreign nationals);
- article 57 (diplomas and self-employed occupations);
- article 75 (common transport policy);
- article 84 (sea and air transport);

– article 87 (competition);
– article 99 (harmonization of tax systems);
– article 100 (harmonization of laws);
– article 103 §2 (conjunctural policy);
– article 113 (common commercial policy);
– article 126 (European Social Fund);
– article 128 (vocational training).

EAEC TREATY
– article 31 (basic standards for protection of health);
– article 76 (adapting chapter VI on supplies);
– article 85 (adapting the methods of safety control laid down in chapter VII);
– article 90 (adapting chapter VIII on the Community's property rights over special fissionable materials).

MERGER TREATY
– article 24 (service regulations of officials).

In the second stage, Parliament would be given a power of co-decision, according to the procedures set out under 4 below, in all matters in list B; naturally, it would continue to exercise its power of co-decision in all matters in list A.

It is necessary briefly to explain, in the light of the principles described above, how the matters on list A and list B were picked.

List A, as already stated, contains the matters which are to be subject to the European Parliament's power of co-decision from the first stage onwards.

It covers questions which materially involve either the Community's constitutive power or its relations with other persons in international law.

The involvement of constitutive power emerges clearly in articles 236 EEC, 204 EAEC, 96 ECSC, concerning amendments to the Treaties. In §4, below, the proposal is made that the Parliament should be given the same power of co-decision as regards articles 201 EEC and 173 EAEC, concerning the Community's own resources. On the other hand, it does not seem that the simplified procedures which, in certain cases, enable very specific points in the Treaties to be adopted or amended to a limited extent (e.g. article 81 ECSC) can be regarded as involving constitutive power. Actually, it is more legislative power that is concerned here, as may be seen from certain items in list B, dealt with below.

It is true that amendment of the Treaties, in accordance with article 236 of the EEC Treaty and analogous articles presupposes democratic endorsement, since ratification in accordance with the constitutional rules of each Member State implies approval by the national parliaments. However, it is highly desirable that the Community's own constituent process should make provision for like approval by the European Parliament, which is the democratic institution of the Community as such. In this way, the amendment procedure would assume its full meaning: approval of the amendment by the Assembly would set the seal of the Community's Parliament on the texts adopted by the Council in pursuance of the proposal made below (§4), before the national parliaments are called upon to speak, and this would undoubtedly make it easier for them to give their assent.

The procedure under articles 235 of the EEC Treaty, 203 of the EAEC Treaty and 95 §1 of the ECSC Treaty, which must be dealt with further in a later chapter, is 'para-constituent', if one can use such a term. As we know, it applies to those cases in which Community authorities take 'appropriate steps' to implement a measure necessary for the functioning of the Common Market without the Treaty having expressly provided the powers for doing so. Article 235 will certainly become more and more important as the economic and monetary union progresses. In any case, this article contains provisions which affect Community tasks and instruments and have a definite influence on the rights of Member States; this justifies the inclusion of article 235 in list A. The European Parliament will thus be able to contribute to the dynamic implementation of this text.

Intervention by the European Parliament, via the process of ratification, in agreements concluded by the Community with persons in international law is in accordance with the constitutional laws of Member States which require international agreements concluded by governmental authorities to be approved by the elected Assemblies in one way or another. (Also in accordance with constitutional practice in most Member States, an exemption must clearly be made in the case of technical and administrative agreements which do not pre-suppose such intervention.) It will be seen that the international agreements which would thus be submitted to the European Parliament for ratification would include the association agreements referred to in articles 238 of the EEC Treaty and 206 of the EAEC Treaty.

Finally, the entry of new members into the Community affects both the constituent power and international agreements. This justifies the Parliament's intervention in the procedure referred to under articles 237 of the EEC Treaty, 205 of the EAEC Treaty and 98 of the ECSC Treaty, not only as a consultative body but also to give its approval to the Council's unanimous decision to admit new members.

It seems that the European Parliament needs to have the power of co-decision in the four matters just described from the first stage onwards. The Working Party did not deem it essential that articles 138 of the EEC Treaty, 108 of the EAEC Treaty and 21 of the ECSC Treaty should be included in list A, since the present text already associates the Parliament closely with the task of achieving election by direct universal suffrage and, in practice, the Council would find it very difficult to adopt provisions which met with determined opposition from the European Parliament.

List B above concerns matters regarding which, during an initial stage, a strengthened consultative role would be conferred upon the Parliament in the shape of a suspensive veto, and which, during a second stage, would be subject to the exercise of a power of co-decision on the part of the Parliament.

According to the Treaties, most of these matters already have to be discussed with the Parliament; but others are exempt from any such compulsory consultation procedure (articles 84, 103 §2, 113 and 128 of the EEC Treaty).

In fact – apart from article 24 of the Merger Treaty (status of Community officials), which, for obvious special reasons, is included in list B – the matters in list B come under one of the two groups described below.

Firstly, there are measures for *harmonization of legislation* which have important effects on national laws and which therefore call for the intervention of a parliamentary body at Community level: take, for example, harmonization measures concerning, notably, the practice of the liberal professions. This group covers those matters referred to in articles 54 §3 g, 56, 57, 99 and 100 of the EEC Treaty.

Secondly, there are the questions of principle affecting *common policies*, which may also involve harmonization measures. Since they are fundamental measures determining one or other common policy, their importance in the life of the Community and the obligations they impose upon Member States justify the strengthening of the Parliament's consultative role during the first stage and its power of co-decision during the second. This is so with matters referred to in articles 43, 75, 84, 87, 103 §2, 113, 126 and 128 of the EEC Treaty.

In both groups, preliminary intervention by the Parliament does not concern implementation measures, which, depending on their nature, will fall to either the Council or the Commission and could be amenable only to control *a posteriori*.

It will be seen that circumstances may bring about inclusion in the list in question of matters which, until now, have not appeared to require such inclusion. For example, articles 49 and 51 of the EEC Treaty concerning the status of workers have not been included in the above proposals so as not to burden them with matters in which the tasks of the Community seem to have been defined quite precisely by the EEC Treaty. One can, however, imagine political situations arising in which the implementation of articles 49 and 51 call for their inclusion in list B. Similarly, implementation of a common regional policy would result in article 94 of the EEC Treaty being included in that list.

§3. FIXING THE TIMETABLE

The first stage mentioned above will, of necessity, begin when the amendments to the Treaties which should result in an extension of the

Parliament's powers come into force. In Chapter VIII we shall see that, as a general rule, these amendments are legally necessary if some of the proposed objectives are to be achieved, although, on certain points, concerted practice between the Council and the Parliament may become an accepted part of relations between them in anticipation of such formal amendments to the Treaties.

As regards the second stage, the Working Party asked itself whether it should be realized in a single step according to a prearranged timetable.

A majority of the Working Party adopted the view that it should. It considers that the second stage should begin with full legal effect at a date prescribed in the treaty of revision. It also believes that this method of fixing a timetable had already proved its worth and that, with due regard to the attractions of gradualness, it prevents any dilatory attitude.

It is true that it is difficult for the Working Party to propose a date for the completion of the second stage, since this will largely depend on the progress made in developing the Community, particularly in respect of the economic and monetary union. Bearing this in mind, it might be considered that the beginning of the second stage could not be delayed beyond 1978.

One member of the Working Party was of the opinion that a much simpler system that could be more easily implemented would be simply to lay down for the second stage a procedure for agreement between the Council and the Parliament which, without any predetermined timetable, would progressively subject matters on list B to the Parliament's power of co-decision.

Conversely, two members of the Working Party consider that, in view of the urgent need to increase the Parliament's normative powers and the time-limits required by the procedure for revising the Treaties, a power of co-decision in matters of common policy should be conferred upon the Parliament from the outset.

§4. PROCEDURES FOR THE PARTICIPATION OF THE PARLIAMENT

For the sake of clarity, mention must be made of the different possible ways in which the Parliament might participate in the first or second stage mentioned above:

A. *Co-decision, consultation and suspensive veto during the first stage*

(1°) During the initial stage the power of co-decision can be exercised in four distinct cases (list A). The procedures envisaged for each of them must be explained:

(a) *Revision of the Treaty*

Article 236 of the EEC Treaty (204 of the EAEC Treaty and 96 of the

ECSC Treaty) makes provision for several procedural phases for revising the Treaty: a proposal made by a government or by the Commission; a Council Opinion in favour of calling a conference of the representatives of the Member States (after consultation with the Parliament and, where appropriate, the Commission); convening of the conference by the President of the Council; determination by the conference of the amendments to be made; ratification of these amendments by the Member States in accordance with their respective constitutional requirements.

Article 201 of the EEC Treaty (173 EAEC) concerns a change of a quasi-constitutional character in the Community rules on the precise point of replacing the financial contributions of the Member States by the Community's own resources. The procedure is appreciably simpler than that under article 236 of the EEC Treaty, since amendment merely presupposes, on a proposal from the Commission and after consultation of the Parliament, a unanimous Council decision whose provisions are submitted to the Member States for adoption in accordance with their respective constitutional requirements.

The mode of revising the Treaties could be based upon the procedure referred to in article 201, which has the advantage of being simpler, since it does not include the holding of a conference of representatives of the Member States, which, moreover, as experience shows, has a formal character. Furthermore, the power of co-decision of the Parliament would naturally fit into this procedure.

Thus, the revision of the Treaties (article 236 of the EEC Treaty, 204 of the EAEC Treaty and 96 of the ECSC Treaty), as well as the very important decision referred to in article 201 of the EEC Treaty and 173 of the EAEC Treaty, would be carried out according to the following uniform procedure:

– Proposal from the governments or the Commission (article 236 of the EEC Treaty, 204 of the EAEC Treaty and 96 of the ECSC Treaty) or from the Commission alone (article 201 of the EEC Treaty and 173 of the EAEC Treaty);
– Consultation of the Parliament;
– Unanimous Council decision on revision or decision (article 201 of the EEC Treaty and 173 of the EAEC Treaty);
– Approval of the Council decision by the Parliament;
– Ratification of the revision or adoption of the decision (article 201 of the EEC Treaty and 173 of the EAEC Treaty) by the Member States in accordance with their respective constitutional requirements.

(b) *Implementation of article 235 of the EEC Treaty*

(203 of the EAEC Treaty and 95, paragraph 1 of the ECSC Treaty)

Implementation of article 235 of the EEC Treaty assumes that the Council, on a proposal from the Commission and after consulting the Parliament, takes the appropriate decisions to give the Community the powers necessary for the functioning of the Common Market, despite the fact that these powers have not been expressly provided for in the Treaty. From the first stage, the Council decision could take effect only after approval by the Parliament. Here the functioning of the co-decision procedure would need to be governed by the same rules as those that will be detailed below in respect of the power of co-decision in general (under B below).

(c) *Admission of new members*

Beginning with the initial stage, the power of co-decision conferred in this matter upon the Parliament would result in the Council decision to admit a new State requesting membership of the Community (article 237 of the EEC Treaty, 205 of the EAEC Treaty and 98 of the ECSC Treaty) taking effect only after approval by the Parliament. In addition, it would be advisable to make provision for the Parliament, like the Commission, to be consulted even before the Council takes its decision. This would be logical and, furthermore, would facilitate implementation of the procedure.

(d) *International agreements concluded by the Community*

The procedures provided for in the Treaties vary according to the hypotheses as regards both the participation of the various institutions and the rules on majority or unanimous voting in the Council (article 113 and 238 of the EEC Treaty and 101 of the EAEC Treaty).
Two common rules should be adopted:

– The Parliament must always be consulted before the beginning of any international negotiations;
– Any international agreement concluded cannot come into force without being approved by the Parliament.

(2°) *Consultation of the Parliament* during the initial stage takes place in one of three possible ways: First, in list A, independently of the power of co-decision, then for matters in list B, where it is accompanied by a suspensive veto, and, finally, for matters not included in either list but for which consultation is already provided for in the Treaties.

Procedural questions concerning the suspensive veto will be dealt with below (3). For the moment, we will look only at what concerns the consultation itself.

The procedure followed at the moment is not without its drawbacks. For example, in law, at least, Commission proposals are submitted to the Parliament only upon a Council decision; the Parliament is not always kept well informed of the amendments the Commission may be led to make to its proposals following dealings with the working parties, the Committee

of Permanent Representatives or the Council, and it is not always given
the opportunity to put forward its own views on amendments which are
nevertheless essential to the initial proposals.

Doubtless, there is no use considering amendments to the Treaties in
order to bring about the desirable improvements on this point.

In fact, in the past, satisfactory practices have been introduced by
agreement between the institutions. Similar procedures might enable
further progress to be made in improving consultation of the Parliament.

First of all, one could go further than the practice whereby the Parliament is 'informed' of proposals submitted to the Council by the Commission. The Council would merely have to duplicate this unofficial
practice by an official and automatic one of reference to the Parliament
which would already integrate it into the institutional procedure.

Secondly, if, once an opinion has been rendered by the Parliament the
Commission proposal is considerably changed as a result of contacts
with the Council, the Committee of Permanent Representatives or the
working parties, the Parliament should be informed of this and be able
to render a new opinion.

Thirdly, if the Council deviates appreciably from the opinion received
from the Parliament, it would be a good thing that it justify this behaviour
in detail. Although it has always reserved the principle that it need not
reply to questions on this point, or has had recourse to purely laconic and
formal replies, the Council has, in certain cases, explained its attitude.

Finally, the situation in which decisions are prejudged by groups of
Council experts before the Parliament has rendered its opinion should be
avoided as far as possible.

(3°) *The suspensive veto* that could be exercised by the Parliament in matters
on list B during the initial stage would result from the right to ask the
Council for a second deliberation.

Without prejudice to the preliminary consultation mentioned above
(2°), the Council should refer to the Parliament any decision taken on
matters in list B. Implementation of the decision would be delayed until
deliberation by the Parliament, which should take place within one
month, at the end of which, in the absence of such deliberation, the
Council decision would come into force. If, within this period of one
month, the Parliament, proceeding in accordance with article 144 of the
EEC Treaty, asks the Council for a second deliberation, the Council must
comply with this request and take a new decision having a definitive and
enforceable character. So as not to complicate the procedure unduly, the
Parliament would always be able to announce that it was dispensing with
the period of one month referred to above and that it agreed to immediate
implementation of the Council decision.

It will be noticed that this procedure would be superimposed on that
under article 149 of the EEC Treaty without, however, taking anything

away from it. This would not adversely affect the role conferred by this text upon the Commission, whose position should never, as a general rule, be weakened by new powers granted to the Parliament.

B. *Co-decision during the second stage*

During the second stage, the power to use a suspensive veto that was granted to the Parliament during the first stage is transformed into a genuine power of co-decision.

There is no reason why this power of co-decision exercised at the final stage of the procedure should not allow the consultation of Parliament at the beginning of the procedure to continue in the terms referred to above. Preliminary consultation of the Parliament on Commission proposals would make it easier for the power of co-decision to be exercised in a harmonious manner. Knowing that approval by the Parliament determines the decision-making process, the Commission and the Council would find it in their interests to be informed in good time of the Parliament's point of view. Furthermore, the Parliament may propose, in advance, amendments to the draft text.

The power of co-decision would mean that a Council decision could not come into force without being approved by the Parliament. There is reason for hoping that, in most cases, the joint tripartite action resulting, as has just been explained, from consultation of the Parliament will lead to a positive vote. If, however, the Parliament refuses to give its approval, the Council, in order to reach a decision, would have to reconsider the matter and resume negotiations with the Parliament.

It has occasionally been proposed that a mediating committee be entrusted with the task of settling difficulties which divide the Council and the Parliament. However, it must be admitted that such mediation is a natural task for the Commission. On the basis of article 149 of the EEC Treaty, the Commission will have to inform the Council of any modified proposal likely, this time, to be approved by the Parliament.

Should one go even further and accept that, in the case of persistent divergences, the definitive decision could, after a certain period, be taken in disregard of the opposition of the Council or of the Parliament, so that Commission proposals that had been approved by one of the other two institutions could be successfully implemented? This idea must be ruled out as being contrary to the concept of co-decision which is to be put into general practice during the second period. One cannot seriously propose the short-circuiting of the Council, even in exceptional circumstances, as this would throw overboard one of the basic elements of the Treaties, or of the Parliament, since it would mean taking away with one hand the power of co-decision just given with the other.

Two members of the Working Party, however, would like to see the Parliament taking its vote before the Council in order to overcome the deadlock. If, within a year, the Council did not take any decision, this would be tantamount to approval. In this case, it could be imagined that the proposal should be given a second reading in Parliament before adoption. The two members who are of this opinion believe that this would make it very unlikely that the Council would systematically give negative replies, given the difficulty of reaching a unanimous 'no' and that, instead, it would be more likely that there would be instituted a system of reference back and forth (*navette*) between the Council and the Parliament.

§5. THE LEGISLATIVE INITIATIVE OF THE PARLIAMENT

The Parliament is already able to propose initiatives affecting legislation by means of resolutions requesting the other institutions of the Community, especially the Commission, to take action.

It does not seem to be advisable to transform this *de facto* facility into a formal power of legislative initiative. It is in the Commission that the Treaties vest the role of initiator and promoter of Community norms. So as not to endanger this prerogative, conferred on the Commission with a view to the Community interest, it would be much better to retain the flexible practice which in fact allows the Parliament to propose initiatives in the legislative field and the efficacity of which can only be strengthened moreover when the Assembly accedes to full parliamentary status.

§6. SCOPE OF ACTIVITY OF THE LEGISLATIVE FUNCTION

In principle, the Parliament is to participate in the normative procedure in the above-mentioned fields when the decisions concerned are similar to those regarded by national laws as normally being of a legislative nature. They are, therefore, important decisions, especially in that they modify the legal order of the Community or of the Member States.

If the Parliament wished to have a say in the mass of measures of application, its work would be overloaded by tasks of secondary importance, which would adversely affect the degree of attention which it should give to fundamental or important decisions. The legislative system in force in the Community already includes a system of 'framework laws' (*lois-cadres*) laying down rules of principle, the detailed implementation of which is left to the Council or to the Commission. Extension of the Parliament's powers should not adversely affect this sensible practice.

In truth, there is no general formula that can be used to find the exact border between the two types of norms just mentioned and of which only one requires the participation of the Parliament, subject to *post facto* control. The distinction will become clearer with practice. Decisions submitted to the Parliament for approval should include express authorization for the Council or the Commission to adopt the implementing measures.

As for the conditions under which the Parliament will be able to exercise a *post facto* check on the way in which the Commission or the Council carries out this task, they are linked with the general problem of parliamentary control, which will be discussed later.

§7. EARLY IMPLEMENTATION OF PROPOSED MEASURES

As we have remarked, even before the proposed reforms are legally ratified by amendment of the Treaties a significant number of them could in fact be implemented by an agreement between the Parliament and the other two institutions and come into force within the shortest possible period (cf. chapter VIII).

SECTION III: PARTICIPATION OF THE PARLIAMENT IN THE FORMULATION OF ECONOMIC POLICY, PLANS AND PROGRAMMES

Quite often the Community institutions, using recommendations and declarations, have made use of the system of programmes for preparing and shaping future Community policies in different sectors and thus prejudging future Community legislation. On three occasions, for example, in 1967, 1969 and 1971,[1] the Council has formulated medium-term economic policy programmes which lay down certain guidelines for the economic policy to be pursued by the Member States. These measures are not binding but their implications can, in fact, be far-reaching.

Once economic and monetary union is achieved, this process of laying down guidelines will assume increasing importance (cf. resolution of 22 March 1971). It goes without saying that, from the initial period, the Parliament should be consulted when these plans or programmes are being formulated.

In principle, the non-compulsory character of these plans and programmes is not necessarily a reason for the Parliament's powers of intervention going as far as co-decision in a matter in which the character of decision is precisely lacking.

In certain cases, however, the programmes may not be purely indicative ones. The Council decision of 22 March 1971[2] concerning the strengthening of co-ordination of the Member States' short-term economic policies provides that the Council may, in one of its three annual deliberations on short-term economic policy, lay down guidelines for the national budgets before these have been finally approved.

These guidelines have at least a *de facto* determining influence on the legislation and the financial decisions of the Community and the Member States.

[1] O.J. No. 79, 25 April 1967, p. 1513; O.J. No. L 129, 30 May 1969, p. 1; O.J. No. L 49, 1 March 1971, p. 1.
[2] O.J. No. L 73, 27 March 1971, p. 12.

If, for the moment, the practice of programmes and plans enables us to be satisfied with the purely consultative role of the Parliament, the possibility must not be excluded of this practice evolving in the direction of a genuine normative power in respect of these programmes and plans. In this eventuality, the Parliament's power of co-decision recognized during the second stage would have to be extended accordingly.

SECTION IV: BUDGETING AND FINANCIAL POWERS OF THE PARLIAMENT

§I. THE COMMUNITY BUDGET AND ITS IMPACT

The whole course of economic and social policy followed in the Community countries, whether under common policies, in co-ordination or independently, is carried out through both the budgets of the Member States and the budget of the Community.

Although Community expenditure looks at first sight to be impressive (the 1972 estimates work out at roughly 4,000 million units of account), it represents in fact quite a small item in public expenditure as a whole – 1% of all the national incomes taken together, as compared with something like 20 or 30% in the budgets of the Member States.

The great bulk of it is accounted for by expenditure in connection with the common agricultural policy, with EAGGF alone accounting for 90%. Very much smaller amounts go in social expenditure (1% for the Social Fund, though its share may well be increased later) and in expenditure on Euratom capital and research projects (1.5%).

Though the impact of Community operations on the national budgets is not always easy to detect, let alone quantify, it undoubtedly exists. It is small in scale as yet, but will necessarily increase with the progress of economic and monetary union and the framing of Community policies on industry, research, energy, the environment and regional development. Even where these policies are aided by Community appropriations, more particularly through the various Funds it is intended to set up, they will have the effect of inducing additional expenditure in the national budget of Member countries. Thus, the Community's budget will only partly reflect the financial implications of its policies on the economic and social side.

Accordingly, it would be both democratic and useful to develop a practice recently approved by the Council for the drawing-up of annual, and in particular of pluriannual, Community estimates.[3]

The scope of these should be extended to provide data in regard to the budgeting impact of Community policies in the national as well as in the Community context. The preparation of the estimates should be the

[3] Council Decision of 21 April 1970, O.J. No. L 94, 28 April 1970, p. 23.

occasion for concerted action between Council, Commission and Parliament, which could thus form an overall picture of the economic and social policy pursued and/or promoted by the Community. This procedure is politically and economically a more important affair than drawing up a single, detached budget. It will incidentally fit into place among the assortment of procedures which will grow up for governing and managing the economic and monetary union.

This is an aspect fundamental to the whole function of Parliament, which includes participation by the Assembly in the determination of the medium- and long-term guidelines for all Community policy, whose financial implications are reflected in the Community and national budgets.[4]

§2. THE LIMITS OF BUDGETING POWER

Power to establish a budget is not co-extensive with power to take the economic and social policy decisions which govern the budget. Thus the expenditure of the Guarantee Section of EAGGF, which accounts for far and away the largest slice of Community expenditure as a whole, flows automatically from the Council's prior decisions on agricultural prices. And even where not automatic to quite the same extent, expenditure from the Community budget is primarily dictated by earlier Council decisions fixing maximum or minimum levels or authorizing the Commission to lay out such and such amounts for such and such purposes.

Correspondingly, the revenue of the Community is likewise automatic and indeed obligatory. It consists for the most part of the agricultural levies, plus, from 1975 on, all duties charged at the frontiers of the customs union. The third source of Community revenue after 1975, i.e. the proportion of the harmonized V.A.T. (up to a maximum of 1%), will be in some measure automatic as to its total, since to balance the budget this total must meet that portion of expenditure which is not covered by the agricultural levies and the customs duties. Should the maximum proportion of V.A.T. yield set aside for the Community prove insufficient for this purpose, either that proportion would have to be increased or new taxes would have to be imposed, which under article 2(2) of the decision of 21 April 1970 in conjunction with article 201 EEC or article 173 Euratom would necessitate a special Council decision and endorsement by the Member States in accordance with their respective constitutional requirements. As noted earlier in connection with article 201 EEC and 173 Euratom, it is necessary that, from the first stage referred to in Section II, Council decisions taken under the provisions just mentioned should come into force only after receiving the approval of the European Parliament.

[4] Cf. Section III above.

All in all, then, the budgetary power and the power of financial decision-making in the broad sense are not co-extensive. On the face of it no doubt this is also the case at national level, where generally speaking there is much rigidity in budgeting inasmuch as the bulk of budget expenditure is governed by situations and decisions predating the presentation and passage of the budget, so that, whether in law or in fact, the role of the Parliament, as the ultimate legal controller of the budget, is much reduced. But even though at national level the Parliament's budgeting powers are thus curbed, at least it is the maker or part-maker of the original decisions underlying the constraints upon it. Under the Community system on the other hand the automatisms and rigidities of the budgeting process are, as the law now stands, imposed by decisions on which the Parliament has been merely consulted, if that. Only by giving the Parliament a greater say in legislation can this anomaly be corrected.

§3. THE BUDGETARY POWER OF THE EUROPEAN PARLIAMENT

Since there is the gap between the budgetary power properly so-called and the power of taking decisions with financial implications, it is understandable that the Treaty of 22 April 1970, although investing the Parliament with the power of adopting the budget from 1975 onwards, does not give it the last word on 'expenditure necessarily resulting from the Treaty or from acts adopted in accordance therewith'. Only in respect of expenditure not of this kind can the Parliament's wishes override the Council's.

The phrase just quoted is far from clear. The Council, acting on a classification contained in an unpublished document, construes it as meaning that the Parliament has the last word only on expenditure the basis of which is to be found exclusively in the budget itself – i.e. only the heads of administrative expenditure and a few items of operating expenditure.[5]

If this construction is the right one, it limits the right of the Parliament to have the last word on no more than 3–4% of total Community expenditure.[6]

[5] The declaration annexed to the Treaty of 22 April 1970 (see 'Les ressources propres aux Communautés européennes et les pouvoirs budgétaires du Parlement européen', published by the European Parliament, 1970, p. 204) notes that the Council 'has based itself on the classification of budget expenditure as exemplified in the list established by the Chair on 3 February 1970, while accepting that this classification may change in accordance with the requirements of the operation of the Communities'.

[6] Over 80% of administrative expenditure is fixed and rigid, being 'necessarily resulting' class (staff salaries, rental and maintenance of premises, telephone charges and so on) (cf. Spenale Report, European Parliament, Doc. No. 42/1970-71, secs. 36 and 42, reproduced in the publication referred to in the footnote, pp. 171 and 172).

However, it is possible to construe the phrase in question in a sense more favourable to the Parliament's budgeting powers, namely that 'expenditure necessarily resulting from the Treaty or from acts adopted in accordance therewith' means only expenditure of which the amount is already *fixed* when the budget is adopted or results *automatically* from an existing arrangement (e.g. the Guarantee Section of EAGGF).

On this reading, the Parliament would be entitled – subject to the quantitative limits set on increases in Community expenditure by article 203(8) EEC, 177 Euratom and 78 ECSC – to vote with final power of decision, appropriations in respect of expenditure not provided for by prior Council decision, and also increases or reductions in appropriations already budgeted for, so long as it observed minima or maxima fixed by prior Council decisions.

It is true that such appropriations made available by the Parliament on its own initiative would have to be expended for purposes falling within the competence of the Community, and more precisely within the powers and responsibilities of a Community institution. Generally speaking, the Council, unless it objected for policy reasons, could find legal warrant in the Treaty – notably in article 235 EEC – for using the funds in question in the manner desired by the Parliament. The Commission – in a way, the natural institution to manage and utilize appropriations – could be given the necessary authorization by the Council to do so.

Two members of the Working Party consider that an increase in the independent financial resources will be inevitable for the implementation of new Community policies to ensure a more effective and complete solution for problems of Community dimensions than any which can be provided by national action. They propose that the choice of sectors for new Community interventions be decided by a qualified majority of the Parliament in a debate having as its object the determination of pluri-annual programmes defining the use of the whole or of a substantial part of the new resources thus placed at the disposal of the Community.

§4. THE REAL PROBLEM

The Parliament strongly defends the idea that Article 203(6) confers on it from 1975 the right 'at the end of the proceedings and in case of serious objection, to reject the whole draft budget in order to secure fresh budgetary proposals'.[7] This interpretation is shared by the Commission and, in the form of motions, by two national parliaments, but despite the stress laid on it by the Parliament, it is not shared by the Council.

The Working Party does not have to reach a decision on this controversy. It must, however, express its doubts on the possibility, by a refusal

[7] Resolutions of 11 March 1970, No. 5, and 13 May 1970, No. 10 – cf. Spenale Report, European Parliament, Doc. No. 42/1970–71, reproduced in the publication mentioned in the footnote to pp. 160, 168 and 189.

of the budget *en bloc*, of advancing the cause of parliamentary participation in Community decisions, particularly in legislative matters. By its very nature a prolonged institutional crisis resulting, should the occasion arise, from such a refusal would endanger the still precarious progress of Community activities, and its outcome would perhaps not be attended by the success desired by the Parliament.

The proper way to present the problem of the participation of the Parliament in Community policy is to consider that, for the reasons given above, purely budgetary powers are a weak means of influence. The direct attribution of a power of co-decision in legislative matters, outlined above, is much more decisive, and it is this reform which, by contrast, will give real significance to the budgetary power of the Parliament.

Since the Parliament will exercise a power of co-decision in the acts which are at the basis of Community expenditure and will be associated with the establishment of pluriannual estimates, it will share with the Council the financial responsibility resulting therefrom. As soon as these powers are in the hands of the Parliament, the hiatus between the budgetary power and the other powers – particularly the legislative powers – will disappear. It will then be necessary to eliminate the distinction between the two categories of expenditure mentioned above, and to give the Parliament a power of co-decision on the budget as a whole equal to that which it will then be exercising in legislative matters.

§5. CONTROL OF THE BUDGET

The Treaty of 22 April 1970 partially adapted control by the Parliament of the execution of the budget to the new powers it will exercise from 1975 regarding its establishment. The new article 206(4) provides that the Council and the Assembly must jointly give discharge for execution to the Commission.

It seems quite logical that the Parliament should also receive, by assimilation, a power of co-decision in two cases closely connected with the execution of the budget: the authorization of expenses exceeding the provisional one-twelfths (article 204 EEC) and the elaboration of the financial texts mentioned in article 209 (a, b, c).

SECTION V: RELATIONS BETWEEN COMMUNITY LAW AND NATIONAL LAW

Whereas, under EEC article 189, a regulation is binding in all respects and directly applicable in all Member States, a directive, which is addressed to the States according to the same provisions, is binding only with regard to the result to be achieved and leaves the decision on ways and means to national authorities.

In certain matters, principally concerning the harmonization of legislation, the directive alone is open to the Community. This is not without
disadvantages in matters in which, for technical reasons, harmonization
means that Community institutions must go into considerable detail, and
where a regulation would consequently seem more appropriate. It is true
that some directives, in order to cope with this difficulty, have taken the
form of very detailed texts, which solves part of the problem, but sur-
prises the national legislator, who wonders what is left of the power over
ways and means which the directive should, in theory, leave to him.

Consideration could be given, if not to the elimination of any distinction between regulations and directives, then at least to a considerable
broadening of the possibility of regulations. The granting to the Parliament of powers of co-decision such as those which have been proposed
would justify this approach by nullifying the argument that the regulation
mutilates national legislative power. In fact, in a system where the European Parliament is associated with the elaboration of the most important
regulations, taking powers from the national parliaments is much less
shocking than if it were done solely to increase the powers of the Council.
Valid as they are, the technical considerations just put forward concerning
the frequent disadvantages of the distinction between regulations and
directives do not appear to justify for the moment the abolition of this
distinction or an extension of the field of application of regulations, which
could be felt, rightly or wrongly, as an assault on the legislative powers
of the national parliaments. On this point, time will do its work: the
practice of co-decision will remove the prejudices against Community
legislative power and its most advanced form, the regulation. The development of Community powers under the auspices of EEC article 235 will
have the effect of progressively extending the field of application of
regulations.

SECTION VI: THE PARLIAMENT'S POWERS OF CONTROL

The extension of the powers of the Parliament does not only concern the
exercise of the normative function, but also that of the control which,
under democratic systems, is one of the fundamental tasks of the Parliament.

§I. UTILIZATION OF PARLIAMENTARY PROCEDURES

The Parliament has endeavoured to strengthen its powers of control
vis-à-vis the Commission and to develop its relations with the Council. To
this end, the most varied procedures have been employed, notably parliamentary questions (very often of great interest) and calling for written or
oral replies (EEC article 140, article 45 to 47 of the standing orders of the
Parliament). It has already been said that the Council has agreed in some

cases to make known the reasons why a decision taken by it diverges appreciably from the opinion rendered by the Parliament. It has even agreed to present a report to the latter from time to time through the medium of its President. These practices should be pursued and developed.

The Parliament's Committees already have real importance which is destined to increase in the future. By multiplying relationships with the other institutions, they can exercise a closer control. The specialization and technical competence of their members enable them to play an important part in the elaboration of programmes and plans and to supervise their execution. Finally, they are in a position to institute very desirable co-operation with the national parliaments (cf. chapter VI).

All these procedures, which are a part of parliamentary techniques, will develop and become consolidated as the Parliament acquires new powers, particularly powers of co-decision. The history of parliaments shows that as soon as a parliament begins to play a real part in the legislative process, it assumes *ipso facto* an authority and an influence which guarantee it the power to watch over the government's actions and to demand the supply of all necessary information.

There does not, therefore, seem to be any point in proposing a revision of the Treaties to endow the European Parliament with a power of control since, for the reasons already mentioned, the sanction of this control, organized *vis-à-vis* the Commission by EEC article 144, cannot extend as far as the Council.

In fact, the Parliament, armed with new powers, notably in the legislative field, will be able to keep itself informed, to judge, and even to warn.

Contributors

Altiero Spinelli *is a member of the Commission of European Communities.*

Denis de Rougemont *is the well-known author, many of whose books have been translated into English. He is Director of the Centre Européen de la Culture in Geneva, Professor in the University of Zürich and a leading European federalist.*

Richard Mayne *is Director of the Federal Trust for Education and Research.*

Étienne Hirsch *is a former President of Euratom.*

Émile Noel *is Secretary General of the Commission of the European Communities.*

Henri Étienne *is Head of Division in the Commission of the European Communities.*

H. Vredeling *belongs to the Netherlands Labour Party and is a member of the Second Chamber of the States General and of the European Parliament, where he is Vice-President of the Agricultural Committee and member of the Committee for Social Affairs and public Health and of the Commission for External Economic Relations.*

Michael Steed *is Lecturer in Government at the University of Manchester.*

J.-R. Rabier *is Director General of Press and Information Services in the Commission of the European Communities.*

Stanley Henig *is a former Labour M.P., and editor of* European Political Parties (*with H. Pinder*). *He is the author of* The External Relations of the European Community (1971).

Helen Wallace *is currently engaged, at the University of Manchester, on research into implications for British policy-making of entry into the Common Market.*

T. Nielsen *teaches political science at the University of Aarhus, Denmark.*

Stephen Holt *is Professor of Comparative European Studies in the University of Bradford.*

Michael A. Wheaton *is Lecturer in Politics at the University of Hull.*

Index

Acheson, Dean, 39
Adenauer, Konrad, 9, 39, 41, 48, 59
Africa, 112, 179, 194, 212
Agriculture, xiv, 14, 58, 92, 95, 104
   n. 2, 202, 203, 209, 215–34
  price-fixing mechanism, 220
  directorates, 217
  divisions, 217, 223, 224, 226, 227,
    230, 231
  interest groups, 218, 219, 227,
    230, 233–4
  consultative committees, 228, 231
    Dutch, 220–1
    French, 220
    Italian, 221
  policy, 99, 106, 108, 124, 208, 217
    decision-making, 221–30
  price mechanism, 216
'Agriculture 1980', 231
Albania, 180, 192
Algeria, 179, 181 n. 4, 189 nn. 13,
  14, 190–2
Allais, Maurice, 14
Ankara Agreement, 112
Aron, Robert, 13, 15
Athens Agreement, 185
Atomic energy, 48
Attlee, Clement, 66, 86–8

Barzel, Rainer, 51
Bech, J., 9
Belgium, 154–8, 160–77
  Ministerial Committee for Econo-
    mic and Social Co-ordination,
    199
  Ministry of Foreign Affairs, 199
  Permanent Representative, 199
Benda, Julien, 16
Benelux Countries, 48–9, 132, 180
Benelux Memorandum, 50
Berdiaeff, Nicolas, 21
Bernanos, Georges, 16
Bernhard, Prince, 23

Bertram, C., 229 and n. 14.
Bevin, Ernest, 40–1, 41 n. 23
Beyen, J. W., 9, 47–9
Bidault, Georges, 39
Bidault Plan, 39
Biggs-Davison, John, 78
Birke, W., 150
Bissery, Jacqueline, 154
Boenants, Paul van den, 51
Bondy, François, 8
Bonn Declaration, 74
Bothereau, Robert, 51
Boyd, Francis, 70
Brandt, Willy, 51
Brentano, H. von, 51
British Supply Council, 35, 37
Brooks, John, 34
Brown, George, 78, 90, 93, 96
Brugmans, Henri, viii, 9, 12–14,
  16–20
Brussels Pact, 23, 25
Buenos Aires Declaration, 112

Callaghan, James, 81, 83–5
Camus, Albert, vii, 8 and n. 4
Canada, 35
Carbonnel, M. de, 206 n. 18
Castle, Barbara, 81
Cattani, Sr., 206 n. 18
Charter of the Rights of Man, 23, 28
Cheshire, Group Capt., 23
Chiesa, Enzo Dalla, 52
China, 34, 35
Chopard, Theo, 14
Churchill, Randolph, 26
Churchill, Winston, 8, 9, 11, 13, 16,
  17, 18, 19, 20, 21, 23, 25, 26, 37,
  66, 67, 71
CIAA (Commission des Industries
  Agricoles et Alimentaires de
  l'UNICE) 218, 232
CISC (Confederation Internationale
  de Syndicats Chrétiens), 218

CISL (Confederation Internationale de Syndicats Libres), 218
Clappier, Bernard, 39
Clay, General, 39 n. 13
COCCEE, (Comité des organisations Commerciales des Pays de la CEE), 218
COGECA, (Comité général de la Coopération Agricole des Pays de la CEE), 218, 227
Collard, Léo, 51
College of Europe, 27
Combat, 8 n. 4
Comissariat du Plan, 211
Comités de Concertation, xiii, 204
Committee of Permanent Representatives, xii, 114, 125, 141, 200, 203–205, 217, 222, 224, 225, 226
Commonwealth, 64, 66–7, 71–2, 76–7, 81–3, 90–2, 94–5, 118
Conrad, Joseph, 23
Conservative Party, 65, 69, 71–6, 80,
Cool, Auguste, 51
Coombes, D., xii, 152
    89, 93
COPA (Comité des Organisations de Producteurs Agricoles), xiv, 215, 218, 219–21, 227, 230–4
Corniglion-Molinier, General, 49
Council of Europe, 10, 25, 27–8, 39, 86–8
Council of Ministers, vii, x, xi–xiii, 43, 44, 57, 58, 73, 99, 100 n. 1, 102–7, 110–13, 115–19, 120–1, 123–7, 129, 134, 139, 141, 190, 194, 201, 204, 217, 221–29, 233–4
    General Secretariat of the Council, 114
    President of the Council, 103, 110, 112, 114, 118
Court of Justice, 44, 134, 141 n. 10
Cousins, Frank, 93
Crosland, C. A. R., 83
Crossman, Richard, 92, 96
Cyprus, 190–3

'D'66', 134
Dahrendorf, Ralf, xiii

Dalton, Hugh, 86
Dangerfield, Elma, 70
Dautry, Raoul, 11, 17
Davignon Committee, xiii, 125
Davignon Report, 74
Dehousse, Fernand, 139, 140, 142, 150
Denmark, 136, 165
Deutsch, Karl, ix
Deutsche Gesellschaft fur Auswärtige Politik, 197 n. 1
Deutscher Gerwerkschaftsbund, 210
Douglas-Home, Sir Alec, 68, 75
Druon, Maurice, 16
Duchêne, François, 34
Duisburg, 216

East Bengal, 147
Easton, D., ix
Ecumenical Council of Churches, 7
Egypt, 192–3
Einfuhrstellen, 216
Eliot, T. S., 21
Elizabeth II, Queen of Great Britain, 66
Erhard, Ludwig, 207
Erler, Fritz, 51
Esprit, 12, 15–16
Étienne, Henri, xii, xiii, 204 n. 13
Euratom, viii, 50, 53–4, 58, 61
    Treaty, see under Treaty, Euratom
European Coal and Steel Community, viii, 38, 46–9, 53 n. 55, 54, 58, 61, 87–8
    Common Assembly, 45, 139
    High Authority, 27, 35, 42–5, 47–51, 56, 59
European Defence Community, 46–7, 53 n. 55
European Economic Community, Commission, viii, x, xi, xii, xiii, 10, 13, 50, 178 n. 1, 220–8, 229 n. 14
    agriculture, 215–34
    Community measures adopted, 1970, 100 n. 1
    Community of the Ten, 135
    Directorate General VI, 217, 223–224, 226, 228, 230–3·
    input of telex-messages, note 14, 229

European Economic Community,—
(*contd.*)
  General Secretariat, 113, 217
  Legal Service, 217, 224, 228
  Press and Information Services, 153
  Statistical Office, 217
European Economic Community,
  Committees, 217
  Association Council, 111, 113, 184-6
  Budget Policy Committee, 119
  Economic and Social Committee,
    210, 222, 224, 232
  interest groups, access to EEC, 233
  Latin American Special Co-ordinat-
    ing Committee, 112
  Management Committees, 203
  Medium-Term Economic Policy
    Committee, xii, 101, 119, 231
  Monetary Committee, 101-2, 119
  Short-Term Economic Policy
    Committee, 119
  Special Committee on Agriculture,
    104 n. 2, 217, 222, 224, 225
    Committee of National Experts,
      227-8, 230-3
    Management Committees, 222,
      227-8, 229-30, 232
    Permanent Committee of Animal
      Feedstuffs, 229
    Permanent Committee of
      Foodstuffs, 229
  Working Group on Scientific and
    Technical Research Policy, 119-
    120
European Federalism, 1, 5-9, 14,
  16-17, 24, 30, 70, 72-3, 76, 86,
  88, 91-2, 138
  European Federalist Conference, 8
  European Federalist Movement,
    6, 141
  European Union, 15
  Estates General of Europe, 17-19,
    25, 31
  Union Européenne des Fédéralistes,
    8, 9, 12, 17-20
European Movement, 9, 16-18, 26,
  140, 143 n. 11, 149
  European Centre of Culture,
    23-4, 27

European Movement,—(*contd.*)
  European Congresses, Amsterdam,
    15
    Hertenstein, 15
    Lausaune, 27
    Luxemburg, 15
    Montreux, 12-13, 15-16, 18, 20
    The Hague, 11, 18-19, 21-8,
      86, 138
    The Hague Congress Cultural
      Commission, 20-2
European Free Trade Association,
  64, 71, 89, 91, 95, 183
European Fund for Agricultural Guid-
  ance and Guarantees (FEOGA),
  217
European Laboratory of Nuclear
  Research, 27
European League of Economic Co-
  operation, 16, 17-18, 20
European Parliament, x, xi, xiii, 57,
  60, 63, 70, 73, 99, 104-5, 117,
  121-2, 125-6, 130-4, 136, 138-52,
  139 n. 4, 160-1, 167, 190, 193,
  204, 208-9, 222, 227, 232
  agricultural policy, 224
  Socialist Group, 127, 134, 137
European Social Fund, 103, 124
European Union of Socialist and
  Allied Parties, *see* Union

Fanfani, Amintore, 51
Faure, Edgar, 47-9
Faure, Maurice, 51
Figaro, 29
Flora, F., 16
Fontaine, François, 34
Foot, Michael, 86, 95
FORMA, 216
Fouchet Committee, 74
Fouchet Plan, 29, 74
France, 16, 25, 27, 36, 39, 40-1, 66-8,
  131-2, 139, 146, 154-8, 160-6,
  168-9, 170-7, 179, 188, 190,
  192, 194, 199, 208, 211, 216
  Committee for European
    Federation, 7
  Council for United Europe, 17

France—(*contd.*)
Fifth Republic, x, 151
Inter-Ministerial Committee for Questions of European Economic Co-operation, 199
National Assembly, 46, 47
National Liberation Committee, 35
Radical Party, 134
Socialist Party, 53 n. 55
Technical Inter-Ministerial Committee for Questions relating to the Application of the EEC and ECSC Treaties, 199
Franco-British Committee for Economic Co-ordination, 35, 38
Franco-Saar Conventions, 39
Free Trade, 69
Free Trade Area, 89, 181–2
Freitag, Walter, 51
Frenay, Henri, 9
French Note, 41, 42
French Plan, 35, 37, 45
Functionalists, 8, 9

Gaitskell, Hugh, 76–7, 89–92, 95
Gallup International, 77–8, 153
Gasperi, A. de, 9
Gaulle, General C. de, viii, xi, 37, 54, 64, 78, 96, 127, 142, 205, 207
Gegner Group, 15
General Agreement on Tariffs and Trade, 181, 185 n. 9, 185, 187–8, 189, 190–1
Gerbert, Pierre, 197 n. 1
German Democratic Republic, 133, 165
Germany, 3, 5, 7, 15, 16, 27, 38–9, 39 n. 13, 41, 50, 66, 68, 129, 132–3, 154–8, 160–9, 170–7, 179, 188, 199, 207–8, 209–10, 216, 225
Chancellery, 199
Foreign Office, 199
Ministry of Agriculture, 199
Ministry of Economic Affairs, 199
Ministry of Finance, 199
Swiss Relations, 201
Social Democratic Party, 128–9, 133
Socialist Party, 45, 53 n. 55
trade union organization, 210

Gibraltar, 192–3
Gilson, Étienne, 21
Giraud, General, 37
Godkin Lectures, 75
Great Britain, viii, x, xi, 3, 16, 21, 25, 32, 36, 37, 39, 41, 42, 46, 64–7, 70–1, 75–8, 80, 82, 85, 88–90, 93–4, 96, 118, 136, 147–8, 150 n. 14, 164–5, 186, 198, 202
Greece, 181, 182, 184–5, 185 n. 8, 190–1, 191 n. 16, 194–5
Grimond, Jo, 65
Guardian, 70
Guéhenno, Jean, 16

Haas, E. B., xi
Haight, John M., 35
Hallstein, Walter, xi, 58
Harriman, Averell, 46
Hayes and Harlington, 148
Healey, Denis, 83, 85
Heath, Edward, 72–3, 75, 85, 94
Heer, Friedrich, 65
Heide, Harry Ter, 130
Henig, Stanley, xi
Hill, E. J., 93
Hirsch, Étienne, viii, 40
Hitler, Adolf, 3–5
Hitler–Stalin Pact, 67
Holmes, Oliver Wendell, 33
Holt, Stephen, viii
Hooft, Visser 't, 7
Houghton, Douglas, 84
Hunter, Leslie, 41 n. 23
Hynd, John, 8

Imig, Heinrich, 51
Indo-Pakistani War, 95
Inglehart, Ronald, 153
Inter-Allied Maritime Commission, 34, 37
International Research Associates, 153
International Ruhr Authority, 38
Investment Bank, 184
Iran, 181–2, 186
Ireland, 147
Israel, 180, 181, 183, 185 n. 10, 186, 187–9, 189 nn. 13, 14, 190, 191 n. 16, 193–4

Italy, 15, 27, 32, 50, 134, 141, 146,
    148, 154–8, 160–77, 180, 186,
    189, 226
  Committee of Directors General,
    200
  Committee of Ministers for Inter-
    national Action on Economic
    Policy, 200

Jaspers, Karl, 16
Jay, Douglas, 79
Jenkins, Clive, 89
Jenkins, Roy, 83–4, 90
Journal of Common Market Studies, viii
Juliana, Queen of the Netherlands,
23

Kaiser, Karl, 197 n. 1
Kennedy, John F., 54
Kennedy Round, 187–8, 192
Kerstens, Senator, 11, 26
Kiesinger, Kurt, 51
Koenig, General, 49
Kogón, Eugen, 9
Kohnstamm, Max, 45, 52

La Malfa, Ugo, 52
Labour Party, viii, 64–5, 75–6,
    80–6, 88–95, 128, 196
  Cabinet, 84, 88, 94, 96
  Committee for Europe, 80
  Government, 68, 73, 85–8, 93–6
  Members of Parliament, 85, 94–5
  Ministers, 206
  National Executive Committee, 76,
    81–6, 88–9, 91
  Parliamentary Labour Party, 80, 82,
    84, 85–6, 90
  Party Conference, 75
    1960, 89
    1961, 89
    1962, 92
    1969, 76
    1971, 80, 82, 84–6
  Victory for Socialism Group, 90
  view of federation, 76
  Whips Office, 96
Lall, B. K., 91
Landbowschap, 221

Latin America, 112
Layton, Lord, 23
League of Nations, 34, 37, 38
Lebanon, 181, 186, 192, 194
Lend-Lease, 37
Lenin, V. I., 1, 19
Liberal Party, 69, 70, 71, 73, 93
Libya, 180, 181 n. 4, 192, 193
Lindberg, L. N., ix
Lindsay, Kenneth, 23
Lipgens, W., 5 n. 1
Lukacz, Georgy, 16
Luxemburg, 154–6, 157–8, 160–77
  Ministry of Foreign Affairs, 200
  Permanent Delegation, 200

Macmillan, Harold, 71, 73, 89, 92,
    93
Madagascar, 112
Madariaga, Salvador de, viii, 21, 27
Malagodi, Giovanni, 52
Malta, 188, 191, 192
Mansholt, S., 223, 226, 230, 231–
    232
Marc, Alexandre, 12, 16
Marshall Plan, 13
Mason, Roy, 84
Massigli, René, 40
Maudling, Reginald, 89
Mayer, René, 49, 50
Mayne, Richard, viii
Mende, Erich, 51
Menderes, A., 184
Mendès-France, Pierre, 47–8
'Message to the Europeans', 22, 23
Messina Resolution, 50, 51
Mikardo, Ian, 81, 86
Miller, J. D. B., 72
Ministers
  Agriculture, 116, 206, 206 n. 16,
    208
  Economic Affairs, 206 n. 16, 206,
    207
  Finance, 116, 206, 207–8
  Foreign Affairs, 116, 118, 206
    n. 16, 206, 208, 213
  Science and Research, 116
  Transport, 116, 206
Mollet, Guy, 51

Monnet, Jean, viii, 8, 9, 14, 27, 32, 33,
    34, 34 n. 5, 35, 37, 40–55, 87–8
  Plan Monnet, 14 n. 4
Moral Rearmament, 23
Morgan, Charles, 23
Moro, Aldo, 51
Morocco, 187, 189, 191–2
Morris, Alf, 83
Morrison, Herbert, 41 n. 23
Moselle, river, 48, 201
Motz, Roger, 52
Mounier, Emanuel, 8
Mozer, Alfred, 9
Munich, 67
Mussolini, B., 6

National Executive Committee, see
    Labour Party
NATO, 39, 46
  Temporary Committee, 46
Netherlands, 42, 128, 134, 140, 154–8,
    160–8, 170–7, 180, 188–9, 209, 216
  Commission of Co-ordination, 200
  Council of the European
      Movement, 48
  European Committee, 200
  General Trade Unions Movement,
      130
  Labour Party, 133
    National Congress, 128
  Ministry of Economic Affairs, 200
  Ministry of Foreign Affairs, 200
  Parliament, 132
  Second Chamber, 209
  Socialist Party, 137
    Party Executive, 136
    Resolution, 136
Neunreither, K., 224 n. 9, 224
New Statesman, 96
New Zealand, 81–2, 84, 118
Newhouse, John, 207
Newton, Isaac, 65
Niblock, Michael, 208
Nielsen, Terkel, xiv
Nigerian Federation, 145
Noel, Émile, xii, xiii
Nord, H., 204 n. 13
Northern Ireland, 146, 151 n. 14
Norway, 136, 152

Nuffield Study
  1969, 68
  1970, 69

OEEC (Organization of European
    Economic Co-operation), 28
Ogmore, Lord, 70
Ollenhauer, Erich, 45, 51
O'Malley, Brian, 80, 96
ONIC, 216
Oppenheimer, Peter, 212 n. 32
l'Ordre Nouveau, 12, 15–16, 17, 28
Orwell, George, 8

Pakistan, 147
Palewski, Gaston, 49
Pastore, Giulo, 51
Pepy, Daniel, 197 n. 1
Permanent Representatives Commit-
    tee, 98, 104–6, 108–13, 115–21,
    141, 202
  Chairman, 112–13
  Conference of Representatives of the
      Member States, 103
  Delegations, 199, 201–2, 206, 208,
      225–6, 229
  Representatives, 111–13, 117–18,
      121, 201, 206 and n. 18
  The Hague Conference, 101–2,
      118, 120
'Personalist Movement', 12, 15
Pflimlin, Pierre, 51
Philip, André, 8, 27
Pinay, Antoine, 48, 52
Pleven, René, 46, 52
Pleven Plan, 46
Plowden, Sir Edwin, 46, 88
Poland, 30, 165
Pompidou, Georges, 85
Price, Roy, 140
Produktschappen, 216
Progressive European Party, 128

Rabier, Jean-Jacques, xiv
Ramadier, Paul, 11, 17
Renard, André, 51
Rencontres Internationales, 16
Resistance, 4, 5, 7–9, 13, 15 n. 5
  Draft Declaration of the European
      Resistances, 7

Resolutions of The Hague, 24
Retinger, Joseph, viii, 11, 13, 16, 18, 20–3, 26
Revolution of 1848, 10
Reynaud, Paul, 17
Rhine, river, 201
Rhodesia, 95
Rhodesia and Nyasaland, Federation of, 147
Rippon, Geoffrey, 73–4, 81
Romains, Jules, 21
Roosevelt, Franklin Delano, 37
Rosenberg, Ludwig, 52
Rossi, Ernesto, 5 note 1, 6
Rougemont, Denis de, vii, 11, 16, 23
Ruhr, 38, 39, 88
Rumania, 30
Russell, Lord, 24

Saar, 39, 48
Salis, Jean de, 16
Sandys, Duncan, 13, 16, 18, 20, 25–6, 26 n. 10
Saragat, Giuseppe, 51
'Schachtian' Decade, 43
Scheingold, S. A., ix
Schiller, Prof. Karl, 207
Schulze-Boysen, Harro, 15
Schumacher, Kurt, 45
Schuman, Robert, 9, 39, 40–2, 87
Schuman Declaration, 43
Schuman Plan, 39, 40, 41 n. 23, 42, 68, 88
Scotland, 32
Serruys, Daniel, 14, 17
Servan-Schreiber, Jean-Jacques, 134, 144
Sidjanski, D., 210
Siegfried, A., 17
Sikorski, General, 16
Silkin, John, 80, 82
Silone, Ignazio, 21
Silva, Raymond, 12–13, 17
Singapore, 145
Smith, Ian, 95
Social Democratic Parties, European Congress of, 136–7
Social Surveys (Gallup Poll) Ltd, 77

Socialist International, 127, 134
    Liaison Office, 128, 134, 137
Socialist Movement for the United States of Europe, 18
Socialist Party, 131
Southern Rhodesia, 78
Spaak, Paul-Henri, 9, 27, 47, 48, 49–50, 90–1
Spaak Report, 50
Spain, 165, 187–8, 190, 191 n. 15, 192
Spender, Stephen, viii, 16
Spinelli, Altiero, vii, viii, 6, 8, 9
Stalin, Joseph, 26
Steed, Michael, xiii
Stewart, Michael, 93, 96
Stonehouse, John, 89, 90
Strachey, Lytton, 32
Strasbourg Assembly, 26 n. 10
Suez, 78, 179
Supreme Court, 7, 24 and n. 7
Sweden, 68
Switzerland, 6, 29, 68, 156
Syria, 180, 193

Thompson, George, 96
Trade Union Committee for Europe, 80
Trade Union Congress, 130
    Trade Union Congress, General Council, 93
    1962 Conference, 93
Trade unions
    Agricultural Workers, 83
    ASSET, 89
    Bleachers, 85
    Clerical Workers, 85
    ETU, 82
    General and Municipal Workers, 85
    Iron and Steel Trades, 85
    NUM, 82–3
    Post Office Workers, 83
    Transport and General Workers, 82, 92
Trade unions and agricultural workers, 221
Trade unions attitude towards EEC, 82–3, 130–1
Treaty of Athens, 183

Treaty, Euratom, 53, 102, 110 n. 3
Treaty of Paris, 61, 98, 200
Treaty of Rome, viii, 50, 53, 58, 72–4, 98–106, 108, 109–13, 115, 118–21, 124–5, 131–2, 135, 139, 139 n. 3, 140–1, 141 n. 10, 178 n. 1, 178, 180, 181 n. 4, 186–7, 192, 194, 200, 222, 228
  Merger Treaty, 104
  Standing Employment Treaty, 103
Tribune, 95
Tribune group, 80
Tunisia, 187, 189, 191
Turkey, 112, 182, 184–5, 185 n. 8, 187, 190–2, 194–5

Union Européenne des Fédéralistes, 8–9, 15–20
Union des Industries de la Communauté Européenne, 210, 218
Union of Socialist and Allied Parties, 134–5
  European Congress, 135, 136
  European Union Board, 135–6
  European Executive, 135–6
L'Unitá Europea, 15
United Nations, 38
United Nations Conference on Trade and Development, 191
United States, viii, 29, 39, 54, 63–4, 67, 77, 145, 158, 168, 188, 213
Uri, Pierre, 40, 50
USSR, 1, 2, 3, 16, 66, 165, 168

Ventotene, 6
Ventotene Manifesto, 6, 15
'Victory Program', 37
Vietnam War, 29
Voisin, A., 17
Vorratstellen, 216
Vredeling, H., xiii

Walker-Smith, Sir Derek, x
Wallace, Helen, x
Wall Street, 26
'Way of Federalism', 12
Wehner, Herbert, 45, 51
Werner Plan, 212, 212 n. 32, 214
West Indies, 82
Western European Union, 74
Westerterp, T., 132
Wheaton, Michael, viii
White Paper of August 1962, 91
White Paper on the EEC, 82
Williams, Allan A., 80
Williams, Shirley, 84
Wilson, Harold, 64, 76–7, 81–6, 92–7
World War I, 1, 36
World War II, 1, 2, 33, 35–6, 38, 66–7, 138,

Yaoundé Convention, 111
Younger, Kenneth, 41 n. 23, 42, 88
Yugoslavia, 187, 192

Zeeland, Paul van, 16–17, 26